PROPOSED AIRBORNE ASSAULTS IN THE LIBERATION OF EUROPE

PROPOSED AIRBORNE ASSAULTS IN THE LIBERATION OF EUROPE

CANCELLED ALLIED PLANS FROM THE BATTLE OF NORMANDY TO MARKET GARDEN

JAMES DALY

FRONTLINE
BOOKS

First published in Great Britain in 2024
by Frontline Books
An imprint of
Pen & Sword Books Ltd
Yorkshire - Philadelphia

Copyright © James Daly, 2024

ISBN 9781399036214

Typeset by Lapiz Digital
Printed and bound in the UK by CPI Group (UK) Ltd,
Croydon, CR0 4YY.

Printed on paper from a sustainable source by
CPI Group (UK) Ltd, Croydon, CR0 4YY

Pen & Sword Books Limited incorporates the imprints of
Archaeology, Atlas, Aviation, Battleground, Digital, Discovery, Family
History, Fiction, History, Local, Local History, Maritime, Military,
Military Classics, Politics, Select, Transport, True Crime, Air World,
Claymore Press, Frontline Publishing, Leo Cooper, Remember
When, Seaforth Publishing, The Praetorian Press, Wharncliffe Books,
Wharncliffe Local History, Wharncliffe Transport, Wharncliffe True
Crime and White Owl.

For a complete list of Pen & Sword titles please contact
PEN & SWORD BOOKS LTD
47 Church Street, Barnsley, South Yorkshire, S70 2AS, England
E-mail: enquiries@pen-and-sword.co.uk
Website: www.pen-and-sword.co.uk
or
PEN & SWORD BOOKS
1950 Lawrence Rd, Havertown, PA 19083, USA
E-mail: uspen-and-sword@casematepublishers.com

MIX
Paper | Supporting
responsible forestry
FSC
www.fsc.org   FSC® C013604

Dedication

For Grandad: Private Henry Miller, 11th Parachute Battalion

CONTENTS

ACKNOWLEDGEMENTS

Like the previous volume which examined planned airborne operations in Normandy and Brittany, this book was inspired by Simon Trew's talk in 2014 at The D-Day Museum's annual conference.

As before, much of the writing was carried out during the Covid-19 pandemic, when having thousands of images to interrogate was a godsend. We take access to archives for granted at our peril. I would like to thank the staff at The National Archives, the Imperial War Museum and the Eisenhower Library for their assistance in producing documents for research. The National Archives' enlightened policy around photography of documents was invaluable in writing a book that is so reliant on official sources.

As ever, colleagues and friends have very kindly commented on and informed the research for this book as well as suggesting sources. I am very grateful to Al Murray and James Holland for allowing me to talk about my research on their We Have Ways podcast and Paul Woodage for allowing me to present on WW2TV. I am also grateful to those who attended talks based on early versions of this research whose questions were very helpful.

I would like to thank John Grehan and Lisa Hooson at Pen and Sword for their assistance, Stephen Chumbley for proofreading and Paul Hewitt at Battlefield Design for designing the maps. Any mistakes are entirely my own.

Finally, and most importantly, I must once again thank my wife Becci for her unfailing support during the significant time that it took to research and write these books.

October 2023
Portsmouth

LIST OF MAPS

LIST OF PHOTOGRAPHS

1. Generals Bradley, Marshall and Arnold meeting in France, 12 June 1944. (USNA 111-SC-2064)
2. Bomb damage to Rouen-Sotteville Bridge over the River Seine. (USNA 342-FH-3A18269-54839AC)
3. The bridge at Mantes-Gassicourt was a key choke point for German forces fleeing the Paris-Orleans Gap. It was bombed on 21 August by B-26 Marauders. (USNA 342-FH-53378AC)
4. US Ninth Air Force bombing in Rouen, trapping German forces attempting to cross the Seine. (USNA 342-FH-3A19136-116475AC)
5. Lieutenant General Brereton greeting Major General Urquhart on his return from Arnhem. (USNA III-SC 194694)
6. Nijmegen and the bridge over the River Waal. (USNA 111-SC-194568)
7. Allied airborne troops landing during Operation Market Garden. (USNA111-SC-354702)
8. Brigadier General James B. Newman, Jr. explains how an airborne bulldozer is used to build and repair airstrips in liberated France. (USNA 342-FH-3A17269-53187AC)

INTRODUCTION

At the end of the previous volume, we left the Allied armies as they were beginning to advance in Normandy. A number of planned airborne operations had been considered and cancelled for a number of reasons – either the contingency for which they were envisaged did not occur, they were turned down by the air forces, or it was felt that their objectives could be achieved just as effectively with a conventional ground operation.

As the Allied advance continued towards the Seine and then on towards Germany itself, airborne operations continued to be a valuable option for Allied commanders and as the battle gained momentum there were several circumstances in which airborne landings could assist. North-west Europe possessed a significant number of formidable water crossings – indeed, even before D-Day the Seine had been identified as a key geographical feature. There were also numerous rivers and canals in Belgium and Holland, and further west the Rhine, the most formidable river of all.

While the relatively static warfare in the early phase of the Normandy campaign gave very few opportunities for airborne operations, as the campaign became more fluid the potential of airborne forces to aid in the advance weighed heavy on the Allied command. Many of the plans considered would have used airborne operations to capture ground ahead of the advancing Allied armies. After the capture of so many prisoners of war in Normandy, the theme of trapping German forces by envelopment was also ever-present.

The formation of the First Allied Airborne Army complicated what was already a difficult command structure, and the increasing dominance of US forces added a further level of complexity to what was already a fraught Allied leadership. Airborne planning was taking place in a less-than-united Allied strategy, and the period after the Battle of Normandy saw sharp differences of opinion.

As with the previous volume, operations have been considered separately, and in places chronologies may appear confusing as often more than one plan was being considered at the same time. If anything, this should indicate what a frenetic period August and early September 1944 was. It certainly was for the airborne planners, who must have been mentally exhausted. Yet it was a slightly different picture for the other ranks, who would not have known about many of the operations. Several ideas did not even reach Major General Urquhart, the commander of the British 1st Airborne Division. As we have seen previously, there is a prevailing conception that for every operation that was considered full plans and orders were drawn up and troops assembled at airfields, only to be cancelled at the last minute. As we will see, events were much more nuanced.

Yet it is still crucial to consider the impact on the rank and file – even though they may have not known about operations, they would have known that they had not yet been used. I should at this point declare something of a family interest, as my grandfather, Private Henry Miller of the 11th Parachute Battalion, was one of the men standing by in England.

As often in military histories many of the individuals featured held higher ranks after the war. For simplicity they have been referred to by the ranks that they held at the time in question.

The intention over these two volumes has been to bridge something of a gap between D-Day and Arnhem. It is not proposed to write about Operation Market Garden here, as it has been extensively covered by historians, and it will only be mentioned in as much as it informs our views of other operations, particularly Operation Comet. Nonetheless it should be clear, for a wide range of reasons, that the roots of what occurred at Arnhem can be found long before September 1944.

ABBREVIATIONS AND GLOSSARY

ADGB	Air Defence of Great Britain
AEAF	Allied Expeditionary Air Forces
AFDAG	Airborne Forward Delivery Airfield Group
AIR	Records of the Air Ministry
ANXF	Allied Naval Expeditionary Forces
ASSU	Air Support Signals Unit
BGS	Brigadier General Staff
CATOR	Combined Airborne Transport Operations Room
COMZ	Communications Zone
CSO	Chief Signals Officer
DD Tank	Duplex Drive 'swimming' tank
DEFE	Records of the Ministry of Defence
DUKW	Six-wheeled drive amphibious truck
ETOUSA	European Theatre of Operations United States Army
FAAA	First Allied Airborne Army
FFI	French Forces of the Interior
FUSAG	First US Army Group
G	General Staff (British designation)
G2	Intelligence Staff (US designation)
G3	Operations Staff (US designation)
G4	Supply Staff (US designation)
GSO1	General Staff Officer (Grade 1)

GSO2	General Staff Officer (Grade 2)
GSO3	General Staff Officer (Grade 3)
HS	Records of the Special Operations Executive
IWM	Imperial War Museum
Q	Quartermaster Staff (British designation)
SAS	Special Air Service
SHAEF	Supreme Headquarters Allied Expeditionary Force
SOE	Special Operations Executive
TCCP	Troop Carrier Combined Command Post
TNA	The National Archives
USSTAF	United States Strategic Air Forces
WO	Records of the War Office

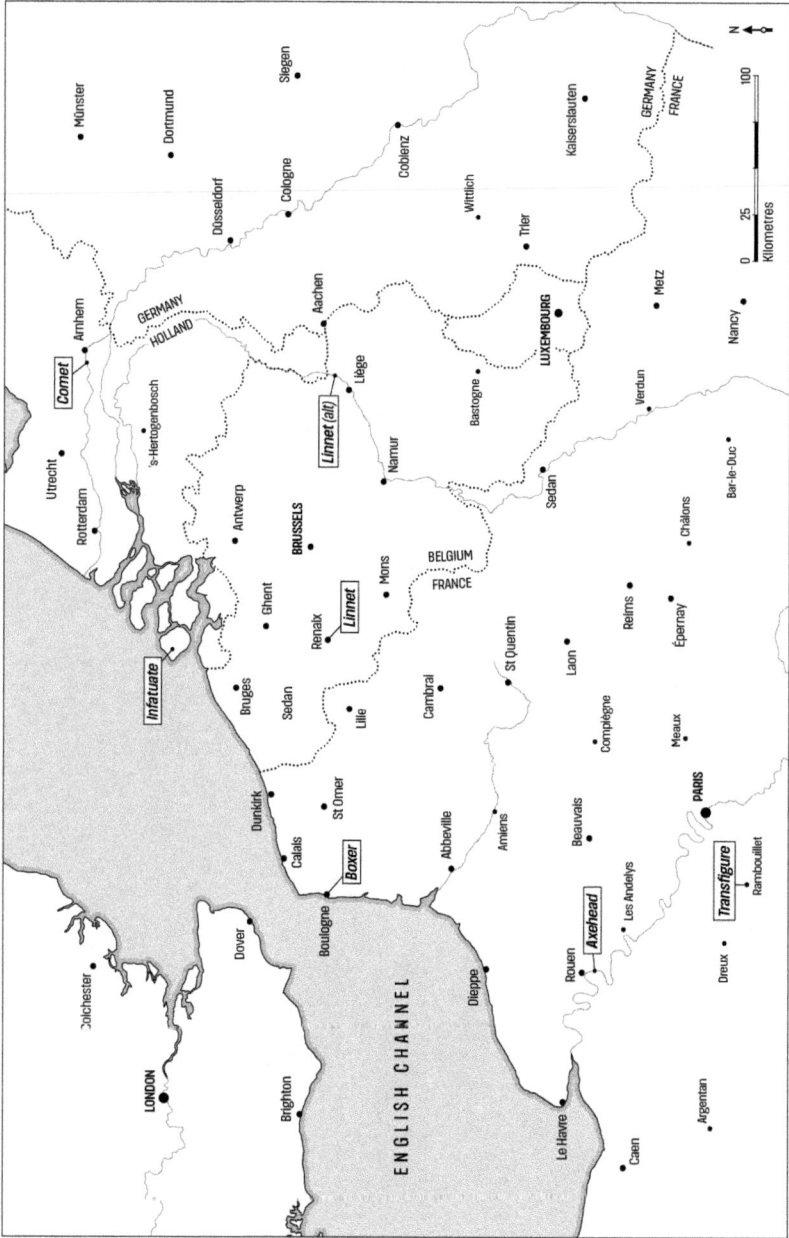

Map 1: Overview of planned airborne operations in North East France, Belgium and Holland. (Source: IWM Urquhart Papers)

Part I – First Allied Airborne Army: August–September 1944

We have previously seen how the First Allied Airborne Army was much longer in gestation than has commonly been thought. Whilst in many accounts it appears in late August 1944, its roots can be found long before D-Day. In the previous volume the new headquarters was in the process of forming after some stiff arguments between Allied commanders as to its worth.

After a great deal of negotiation since before D-Day, and not a little pressure from Washington, the Supreme Commander General Eisenhower had decided in late July 1944 to form a combined airborne headquarters for the Allied forces in North-west Europe. On 2 August Eisenhower wrote to his Chief of Staff, Lieutenant General Walter Bedell Smith. He wanted the new airborne headquarters to begin work immediately:

> In accordance with our conversation this morning, Brereton should be working on his new job instantly. Please inform him that I am particularly anxious about the navigational qualifications of the Transport Command crews. He is to get on to this in an intensive way. He is to keep me in touch with his progress. There is nothing we are undertaking about which I am more concerned than this job of his. I want him on the ball with all his might.[1]

Simultaneously Lieutenant General Lewis Brereton was told by SHAEF that the Airborne Army would be activated immediately. Soon after his new Chief of Staff, Brigadier General Floyd Parks, reported for duty from the United States having discussed the new organisation with the US Army Chief of Staff General Marshall and General Arnold, commander of the United States Army Air Forces, in Washington before his departure.[2]

The next day Lieutenant General Frederick Morgan at SHAEF wrote to the War Office and the Air Ministry to inform them of the formation of what he called the 'Combined Airborne Headquarters'.[3] He told them that the British increment of the new headquarters would be 13 officers and 101 other ranks from the Army and three officers and three other ranks from the RAF. The headquarters would include a Major as the British camp commandant, one Military Police officer and eighty-two other ranks including military policemen, batmen, a butcher, clerks, cooks, orderlies and medical staff. Although the British Army was low on manpower reserves it was still a relatively small complement for an Army-level headquarters. It is not surprising that FAAA was dominated by US personnel, given the relative manpower situation in 1944.

On 4 August Brereton agreed that Lieutenant General Frederick Browning, the commander of the British HQ Airborne Troops, would be his deputy commander. Brereton had first met Browning in North Africa and they had previously worked together. Brereton described Browning as 'a distinguished officer of the British Guardsman type' – it is not clear whether this was intended as a compliment.

Meanwhile Brereton was considering the name of his new formation. Even though he had previously sought to Americanise his new command on 4 August suggested to Eisenhower that as his new command included American, British and Polish troops and was likely to include personnel from other nations it should be re-designated as the First Allied Airborne Army.[4] Brereton thought that an Allied title would enhance the prestige of the force and its *esprit de corps*. Bedell Smith rejected Brereton's proposal on 8 August as the command was not intended or equipped to operate in the field as an army headquarters. Soon after on 9 August Major General Harold Bull told Bedell Smith that he thought that Eisenhower might not have the authority to rename the formation in any case as the Combined Chiefs of Staff had named it. Bull also argued that the force would lack many of the attributes of an Army as it was organised as a planning and co-ordinating headquarters, had no capability to function as an Army Headquarters in the field, and there was no intention to use it as such. However, a pencil note added to Bull's memo states '10/8/44 – Disapproved – Name Allied Airborne Army authorized' and with Bedell Smith's initials, suggesting that Bull's objections were not acceded to, and a further note 'C/S disapproval of basic recommendation and approved name 14/8/44'. These notes suggest that Bedell Smith agreed with Bull, but that both were overruled, almost certainly by Eisenhower.

On 16 August SHAEF informed the War Office, Air Ministry and all headquarters in theatre that the Combined Airborne Forces had been re-designated as the First Allied Airborne Army. Then on 23 August FAAA General Order No. 3 announced the redesignation effective from 16 August and the appointment of Brigadier Robert Sixsmith as the British Deputy Chief of Staff. The acceptance of a more operational sounding name may have been influenced by the pressure that Marshall and Arnold were exerting on Eisenhower.

Meanwhile the new staff were getting on with planning. On 3 August Brigadier General Cutler, the Deputy Chief of Staff, sent a memo to Brereton regarding the availability of airborne formations.[5] Cutler stressed four factors that would affect the number of future operations – the availability of troops, equipment, aircraft and crews and supporting air forces. The 82nd Airborne Division had suffered approximately 50 per cent losses in Normandy, and although replacements were currently being received the division was still short by about 500 men. The 101st Airborne Division had suffered approximately 33 per cent casualties and was still short by 300 men. It was estimated that the two divisions would reach 80 per cent efficiency by 1 September and 100 per cent by 1 October. The 504th Parachute Infantry Regiment, which had seen considerable fighting in Sicily and Italy but had arrived too late to be used in Normandy, was at 100 per cent strength and ready for action. The 17th Airborne Division, which was due to arrive in Britain at the end of August, had completed training in the US and would be ready for operations 30 days after its arrival.

The British 1st Airborne Division had been held in readiness since D-Day and Cutler described it as a well-trained division. The Polish Parachute Brigade was undergoing tactical training and would be ready for operations from 15 August and the 52nd Lowland Division, being trained to be air transported, would also be ready from 15 August.

While equipment was plentiful, the personnel situation was more of a concern. Approximately 1,000 transport aircrews were available in the UK on 1 July, but of these 384 had already been allotted to Operation Anvil in the South of France. One hundred and seventy-six replacement crews were due to arrive in July and another 176 in August. Training attrition was estimated to be 3 per cent, or approximately 33 crews. This would give a total of 1,259 aircrews available by 1 October, enough to lift two airborne divisions on a reduced scale and then lift the balance of all US airborne forces within 48 hours. There were enough gliders to lift three US airborne divisions and 1,701 glider crews available as of 3 July, with 125 crews arriving every month: 225 had been allocated to Anvil. It was estimated that there would be 2,030 crews available by 1 October which would be sufficient to life two divisions at full strength, while a third could be carried soon after if the glider crews returned quickly. There were enough British aircraft and crews to lift approximately two-thirds of a division at any one time, on which basis a complete division could be carried within 36 hours. There were about 700 British gliders available, with 30 to 40 arriving each month.

Brereton's appointment was not without controversy, even before it had been announced. On 9 August rumours spread among American journalists that his transfer from Ninth Air Force was due to the accidental bombing of American ground forces at Saint-Lô. Brereton asked SHAEF to announce his new appointment to counter what he described as 'malicious gossip.' Bedell Smith told him that this would not be possible as the formation of the Airborne Army was still top secret.[6] However, the next day Eisenhower and Brereton visited the 101st Airborne Division at Membury and in a speech Eisenhower announced the formation of the First Allied Airborne Army.[7] Eisenhower told his audience that 'In the airborne operations lies one of the great futures of our success ... for we have an opportunity to end this war far, far quicker than we could do without you'. Not for the first or last time Eisenhower had overruled his staff on airborne matters.

Brereton's new command comprised all US airborne formations, US IX Troop Carrier Command, Headquarters British Airborne Troops along with 52nd (Lowland) Division, British 1st Airborne Division, SAS troops and 1st Polish Parachute Brigade. The Combined Air Transport Operations Room – CATOR – also came under Brereton's new command. 38 and 46 Groups RAF would only be under Brereton's command for airborne operations specifically. The new command's functions were described as the supervision of training and allotment of facilities, studying and recommending improvements in airborne equipment, co-ordinating supply, consulting with the Allied Naval Expeditionary Forces on routes over sea, consulting with Allied Expeditionary Air Forces and assembling troops, equipment and supplies at designated air bases. FAAA would also prepare and examine outline plans for airborne operations in conjunction with SHAEF planning staff and with army and air force commanders.

It was increasingly apparent that the Americans lacked an airborne corps headquarters. They therefore decided to convert an existing infantry corps to the role, and on 9 August SHAEF informed Washington that XVIII Corps would be re-designated as an airborne formation.[8] The corps headquarters was still in the US preparing to embark for Europe but the Deputy Chief of Staff, Assistant Chief of Staff G2, Adjutant General, Quartermaster, Signals Officer and a number of other ranks were rushed across the Atlantic to begin adapting to its new role, and departed Washington on 10 August. Ridgway appointed his own Chief of Staff, G1, G2 and G4 staff, Inspector General, Judge Advocate, Camp Commandant and Surgeon and the corresponding personnel from XVIII Corps were left behind in the United States. He took over command on 27 August 1944 and on 31 August SHAEF asked the War Department in Washington to redesignate the existing XVIII Corps troops as parachute units, including the headquarters and headquarters company, the Military Police platoon and the corps artillery headquarters.[9]

In London there were still concerns about the new Allied headquarters. On 9 August the Director of Air at the War Office, Major General Kenneth Crawford, wrote to the Director of Staff Duties, Brigadier James Steele, concerning SHAEF's letter of 3 August about the formation of FAAA. He started his letter by saying 'there are several points about which I am not at all happy'. Crawford felt that the proposed establishment bore little resemblance to the function of the new headquarters. He thought that the G3 staff would not be able to perform all the tasks expected of it but accepted that the War Office would not be able to do much about it. SHAEF had also proposed transferring functions to FAAA, including reinforcements, which were currently the responsibility of the War Office where British airborne forces were concerned, and Crawford argued that the War Office should continue to deal directly with 21st Army Group. He also felt that the RAF was inadequately represented and suggested that FAAA should have two British Deputy Chiefs of Staff, one Brigadier and one Air Commodore. Subsequently on 18 August the Director of Staff Duties wrote to Eisenhower, the Commander of 21st Army Group General Sir Bernard Montgomery and Browning about the war establishment of the British increment of FAAA and from 15 August the British staff consisted of fifteen officers and fifty-five other ranks, who would join the G1, G2, G3 and G4 staffs.

One of the most important elements of any headquarters – and one that is often overlooked – is that of signals support. Throughout the campaign in North-west Europe airborne signals were found to be inadequate and FAAA's signals were slow to develop. On 22 August the Chief Signal Officer at 21st Army Group, Major General Cecil White, signalled his counterpart at SHAEF regarding the lack of a British Signals Officer at FAAA and asked for the appointment of a

Royal Signals Major with airborne experience. Days later the Chief Signals Officer at SHAEF replied that the war establishment of FAAA included a US Colonel as Chief Signals Officer, a US Lieutenant Colonel and a Royal Signals Major. On 5 September, just over a week before Operation Market Garden and far too late to influence events, SHAEF ordered the attachment of 116 US signals personnel.[10]

On 13 August Air Marshal Sir Trafford Leigh Mallory, the commander of AEAF, wrote to Eisenhower in response to the announcement of the new headquarters.[11] Leigh Mallory was not happy with the wording of the announcement and also felt that it did not reflect his discussions with Eisenhower regarding the command of air forces:

> I would be grateful if I could have a more precise definition than the present directive contains of my responsibilities in regard to their air aspect of airborne operations . . . In all discussions I have had with SHAEF it has always been affirmed that the Commander of Airborne Forces would control only the air lift of the Allied Airborne Forces, and that the responsibility for all supporting air operations to get the airborne expedition to its landing area and back to base would be entirely mine as Air Commander-in-Chief.

Leigh Mallory asked for a further directive clarifying these issues to avoid any misunderstandings. His letter prompted a flurry of communication. Bull told Bedell Smith that Leigh Mallory had already been informed of his responsibilities regarding air support in a letter dated 31 July. Bedell Smith replied to Leigh Mallory on 19 August confirming that the troop carrier forces would be commanded by FAAA while the Air Commander-in-Chief would command the supporting air operations. He was also informed that although the Combined Air Transport Operations Room had been placed under FAAA:

> You will note that Royal Air Force Transport and Troop Carrier formations are placed under the Commanding General, First Allied Airborne Army only when allocated. As the Combined Air Transport Operations Room is in continuous operation and the training of airborne troops requires the use of these aircraft, this allocation should be made promptly in response to the request of the commanding general, First Allied Airborne Army.

Of the eight senior staff officers for FAAA announced on 8 August all were American, including the Chief of Staff (Parks), Deputy Chief of Staff (Cutler) and the Assistant Chiefs of Staff for G1, G2 and G4. Although Brereton had initially accepted the SHAEF formula of a

50:50 ratio for American and British staff he subsequently changed this policy and insisted that an aviator should head the G3 section. This was influenced by Brereton's air background and his view that airborne planning was an air matter until the airborne troops had been delivered and that as FAAA would not command troops on the ground, air planning would take primacy.[12]

Despite the formation of the new headquarters Washington was still pressing for action. On 14 August Brereton was copied into a message sent from Arnold in Washington to Eisenhower at SHAEF: 'In view of the situation in France today, what is your plan in very broad outline for the employment of the Brereton Command? Troop carrier planes are not comparing at all favourably with combat plane missions (other than supply and training) accomplished and hours in the air.'[13] It is hard not to conclude that Arnold and Marshall were exerting an unhelpful level of influence on Eisenhower, particularly from such a distance across the Atlantic.

From mid-August SHAEF began to issue directives to the First Allied Airborne Army, and FAAA was ordered to prepare six contingency plans on a short timescale. FAAA's 'Priority I' was to consider an operation north of the Lower Seine between the Oise and Rouen to facilitate the crossing of the Seine, a proposal that shared strong similarities with Operation Axehead. 'Priority II' was an operation to seize the crossings over the Oise between the Seine and Compiègne to protect the right flank of the advancing Allied forces. 'Priority III' was an operation north of the Upper Seine between Fontainebleau and Juvisy to facilitate the crossing of the Seine. 'Priority IV' would be an operation north of the Somme between Peronne and Abbeville to facilitate the crossing of the Somme. 'Priority V' would be an operation north of the River Aisne close to Soissons to facilitate the crossing of the Aisne to the south. And finally 'Priority VI' would be an operation to capture the St Omer area with a view to hindering the withdrawal of enemy forces from the Pas de Calais coast.[14] Planning for these operations would be completed by 25 August, except for the operation north of the Seine, which was to be completed by 7 September or later.[15] As a result of this pressure from Washington on 26 August Brereton told his staff that General Eisenhower wanted the airborne divisions to be used in mass and that he believed that if used in this way they would have a devastating effect on German morale.

These directives show that FAAA found itself supporting two cliques. It was being handed directives from SHAEF, who were under pressure from Washington to use it strategically, but it had been detailed to support Montgomery's 21st Army Group. Even though airborne planning had theoretically been placed at a theatre level and further from 21st Army Group, Montgomery still saw utility in airborne forces and kept his chief planner, Brigadier Charles Richardson, in contact with Browning's staff. Montgomery seems to have considered Browning to be his own airborne planner and was comfortable bypassing SHAEF and FAAA, a situation which was further complicated by Browning's 'dual-hatting' as commander of the British Airborne Corps and as a deputy commander of FAAA.[16] This also highlights the difficulty with Browning acting as both an advisor and an operational corps commander.[17]

On 23 August the Staff Duties Division at the War Office wrote to Crawford, the Director of Air, regarding the formation of FAAA.[18] The War Office had heard that the formation would be called the First Allied Airborne Army but had not received an official notification or a date for its activation from SHAEF, and naturally wanted to clarify the position of HQ British Airborne Troops. Formerly the headquarters had come under 21st Army Group but also had access to the War Office on technical matters. FAAA, however, had no British personnel on its staff and would not be able to carry out the administrative functions that were currently performed by 21st Army Group. Crawford was asked to clarify several points, particularly around the chain of command for administrative matters and reinforcements. On 24 August SHAEF informed the Crawford that the Combined Airborne HQ would indeed now be called the First Allied Airborne Army and would have its headquarters at Sunninghill Park in Ascot.[19] On the same day SHAEF messaged 21st Army Group that HQ Airborne Troops, with 52nd Infantry Division, 1st Airborne Division, SAS Troops and 1st Polish Parachute Brigade, had been placed under the command of FAAA.

Leigh Mallory, meanwhile, was still far from happy. On 26 August he sent a curt letter to Brereton complaining that although he could request operational resources from 38 and 46 Groups, these still needed to be reported to AEAF.[20] Leigh Mallory also reminded Brereton that 'administrative control' of both groups would rest with their respective RAF Commands. He would also later complain that his planners were being ignored.[21] Despite Leigh Mallory's objections on 1 September US Strategic Air Forces Europe General Order No. 59 announced that IX Troop Carrier Command was relieved from its assignment to Ninth Air Force and was to be placed under the 'administrative control' of the Strategic Air Forces in Europe from 25 August, and under the operational control of FAAA.[22]

On 1 September Parks wrote to Eisenhower on behalf of Brereton.[23] He thought that the authorised establishment of 30 US officers and

142 men for the Headquarters and Headquarters Company of FAAA was already inadequate. He asked for the transfer of fifteen officers, three warrant officers and twenty-three enlisted men who were surplus after the conversion of XVIII Corps. He also asked for the assignment of nine officers and fifty men from US Strategic Air Forces and two men from theatre overheads. It is striking that FAAA was requesting more men so soon after its establishment and after being involved in planning only two operations. This suggests that its establishment and its intended role were out of balance from the start. On 1 September the British element at FAAA numbered 16 officers and 101 other ranks, the majority of whom had been loaned by other British units who reduced their own strengths to assist. Many of these were additional to the nine officers allowed in FAAA's table of organisation and could only be attached temporarily. They were therefore liable for recall at short notice, which meant that FAAA might have to rebuild its staff sections during an operation. Parks requested an increased war establishment urgently. The amount and detail of the staff work required had become more complicated due to the novel requirement for FAAA to be both an air force unit and a ground forces unit at the same time, which called for more staff officers in each section than might normally have been required.

Parks mentioned two other problems. FAAA had been sharing its headquarters at Sunninghill with Ninth Air Force which was expected to move to the Continent shortly, taking its headquarters signals unit – which FAAA had been sharing – with it. To provide FAAA with its own signals unit would require 400 men. In addition fifteen officers and twenty-four men who had been made available by the reorganisation of XVIII Corps were liable to be recalled after it had been reactivated as an airborne corps. FAAA had found that each operation required around twelve officer courier trips to the various headquarters involved, to carry documents which could not be sent through normal mail. This meant that there was a need for additional staff officers. Operations also required daily trips for planning conferences, which in turn increased the need for motor transport and driver personnel which had previously been borrowed from Ninth Air Force. Parks suggested that FAAA would require the attachment of one Car Company and one Quartermaster Truck Company. Ninth Air Force was also currently providing military police, with two Military Police Companies patrolling seven towns in the Sunninghill area. Thirty MPs were on duty day and night and fifty men were needed for gate and guard duty. Parks estimated that although the requirement would be less once Ninth Air Force left, FAAA would still need one

Military Policy Company. FAAA was clearly not staffed adequately for the ambitious role given to it.

Well into September there were misunderstandings about which of the Allied air commanders would command the troop carrier element of airborne operations. On 31 August Hollinghurst, the commander of 38 Group, wrote to Leigh Mallory expressing his concerns about the division of responsibilities for planning for airborne operations after the establishment of the First Allied Airborne Army.[24] He felt that 38 Group had been excluded from the planning of recent operations. It had not been consulted at all in preparing the air plans for Linnet and had not been invited to a meeting at Leigh Mallory's headquarters, while IX Troop Carrier Command had. He felt that the route proposed for Linnet was sensible, that the planners had given too much emphasis to avoiding flak and that the prospect of enemy fighters had been ignored. Hollinghurst did not feel that the importance of fighter cover had been fully appreciated by those responsible for 'laying it on'. Hollinghurst also suggested to Leigh Mallory that he would have landed the glider elements first as the most vulnerable part of the operation. He had also been candid with Williams regarding his dislike for aspects of the plan for Linnet but accepted that as the plan had already been finalised no changes would be forthcoming. Hollinghurst grudgingly accepted Williams' apparent primacy in commanding Allied troop carrier forces and it was fortunate that Hollinghurst and Williams, along with their respective staffs, got on well together. However Hollinghurst seems to have been unhappy with how the RAF Transport Groups had been treated since the formation of the First Allied Airborne Army:

> Rightly or wrongly, I feel that I – and not FAAA or the Troop Carrier Command designate for a particular operation – am responsible to you (and through you to the Air Ministry) that the aircrew of 38 Group (and 46 Group whilst working under our operational control) have the best chance of carrying out their tasks successfully and as safely as is possible in war. I also feel that we have a responsibility towards our soldier passengers. I therefore ask that arrangements be made that in future operations AOC 38 Group is consulted parri passu with CG IX Troop Carrier instead of being presented with (as in this case) a more or less finalised plan.

Hollinghurst's comparison of 38 Group's declining involvement with that of IX Troop Carrier Command and its commander Williams is perceptive. Was the latter being brought into the fold more as most officers at FAAA were American? Or was it because Brereton, in his previous post, had been Williams' commanding officer?

Leigh Mallory wrote to Brereton on 6 September amplifying Hollinghurst's concerns. With his characteristic directness Leigh Mallory argued that for any future operations in which 38 or 46 Groups were to be involved their commanders should be invited to take part in the planning. Leigh Mallory went further and challenged Brereton over the appointment of the troop carrier commander for airborne operations. In their earlier discussions it had been agreed that the commander of the troop carrier aspect should come from the nation 'principally interested'. As the airborne operations planned immediately after D-Day would only have used British and Polish formations Hollinghurst was the appointed commander. Leigh Mallory reminded Brereton that on one of these occasions – it is not clear for which operation – he appointed Williams as the troop carrier commander to give him a turn. He therefore made a plea for Hollinghurst to be 'given a chance' to command an operation, 'as I know he would do you very well'.

Brereton replied to Leigh Mallory on 10 September. He explained that not including Hollinghurst in the planning for Linnet was an oversight, but attempted to deflect some blame by arguing that as the conference in question was organised by AEAF those in attendance had been invited by Leigh Mallory's headquarters. He did concede, however, that AEAF 'might have felt' that FAAA would ask the British Troop Carrier commanders to be present as well as their American counterparts. Brereton went on to indicate that on two previous occasions Hollinghurst had been invited to similar conferences, not receiving the invitation on one occasion and on the other sending a representative of a rank below the level required. On the question of who would command the Allied troop carrier effort, Brereton gave Leigh Mallory's suggestions short shrift. He reminded him that Browning had been in command of all airborne troops, and that as most troop carrier aircraft were now coming from IX Troop Carrier Command that Williams would be placed in command.

This frosty exchange clearly failed to resolve the issue. As late as 13 October – a month after Market Garden – Leigh-Mallory wrote to Eisenhower stating that he was unclear what of 38 Group's resources First Allied Airborne Army would have at any given time. The difficult relationship issues between the RAF and FAAA was clearly at risk of affecting coordination.[25]

Into September there were still wider concerns over FAAA's reporting lines. On 4 September Steele at the War Office wrote to SHAEF G3 requesting clarification on its functions.[26] He asked SHAEF to clarify how HQ Airborne Troops could report to FAAA on administrative matters when the latter had no British staff. Steele also reminded SHAEF that the movement of troops in Britain was controlled by the War Office and that this could not be changed. The War Office had also set up an Air Despatch Group to supply airborne forces and ground forces by air, the commander of which was under the direct command of the War Office and HQ Airborne Troops had access to the commander during airborne operations. The War Office was also responsible for reconstituting British airborne forces after operations, controlling accommodation, the issue of equipment and stores and the posting of reinforcements. The reinforcement of airborne forces, Steele argued, could only be dealt with as part of the whole manpower problem, no doubt due to Britain's chronic shortage of reinforcements. Steele suggested that a conference should be held to discuss the responsibilities of FAAA as soon as possible. SHAEF replied on 8 September. They agreed with the need for a conference, which they thought that FAAA should have already organised. SHAEF therefore suggested that the War Office should call the conference instead and that SHAEF, 21st Army Group, 38 Group, HQ Airborne Troops and FAAA should be represented.

Meanwhile the progress of the Allied campaign after the Battle of Normandy was stretching logistics to the limit. By late August and early September Troop Carrier units began to move to the continent. On 6 September the US Army's Communications Zone asked SHAEF to order two Troop Carrier Groups, consisting of 220 C-47 aircraft, to begin operations from airfields A-62 at Reims, A-63 at Villeneuve in Champagne and A-68 at Juvincourt in Aisne.[27] The aircraft were urgently required to carry fuel forwards from the Omaha area for 12th Army Group and were to begin operations by 0700 on 8 September. They would be based at A-23 Querqueville near Cherbourg and fly fuel forwards from A-22 at Colleville-sur-Mer and A-11 at Saint-Lambert. Each plane would make two cargo runs a day. This air lift would constitute the major contribution of petrol to 12th Army Group and had been agreed between SHAEF, CATOR, 12th Army Group, Ninth Air Force and 302nd Transport Wing. This fait accompli was presented to FAAA who were asked to issue orders to the Troop Carrier Groups. Two days later this order was confirmed by Lieutenant General John C.H. Lee, the commander of COMZ. Eisenhower's authorisation of Lee's request mentioned air supply 'during present emergency' and problems with 'Channel weather' closing French ports, but it would be reasonable to question whether the 'emergency' had been caused by the Allies' uncoordinated advance rather than the weather. On 9 September Williams signalled FAAA, SHAEF and COMZ to confirm that three Groups of 50th Troop Carrier Wing – the 439th, 440th and 441st – along the with Wing Headquarters, had moved to the continent the previous day.

On 7 September Tedder visited Brereton to discuss what the latter described as 'airborne problems'.[28] Brereton told him that the biggest obstacle to the employment of airborne forces was the refusal of commanders to use the Troop Carrier air forces in their primary mission of carrying airborne troops. The Troop Carriers were being used to supply the ground forces but could not do this and support airborne operations. Army commanders had strongly opposed releasing aircraft for airborne operations, and Brereton told Tedder that this made it impossible to take advantage of opportunities for using airborne forces as their transport aircraft were not immediately available for use. His suggestion was for the Troop Carrier aircraft to be controlled by the Supreme Commander rather than his Army Group or Army commanders who were likely to use the transport aircraft to improve their supply situation. Brereton saw the airborne army as a strategic reserve to be planned on a Supreme Command level and thought that when airborne operations were planned below Army Group level time was usually wasted as the operations were not feasible or had to be re-planned.

On 13 September Wing Commander D.A. Catesby of the AEAF Staff wrote to Lieutenant Colonel Bird in the Staff Duties Directorate at the War Office to submit agenda items from the air force perspective.[29] AEAF were particularly interested in discussing the channels of communication between 38 and 46 Group and the Air Ministry regarding the allocation of aircraft and airfields, accommodation and airborne equipment. Catesby also queried FAAA's responsibilities for administrative and equipment planning, and the submission of requirements, and questioned whether the RAF G4 element of FAAA would be adequate to undertake the work expected of it. In the event the Air Ministry did not submit any comments or questions and only attended the conference with what Bird described to Catesby as a 'watching brief'. 21st Army Group raised the issue of Military Secretary matters, airborne war establishment, the provision of personnel, specialist equipment – common-use and nationality-specific – the mounting of operations, resupply, discipline, signals and the reforming of units after operations.

Even while Market Garden was being launched and fought issues abounded around FAAA's formation. Ironically, on 16 September the Major General for Staff Duties at SHAEF wrote to the Air Ministry, 21st Army Group, SHAEF G-3, First Allied Airborne Army and

Headquarters Airborne Troops suggesting a meeting to discuss problems in staff work and administration in connection with the formation of the Airborne Army. The meeting would take place on 22 September, when grave events were unfolding in Holland.[30] On 16 September Brigadier Sixsmith, on behalf of Major General Steele, wrote to invite attendees to a conference to discuss staff duties and administrative matters arising from the formation of FAAA. Sixsmith stated that the conference had been called at the request of Eisenhower and would take place at the War Office. The agenda included clarification of the functions of FAAA and the relationship between HQ Airborne Troops, FAAA and the War Office. The agenda also included administrative matters including reinforcements, the control of movements, supply and function of British air-transported forces. Organising a conference at such a critical point in the battle and with attendees from headquarters in Britain and on the continent was far from simple. 21st Army Group replied to the invitation that although it was 'vitally interested' in any decisions reached, in view of the strain on communications it needed six days' notice of the meeting and full agenda.

The conference on 22 September was chaired by the Director of Staff Duties at the War Office, Major General Steele. The conference agreed that FAAA's functions would be limited to outline planning and the exercising of operational command. HQ Airborne Troops would be under the operational command of FAAA, but for administrative purposes would have direct access to 21st Army Group or the War Office. It was agreed that there was no need for a direct channel between FAAA and the War Office, who would deal only with SHAEF or HQ Airborne Troops. Air-transported forces – such as 52nd Division – would remain under the command of the ground forces concerned but would be placed under HQ Airborne Troops when necessary.

In terms of how this division of responsibilities would work in practice, the minutes of the conference included a table delineating which headquarters was responsible for supporting British Airborne Forces for various subjects. Military Secretary matters would be dealt with by the War Office through 21st Army Group, Records by 21st Army Group, reinforcements by the War Office for units in the UK and 21st Army Group for units on the Continent, discipline by 21st Army Group in Europe and the home commands while units were in the UK, supply by the Air Despatch Group, RAF equipment by the Air Ministry through AEAF and then ADGB once AEAF had been disbanded. Movements were the responsibility of the War Office, through FAAA and SHAEF.

Roger Cirillo has argued that even after the formation of FAAA the 'trigger' for airborne operations remained with Montgomery, but the complicated machinery in place, the proliferation of headquarters and staffs and conflicting personalities meant that pressing the trigger was anything but straightforward.[31] During the planning for Operation Comet it was clear that having multiple headquarters in different countries was causing communication problems and lengthening the planning process. The coordinating conference prior to the operation was eventually held by FAAA at the War Office on 8 September, with three days' notice to organise. Some of the infrastructure set up in Britain prior to D-Day was functioning less effectively as the Allied armies advanced further east. On 10 September after a discussion between Crawford at SHAEF and Parks at FAAA, SHAEF asked FAAA to attach an Advanced Echelon of CATOR to SHAEF Forward from 12 September.[32] In early December FAAA proposed to form a Tactical HQ. Market Garden had shown that there was a lack of communication between the ground forces and FAAA, which was back in England. A small tactical headquarters was therefore proposed to join the relevant Army headquarters for operations. It can only be speculated how this might have affected Market Garden, but it could well be argued that FAAA was out of the loop once the operation commenced. The Deputy Chief of Staff would head the Tactical HQ, with four other officers.[33]

In hindsight FAAA was a compromise that nobody in the European Theatre really wanted or needed, apart from Eisenhower. Even then, Arnold and Marshall in Washington had clearly influenced the Supreme Commander. The new headquarters was strongly opposed by Bradley, Ridgway and Gavin who were worried about the British taking control of airborne operations. Brereton did not want the new appointment and was chosen a compromise, and Browning was unhappy at being passed over.[34] Personality clashes might not have been the sole cause of the Allies' airborne problems in 1944, but they made it impossible for them to overcome the other challenges facing them. FAAA complicated what was already a difficult situation.

Part II – Breakout

OPERATION LUCKY STRIKE

Not all the operations considered for the Allied airborne forces in 1944 were devised during the battle. In fact, some of them had their genesis long before D-Day. The roots of one such operation, Lucky Strike, can be found in the pre-invasion strategic planning for subsequent phases of Operation Overlord. Lucky Strike also demonstrates how airborne planning always took place within a much broader strategic context.

21st Army Group's strategy for the campaign after D-Day was circulated on 7 May 1944, shortly before Montgomery's Thunderclap briefing on 15 May 1944.[1] This included an 'Appreciation on possible development of operations to secure a lodgement area' with the object of studying the implications of the terrain in the Normandy area, alongside an intelligence assessment of the Germans' capability to resist. 21st Army Group was already aware of the importance of moving out of the difficult bocage terrain before attempting a major offensive. This report concluded that one of the options available to the Allies was to advance south from the Normandy beachhead towards Rennes and from there either to direct the main advance towards Brittany or the Seine.

On 14 June the Chief of Staff of 21st Army Group, Major General De Guingand, wrote to Montgomery. He explained that 21st Army Group staff were currently examining how if the Germans had to withdraw from Normandy, the Allies could concentrate forces to pursue and defeat them west of Paris. De Guingand's concept of Lucky Strike would have given operations to clear Brittany a lower priority. He estimated that Lucky Strike would consist of Second British, First Canadian and First US Armies. He also suggested that as the bridges over the River Seine had been blown a strong force advancing on the axis of Le Mans, Orleans and Chartres would cut off the German retreat south of Paris. An armoured force on this route, which effectively amounted to a long hook, would also avoid the difficult bocage terrain further north in Normandy.[2]

Two days later 21st Army Group's G(Plans) staff submitted an 'Appreciation of the development of Operations' to De Guingand.[3] This considered the possibility of driving for the Seine instead of securing the Biscay ports, very much from a logistical background, weighing up the relative merits of different ports and their ability to support the Allied build-up. The main motivation for Lucky Strike at this stage appears to have been a school of thought that Le Havre would need to be captured by D+60 and to be in full operation by D+110. In this context Operation Axehead, the crossing of the Seine, would have been the final phase of Lucky Strike. As it would take 15 to 20 days to assemble the required bridging equipment to cross the Seine, working backwards the planners estimated that the Seine would need to be reached by D+30 to D+35. 21st Army Group would advance south to Flers and then towards the Seine on a line between Argentan and Laigle, with the inter-army boundary between the Canadian and British Armies on the line of Falaise, Bernay and Elbeuf. First US Army would follow a similar path to the south. This suggests that 21st Army Group were aware of the need to outflank the bocage terrain. On 18 June 21st Army Group's G(Plans) section published an amended version of this appreciation. The aim was to examine the potential tactical development of the operation to provide a basis to allow for the administrative implications to be studied.[4]

At this early juncture Lucky Strike was planned to consist of three phases. It would begin with an initial penetration to the south to create a sufficiently wide front with the objective of securing a line from Avranches to Domfront and Sees. The decision to commence Lucky Strike would be taken around D+35 based on progress of the Allied advance and the intelligence picture. Once a sufficiently wide breakthrough had been made the Allies would drive to the east with a right flank likely to rest on the line of Avranches, Mayenne, Beaumont, Nogent-le-Rotrou and Dreux before reaching the Seine at Vernon. This advance would be carried out by the First US Army and a proportion of US Third Army on a two-corps front, Second British Army on a two-corps front and Canadian First Army on a three-corps front. The inter Army boundary between the Americans and British would run between Brioux, Argentan, Laigle and Evreux, while the boundary between the British and Canadians would run between Morteau, Bernay and Bourgtherolde. This phase was predicted to take place between D+30 and D+70.

To force the Germans into battle and to trap retreating forces against the western bank of the Seine the bridges north of Paris were to be destroyed by air attack and it was hoped that the enemy would be forced to withdraw south-east from Normandy towards Paris. Alternatively, it was suggested that the Allies could follow several alternative courses during the exploitation phase. These included an immediate pursuit with all available forces south-east towards Paris, a follow-up by First US and Second British Armies while the Canadians crossed the Seine and either secured Le Havre, pushed east for the Somme or push east, then south-east and cut off Paris; or First US Army could pursue the German withdrawal. Second British Army could cross the Seine and strike east and south-east to cut off Paris and First Canadian Army would either capture Le Havre or push east towards the Somme. The document predicted that the pursuit might begin between D+60 and D+70. The question of Brittany was also considered. It was estimated that if the conditions that would make Lucky Strike possible existed it would also be likely that the German forces in Brittany would be reduced to static garrisons. In this scenario it was estimated that one US corps could clear Brittany, freeing up the rest of US Third Army for Lucky Strike. This emphasises the range of options that were available to the Allies in Normandy.

One major consideration faced by the 21st Army Group planners was the issue of administration and its effect on decision making. If Lucky Strike were to succeed it was likely that from D+30 to D+70 the bulk of the Allied armies would be fighting major battles west of the Seine. Would it be possible to maintain these forces from the existing Mulberry harbour, small Normandy ports and beach facilities? And did these logistical constraints make Le Havre a necessary objective of the pursuit? Any general pursuit after D+60 would also increase the Allied lines of communication over the Seine and subsequently west, north-east, south-east or a combination of all three.

On 20 June SHAEF's plans division began to examine the implementation of Lucky Strike, particularly from a logistical perspective.[5] Lucky Strike was defined by SHAEF as the 'exploitation of a deterioration in German capability to resist'. SHAEF expected it to take the form of a drive towards the Seine with maximum force from the Neptune bridgehead in an effort to divide the German forces. The Allied would then cross the Seine and capture the ports of Rouen and Le Havre. SHAEF understood 21st Army Group's concept of Lucky Strike to include a British and Canadian drive for the Seine while the US forces protected the southern flank, with the dividing line being between Argentan, Ligix and Evreux. SHAEF's understanding was at odds with the plan that 21st Army Group had developed, which placed the main breakthrough effort in the hands of the US forces, both in terms of a drive south to Avranches and a turn and advance to the east. Different headquarters could clearly interpret the same plans in different ways.

SHAEF would only consider Lucky Strike if German resistance began to lose co-ordination and drive, units were short of equipment, were in a lower state of training and if there were delays in moving up reserves. It would also aid Lucky Strike if the Germans attempted to fight a defensive action in the Normand bridgehead, which would give the Allies with the opportunity to exploit their success rapidly and turn retreat into rout. The SHAEF planners saw considerable logistical difficulties with 21st Army Group's plans. They questioned when a major crossing of the Seine could take place, how US forces would be maintained over the Seine, the extent to which airborne and armoured forces could be used to prevent a German withdrawal to the south-east and the extent to which US forces could exploit south-east of Paris.

At a planning meeting chaired by De Guingand on 22 June the Major General Administration, Miles Graham, envisaged that 21st Army Group would retain operational control, but that First US Army Group would support the US First and Third Armies administratively. He also thought that the possession of Brittany and Quiberon Bay would be essential.[6]

On 26 June Major General Drummond-Inglis, the Chief Engineer at 21st Army Group, shared an Engineer Appreciation for Lucky Strike. For Lucky Strike bridging material would need to be brought up to the Seine during the period between D+40 and D+55. This would mean a reduction in the number of routes that could be bridged unless additional bridging materials could be made available, and the amount of bridging material required in the US sector would depend on how wide the flanking movement was. Heading towards Chartres would avoid serious water obstacles but would cross the bocage country, and the tributaries of the Loire, Mayenne, Sarthe and Orne were wider than many English rivers.[7]

Rapid progress between the beachhead area and the Seine would also make airfield sites available in a favourable area west of the Seine and a prompt decision would be needed regarding whether the air force build-up would be accelerated to take advantage of this. If the air forces were prepared to accept untracked airstrips and a lower standard of smoothness it would be possible to build airfields quickly with little more than a reconnaissance and marking out.

In the US sector there were ample roads leading towards the Seine but bottlenecks at Coutances, Torigny-sur-Vire and Vire, and there was a lack of suitable roads in the British sector. Therefore any British advance as part of Lucky Strike would need to be carefully planned as a move south from Caen would go against the grain of the main roads radiating from Caen and Bayeux which also converged at Villers-Bocage and Aunay. Caen itself would be a serious bottleneck. Much would depend on whether the Germans carried out demolitions on river crossings – it was thought that crossings at Le Havre would be demolished as well as at Dives, Touques and Risle. It was also thought that crossings of the Orne would be demolished.

Lucky Strike would see an exploitation to the north-east and south-east which could not be carried out with any less than four bridges. Bridging materials for three Class 40 and one Class 70 bridge would be required by D+40. The appreciation suggested that work was needed to calculate the number and type of river crossings required, changes to the airfield construction programme, an examination of routes east from Normandy to the Seine and the coordinating of routes and lines of communication between the Allied armies.

On 27 June Montgomery sent a report to Eisenhower and Bradley on Lucky Strike, describing the operation as a course of action for developing Overlord. The paper included alternative plans for operations against stronger enemy resistance than had been expected. The general intention was to exploit enemy weakness by driving to the east as the Germans were at the time of writing engaged in a decisive battle around the beachhead. As intelligence suggested that they were running low on reserves and were being forced to put Panzer divisions into the defensive line rather than keeping them in reserve for a counter-attack, the report proposed that there was an opportunity to exploit this situation and deal the Germans a decisive defeat.[8] The bridges between Paris and the sea had been blown, hence the gap between Paris and Orleans was the only clear route for the German forces in Normandy to withdraw east through. Therefore a bold operation might trap most German units west of the Seine and potentially shorten the war.

First the German forces in Normandy would have to be dealt a heavy defeat to secure the beachhead and to force them to withdraw towards Germany, before the second phase involving a swift drive towards the east. This pursuit could develop in two ways. The first foresaw the Germans having strong forces in the area around Laval, Le Mans and Chartres but the overall situation would have deteriorated. In this scenario the Allies would advance north of Paris with the First Canadian Army, Second British Army and part of the First US Army, with the balance holding the southern flank and trapping the German forces against the Seine. The second option was similar but with the

Germans having no or few forces around Laval, Le Mans and Chartres. In this scenario the Allies would exploit to the south, securing Rennes and Laval before a wide sweep with armoured forces to block the gap between Paris and Orleans. The report predicted that the second option would lead to the greatest destruction of German forces, as a wider encirclement would trap a larger number of units and troops. The third phase once the Allies had destroyed a considerable proportion of the German forces would involve crossing the Seine and clearing the Brittany ports to enable reinforcements to disembark directly from the US. The fourth and final phase would be a continued pursuit of the German forces through the Paris-Orleans Gap.

Several key points emerge from the 21st Army Group briefing paper. At this stage no role was envisaged for airborne forces due to the relatively high-level nature of the strategy being discussed. It is also noticeable that Patton's Third Army is not mentioned at all and that the primary role in the offensive is assigned to the British and Canadian forces. The report also predicted, accurately, that the bocage terrain in Normandy would make it difficult to carry out ambitious armoured offensives.

Meanwhile the SHAEF plans staff had examined options for Lucky Strike alongside plans for Beneficiary and Hands Up. A first draft of their conclusions was completed on 27 June and was discussed at a meeting at SHAEF on 30 June 1944.[9] The SHAEF planners estimated that the Germans would probably fall back to the Seine if defeated in Normandy and that the destruction of the bridges over the river would force them to fall back towards Paris. The Germans were thought to be likely to defend the Seine and to hold Paris strongly. Therefore it was imperative to keep up the pressure on the Germans to prevent them escaping south of the French capital.

In contrast to the report filed on 20 June SHAEF now reported that 'Lucky Strike is in accord with general concept provided capture of Brittany ports is not delayed'. However, it was clarified that logistical demands would force a pause to regroup before the final attack. Time spent regrouping would delay the exploitation and would therefore be kept to a minimum – 15 days was suggested. Lucky Strike would also require all forces other than those engaged in the exploitation to be kept on minimum maintenance – in other words, units not pursuing the Germans would effectively be grounded. SHAEF also suggested that with the air support available airborne troops could prevent the Germans escaping to Paris while 21st Army Group advanced to the Seine. This was the first mention of a possible airborne operation as part of Lucky Strike.

SHAEF also posed some cautionary notes. As of D+20 the forces ashore in France were 30 per cent down on their planned levels of motor transport. The US advance would require the maximum available motor transport, which might include diverting some transport from the British forces. SHAEF also proposed moving supplies by air, although it would be difficult to provide advanced airfields behind the Allied forces.

The pursuit after Lucky Strike would have to be limited in scope due to the logistical situation. SHAEF therefore proposed that US forces would provide flank protection while the British and Canadians advanced to the Somme before attempting to open Le Havre. It is intriguing, especially given post-war debates among historians regarding the roles and performance of US and British formations in Normandy, that in late June SHAEF was advocating for 21st Army Group to make the main advance to the Seine and for the US force to play a supporting role.

A second SHAEF analysis of Lucky Strike, also published on 27 June, was titled 'Appreciation of possible development of operations'.[10] This report outlined possible courses of action for developing Operation Overlord and their implications, with Lucky Strike defined as the general code name for a major exploitation drive to the east.

The Germans' reactions to the Allied landings altered the Allies' estimation of their capabilities compared to their planning before D-Day. Their determination to hold the line in the beachhead area presented an opportunity to trap German forces in Normandy as the bridges over the Seine between the Channel coast and Paris had been blown. The only open route east from Normandy would therefore be the Paris-Orleans gap.

The analysis broke Lucky Strike into four phases, in contrast to 21st Army Group's concept of three. Phase one would begin with inflicting a severe defeat on the Germans in the beachhead and bocage area to establish a firm base and deplete the enemy ability to resist, particularly degrading their mobility. Interestingly this was similar to Montgomery's strategy for Overlord of drawing the German mobile formations onto the British front to wear them down. The second phase would be an advance to the east. This could either consist of a British and Canadian drive straight for the Seine with the US First Army firm to south, or the establishment of a firm base south of Rennes and Laval and then a drive east, simultaneous to a wide sweep with armoured forces along the north bank of the Loire near to Paris to block the Paris-Orleans Gap. Having reached the Seine phase three would see the Allies forcing a crossing over the River with 'the least possible delay' and capturing the Seine ports. The final phase would continue the pursuit of the enemy forces through the Paris-Orleans Gap and immediately north of Paris.

By late June experience in Normandy had shown that the bocage terrain was unsuitable for large-scale armoured operations, and that the hedgerows offered the Germans limitless opportunities for staging delaying actions. Therefore SHAEF accepted that the object prior to launching Lucky Strike would be to drive the enemy out of as much of the bocage as possible prior to the drive east, so that the mobility of Allied forces could be fully exploited. This suggests that well before the US breakout and the establishment of the Falaise Pocket the planning staff at SHAEF understood the background to Montgomery's strategy.

SHAEF envisaged two alternative plans for the drive east. Plan A would take place without an armoured force or a wide envelopment and would be made by First Canadian Army on the left and Second British Army on right. To trap as many Germany forces against the Seine as possible the advance would have to proceed at speed with maximum armoured forces. Plan A was proposed chiefly as the terrain between the Orne and the Seine was relatively open and fair tank country, whereas there were considerable areas of bocage further west in the US sector.

Plan B would involve a wider envelopment, using a strong armoured force to push as rapidly as possible from Laval on an axis connecting La Flèche, Vendome and Châteaudun to an area south-west of Paris, from where it could block the German withdrawal through the Paris-Orleans Gap. First the US forces would drive a firm base south towards Rennes and concentrate an armoured corps at Laval. The speed of advance required by Plan B would call on the use of air resupply. A drive to the Seine would then take place followed by the capture of Rouen, Le Havre and Dieppe.

The Allies' original concept for forcing a crossing over the Seine was code-named Axehead. Studied well before D-Day, Axehead was envisaged as being a deliberate advance to the Seine followed by a three week interval to allow for the dumping of bridging stores. It was expected that the crossing would be strongly opposed. The German strategy in Normandy had clearly changed perceptions, and under the conditions that would make Lucky Strike possible opposition would almost certainly be lighter. Therefore it would be undesirable to give the enemy a chance to catch breath during a pause on the Seine, and a halt for administrative reasons would take place after a crossing was made. The SHAEF report expected that a large part of the German forces would withdraw through the Paris area. As there were no bridges remaining north of Paris the Germans would be forced towards the French capital, and therefore SHAEF felt that Second British Army should be prepared to envelope Paris from the north to close off this avenue of escape.

In conclusion the SHAEF report stated that the possible development of operations depended primarily on how weakened the German forces were after the beachhead battle in Normandy. SHAEF's planners however expected that the Germans would prevent a complete rout and would conduct an orderly retreat. Although they did not say so, the SHAEF planners implied that Lucky Strike was unlikely to be feasible.

The SHAEF planners felt that many aspects of Lucky Strike needed to be examined including the conditions required to launch the operation, the administrative limitations and the possibility of maintaining the advance by air supply. The planners also questioned whether bridging equipment and amphibious vehicles could be made available by D+50, the extent to which Special Forces and the French Resistance could assist, the policy on the tactical and strategic use of air forces and the use of deception. Finally SHAEF raised the question of how best to use airborne forces during Lucky Strike.

On 27 June Colonel Whipple, the Chief of Logistics Plans at SHAEF G4, circulated an unofficial draft administrative appreciation for Lucky Strike to Brigadier Moses, 21st Army Group's Deputy Major General Administration, and Brigadier Rimer of the Q staff at 21st Army Group Main Headquarters. SHAEF G4 Movements & Transportation Branch had re-examined the possibility of moving US reserves up to support Operation Lucky Strike. As the rate of advance had been slower, reserves arriving in Normandy were being held in port areas. The accumulation of stores would not be able to start until the Vire area had been reached. At this point it would require thirty-eight Truck Companies to move 11,400 tons of stores the 40 miles daily from the Normandy ports to Vire. If Alençon was captured by D+40 the Allies would then require the equivalent of nineteen Truck Companies to move reserves on from Vire to Alençon. Railway movements would be able to transport the equivalent of ten Truck Companies – it would be too soon to establish a railhead at Avranches, but the railways would be able to assist moving supplies forward from Cherbourg. By D+40 it was hoped that the Truck Companies would be able to move 3,550 tons a day forward from Vire to Alençon.[11]

At a planning meeting held by 21st Army Group on 28 June a group was ordered to examine possible tasks for airborne forces to assist in capturing crossings over the Seine. Browning's chief of staff, Brigadier

Gordon Walch, took part in this and other syndicates connected with the planning of Lucky Strike.[12]

The question of Special Forces involvement in Lucky Strike arose on 29 June at a meeting at Special Forces Headquarters. The meeting, attended by 21st Army Group G(Plans), HQ Airborne Troops, Special Forces Headquarters and 12th Special Forces Detachment, discussed a paper outlining what support might be possible. The paper outlined that the Resistance was a long-term and strategic weapon and that its effects could be prejudiced by concentrating it too much on a short-term operation. Security considerations dictated that no indications of the wider operations should be given to Special Forces or SAS troops – even officers – until the last moment. It was suggested that Resistance groups in the area could be stiffened with SAS troops and Jedburgh units by adding to their communication channels. They would also be able to pass on any last-minute changes of orders related to a broader operation.[13] It is odd how Special Forces appear to flit in and out of airborne planning in 1944.

Supplying equipment to Resistance groups was thought to be a particular problem, particularly if their involvement in a specific operation would call for different weapons for example, as Resistance groups were only supplied with weapons that they required immediately. There were a limited number of aircraft available for resupplying them and the summer nights were short, giving less time for clandestine dropping. German flak and fighters also limited potential dropping areas. The Resistance in France was being developed with the object of giving maximum support and it was thought that this would be on the general lines required for supporting Lucky Strike. In the north-east of France, the area relevant to Lucky Strike, the aim was to build up the Resistance with the intention of stepping up activities at the vital time to impede German reinforcements moving to the east of the Seine. It was proving difficult to develop this plan, however, due to German fighter and flak defences. In the Orleans Gap specifically resistance was being organised and supplied to achieve maximum sabotage of enemy communications. It was thought that these resistance groups could be switched to more overt action to support Lucky Strike either by covering the flanks of the armoured force south-west of Paris or assisting the lines of communications to move rapidly. To do this however, the resistance groups would need stiffening with Allied Special Forces. Although all resistance groups in France were classified as the French Forces of the Interior (FFI) and were under the command of General Koenig, he was in turn under the command of SHAEF. The relationships between French Resistance groups, and their relationships with the De Gaulle government in Britain and the Allied command, were less than straightforward.

On 30 June the SAS section at HQ Airborne Troops proposed to 21st Army Group to send SAS reconnaissance and base parties to the area of Argentan and Le Mans with an eye on preparing for Lucky Strike. There were concerns however that the French staff at Special Forces Headquarters might object as it would conflict with their plans for the Resistance groups in the field. Experience had shown that it was essential to get bases established before operations commenced.[14]

21st Army Group G(Plans) issued a 'Tentative Tactical Outline Plan' for Lucky Strike on 30 June 1944. The plan was to assist in the destruction of German forces west of the Seine by the rapid movement of an armoured force into the area between Paris and Orleans to prevent the enemy using that route of escape from the Normandy battlefield. Lucky Strike would not take place until German forces had retreated from Brittany and there were no enemy mobile forces south of the Loire. It was felt that the Germans may well reinforce their right flank to prevent the Allies from reaching the Seine north of Paris, and thus may leave their left flank weakened and vulnerable to an armoured attack. No mention was made of airborne forces, even though their involvement had been suggested by SHAEF.[15]

Also on 30 June Richardson sent the Tentative Tactical Outline Plan for the armoured flanking movement in Lucky Strike Plan B to 21st Army Group's American planners. The plan suggested that the armoured flanking movement could only take place if there were no significant German units between the Loire and the area south of Laval, Le Mans and Chartres. Brittany would also have to have been evacuated by all German mobile forces so that no threat would exist in Normandy. The author of the plan accepted that this might be restrictive, but that it might become possible if the Germans had become weakened by fighting in the bocage.[16] The author also accepted that the plan was optimistic in ambition and potential results. The plan suggested that the armoured movement could be achieved in several ways, but that the less-daring alternatives would be less likely to succeed in bottling German forces against the Seine. These options ranged from a plan to reinforce First US Army's advance with an armoured corps spearhead, to a plan to move an armoured corps in a semi-independent mission along the southern fringe of the bocage to Chartres. It was thought that the latter plan would be difficult to support logistically.

On passing Avranches US VIII Corps would move into Brittany to capture St Malo, but the main US forces would move south and south-east to the Loire until Rennes and Laval were captured. If, however, conditions were not suitable for executing Lucky Strike then US forces would instead capture Quiberon Bay first. If the conditions were suitable for the armoured flanking movement to take place the Allied forces would need to be reorganised, to establish an armoured corps around Laval. This would also require the stockpiling of fuel and ammunition. The corps would consist of two armoured divisions each reinforced by a Tank Destroyer Battalion and an infantry division to secure the lines of communications. The corps would also have engineer companies to provide bridging. The plan would see the armoured divisions advancing abreast with the motorized infantry division following closely behind as rapidly as possible until Châteaudun and Blois were reached, when a pause would take place for two or three days to restock. This would also permit resupply via airstrips or airdrops. The corps was expected to hold its final objective for a maximum of five days and if on the fourth day it appeared unlikely that contact could be made it would withdraw to the west. Once the objective was reached the corps would go onto the defensive. It was hoped that the French Resistance would assist the advance by demolishing bridges and culverts and acting as outposts and recce parties.

While the armoured corps was advancing to the Paris-Orleans Gap the rest of the US First Army would curtail its advance if the logistical situation was challenging. The minimum advance would be of one corps advancing with a second corps around Alençon, moving south-east to maintain the lines of communications towards Châteaudun. The leading corps of First Army would have the job of linking up with the armoured corps within five days. Only one corps would advance into Brittany to clear the peninsula with the objective of securing Quiberon Bay and Brest.

It was thought that the start line for Lucky Strike would not be reached until the end of July when it was likely that the US XV Corps – consisting of 5th, 8th and 35th Infantry Divisions and 4th Armoured Division – would be fully landed in Normandy and some of XX Corps – 6th and 7th Armoured Divisions and possibly 28th Infantry Division and 5th French Armoured Division – might be available. Some of the latter armoured formations might have to be moved across the Channel early to create an armoured corps.

The major limitation on the plan would be logistics. The maintenance situation would have to be based on the absolute minimum required to safely carry out the operation, but it was assumed that if the operation was successful it would lead to the annihilation of a significant part of the German armed forces west of the Seine.

A conference was held at 21st Army Group Main HQ on 2 July to discuss the river crossing that would be required as part of Lucky Strike. A paper circulated by 21st Army Group's plans section on 30 June prior to the meeting assessed that the Germans were now likely to continue to resist most strongly go prevent the Allies from reaching the Seine. If the deception measures of Operation Fortitude held and the Germans retained forces in the Pas de Calais it was thought that Lucky Strike would be more likely to take advantage of this situation. The logistical situation would require a pause on the west bank, which would be preferable to stopping on the far bank. An immediate crossing was desirable to allow as many divisions to cross the river as possible. It would be necessary to study availability of usefulness of the equipment and tactics available – particularly Duplex Drive (DD) tanks, Landing Vehicles Tracked (LVT), Canal Defence Lights – tanks fitted with searchlights – and airborne formations and bombing on the far bank.[17]

The SHAEF planning staff – Captain P.N. Walter of ANXF, Brigadier-General K. Mclean of SHAEF G3 and Group Captain T.P. Cleave of AEAF – published their feedback on 3 July after they had examined Lucky Strike from a logistical point of view. The operation was defined as an 'exploitation of the deterioration' of the enemy capability to resist. It would incorporate a drive from the Neptune bridgehead in Normandy towards Seine with maximum forces, followed by a crossing of the Seine and the capture of the Seine ports.[18]

21st Army Group's concept for Lucky Strike was that the British and Canadian Armies should drive for the Seine whilst the US forces acted in support and cleared Brittany. The SHAEF staff felt that 21st Army Group's planning was based on a hypothesis that the enemy would not be stubborn or co-ordinated. This is, however, understandable as Lucky Strike was designed to turn a retreat into a rout.

Until early July the Allies had only considered that operations could take place east of Seine only after Brittany had been secured. The Germans were expected to defend the line of the Seine strongly and were equally likely to attempt to hold Paris firmly. All non-static divisions in Brittany were likely to be sucked into the fighting in Normandy and it was hoped that the French Resistance would be able to capture much of Brittany unaided.

The report concluded that there would be little opposition to an advance into Brittany and that destroying the German army west of the Seine would involve an advance on wide front to prevent the Germans escaping south of Paris. The importance of the Brittany ports was also stressed, namely that the capture of the Seine ports would not compensate for a lack of ports in Brittany. It was estimated that a failure to secure the Brittany ports would reduce the Allied ability to maintain forces by eight divisions, a figure that was 'clearly not acceptable'.

On 3 July Brigadier General Moses, the Deputy Major General Administration at 21st Army Group, shared an estimate of the administrative situation for Lucky Strike based on the Tactical Outline Plan. The appreciation assumed that the Allies would be able to build up enough supplies by 17 July to support all operations but that due to the adverse weather experienced in June the build-up of supplies was behind by 110,000 tons. The delay in capturing Cherbourg had been overcome by developing increased landing capacity over the Normandy beaches but despite this there were critical shortages of 60mm and 80mm mortar ammunition, signal equipment and 4.2in mortar parts. The build-up of US troops was eight days behind schedule, and while the build-up of divisions was slightly ahead there was a deficit of service troops.[19]

The appreciation found that the road network was adequate and that COMZ should move forward as much materiel as possible to avoid delays in launching the operation, by building up reserves in the First Army area while the lines of communications from the beaches were short. The railway network would be hampered by the 12-day delay in capturing Cherbourg. There was sufficient airlift available for a daily resupply of the armoured corps from the UK, including ammunition. Spare parts for vehicles would need to be moved by land and engine and track replacements would have to be stockpiled to enable them to be available. Motor Transport would be critical to make ground supply possible and it was thought that Truck Companies could be moved forward in the build-up plan.

On 3 July G.W. Richards, the Major General Royal Armoured Corps at 21st Army Group, confirmed that 191 Sherman DD tanks were available to 21st Army Group. He thought that only one regiment should cross the Seine in support of the river crossing, but if the disadvantages of a larger force were accepted – regrouping of units, withdrawal for training and movement up to the Seine – all available DD tanks could be used up to brigade strength. However this would leave no DD tanks available for other operations.[20]

Planning for Lucky Strike within AEAF seems to have proceeded slowly. After the planning conference at 21st Army Group on 28 June it was not until 4 July that a study table was distributed. The syndicate delegated to examine possible airborne involvement in Lucky Strike was chaired by Brigadier Walch as Browning's Brigadier General Staff, and included Colonel Bonesteel – a US Army Officer from 21st Army Group G(Plans) – Brigadier Bill Williams – Montgomery's Head of Intelligence – Group Captain McIntyre and Colonel Bagby from AEAF. The syndicate was requested to 'examine possible tasks for airborne troops to assist in the crossing of the Seine and the armoured move in Plan B, the formations likely to be available and relative priorities of tasks'.[21]

On the same day a meeting was held at HQ Airborne Troops to consider the use of airborne formations during Operation Lucky Strike.[22] HQ Airborne Troops considered that the best use of airborne formations would be in conjunction with the move of an armoured force as envisaged in Plan B would be to drop them in the final concentration area of the armoured formation south-west of Paris. Exactly when to drop the airborne forces was discussed at length and two scenarios were considered. Case A, if it were likely that the armoured formation would be short of petrol, would drop the airborne force 48 hours before the estimated time of arrival of the armoured force to secure fuel. Case B, if the supply situation were more secure, would see the airborne force dropped after the armour had arrived to hold a firm base from which it could then operate.

The meeting concluded that it would be impossible to decide the best course of action until the enemy's reactions and positions were known more accurately. The meeting was reminded that around 400 C-47s would have to go to the Mediterranean to take part in Anvil and that therefore until they remained only enough transport aircraft would be available to carry just over one division. The situation would be even more critical if the armoured forces had to be supplied by air, leaving no margin for aircraft losses. The seaborne tail of the airborne division would have to go overland, which would need to be carefully planned to prevent the vehicles being caught up in traffic jams with the armoured forces. HQ Airborne Troops reported that they were anxious to prioritise the numerous operations which they were planning. As of 4 July these included Beneficiary, Hands Up, Lucky Strike B, Axehead and two other unnamed operations in conjunction with the crossing of the Seine. It is hard to escape the conclusion that the number of operations they were being asked to plan for was far more than what an under-establishment and inexperienced corps headquarters could cope with.

On 4 July Browning forwarded a Staff Study of 'possible task for Airborne Troops to assist the armoured move in Plan B'. The Study defined the objectives of the airborne forces as follows:

To assist the armoured force to carry out its task by:
a) Establishing a firm base for the armoured force prior to its arrival.
b) Cutting lateral routes through or in the vicinity of this base. This will have the effect of disorganising enemy movement, and making it easier prey for the armoured force.
c) Repairing an airfield, or constructing strips within the base so that supplies, ammunition and POL can be flown in, and casualties flown out, immediately the armoured force arrives.
d) Holding the firm base when the armour strikes out from it, thus permitting the Motorised Infantry Division to accompany the armour on its sorties.

When the armoured force arrived it would have to be prepared to take 'immediate action' to assist the airborne force by neutralising or destroying enemy flak and field artillery which could otherwise hinder the landing of supply aircraft.

The airborne order of battle would be HQ Airborne Troops, 1st Airborne Division, US 504th Parachute Infantry Regimental Combat Team, 1st Polish Parachute Brigade, 2nd Light Anti-Aircraft Battery, 878th US Airborne Aviation Engineer Battalion and some SAS Troops. It was thought that the airborne divisions that had landed in Normandy – 6th British Airborne Division and the 101st and 82nd US Airborne Divisions – could also be available if they were withdrawn from action immediately and if the operation did not take place before about 1 September. The 17th US Airborne Division might also have been available if it arrived in Britain and was equipped in time.

The size of the airborne force that could be employed would be limited by the airlift that was available. It was probable that 412 aircraft of IX Troop Carrier Command would leave for the Mediterranean Theatre in early August, severely reducing the airlift available. The combined resources of 38 Group, 46 Group and the remaining aircraft of IX Troop Carrier Command would be able to lift the equivalent of one airborne division, two parachute brigades and the airfield construction and maintenance units in two lifts.

Browning stressed that the large-scale resupply of armoured forces before the airborne operation took place would be 'most undesirable' as it would reduce aircraft serviceability and hence availability to a dangerously low level. Browning advised that all air resupply to the armour should cease at least 48 hours before the airborne operation is launched, to allow aircraft to be checked, serviced and marshalled. He felt that the airborne forces should not be launched until the time of arrival of the armoured force in the base area could be forecast with certainty, to reduce the risk of the airborne forces being isolated. It was felt that this forecast would not be possible until 30 hours – at the most – before it was due to arrive.

It was desirable that the airborne force should land 24 hours ahead of the armoured force to organise and prepare airstrips. Browning advised that the airborne force should not land any more than 24 hours before the armoured force, because of the difficulty in predicting the arrival of the armour and because it was likely that the Germans would be able to move up large mobile forces to oppose the airborne landing. Already Browning was advising quite different timescales to those he would give for other operations. It would take approximately three hours to land the airborne force, after a three-hour flight from England. After a six-hour turnaround time in England, the first supply aircraft might be expected to arrive in the area 12 hours after the initial airborne landing.

Once the airborne force had landed two airstrips would be constructed, each 1,200 yards long with dispersal areas for twenty aircraft and the ability to receive twenty aircraft per hour. Assuming no enemy interference the overall tonnage build-up would be approximately 100 tons per hour. Each strip would require one Airfield Control Detachment of approximately sixty air force personnel and six jeeps. Browning suggested that these detachments should move up with the armoured force to prioritise air lift for the airborne force, but they would also – paradoxically – need to be in operation before the armoured force arrived. In addition an Airborne Forward Delivery Airfield Group (AFDAG) would be required for handling stores and casualties as they arrived. The AFDAG did not actually exist yet, but Browning predicted that it might consist of up to 2,000 personnel and 200 jeeps.

The area between Paris and Orleans was thought to contain many suitable areas for landing and dropping zones. It was suggested that it would be possible to land airborne forces wherever the ground forces felt would be the most suitable location to support them in their task. Browning presumed that the armoured forces would want to establish itself somewhere in the area around Étampes and Rambouillet. From there it would be situated in suitable country for infantry defence and at the same time be able to strike north-west, west or southwards across what was thought to be very suitable tank country south of the line Dreux, Etampes and Nemours. Browning suggested that the area around Dourdan would be the most suitable area for the establishment of a firm base by the airborne force. Dourdan had good air landmarks including the forests of St Arnoult and L'Ouvre, a railway line, and six converging roads. It had good landing and dropping zones to the north-east, south-east and south-west beyond the Forest de L'Ouvre. The two forests, railway line and a river would provide good natural defences against tanks and the six radiating roads would provide a good road network for the armoured forces to exploit.

It was thought that the air forces would select a route that would cross the Channel and then take the transport aircraft west of Caen. Browning stated that flights could be made both by day and night, but that it would 'highly desirable' that the operation should take place within the period of six days either side of full moon.

Browning concluded that the proposed operation was feasible and that it would 'greatly assist' the armoured force. He proposed that the first lift would consist of HQ Airborne Troops, 1st Airborne Division, 504th Regimental Combat Team, and the 1st Polish Parachute Brigade Group. The second lift would land the 2nd Light Anti-Aircraft Battery, the AFDAG and 878th Airborne Aviation Engineer Battalion. It is unclear why Browning would propose that his corps headquarters would land in the first lift, given the need to get infantry on the ground quickly with a limited airlift limited airlift, but this showed the start of a pattern.

Airborne formations would need to be concentrated and ready five days before D-Day. Once the armoured force was confident that it would reach the airborne operation area within 72 hours it was to forecast as such. All air supply to the armoured force would then cease, so that that the air forces could reconfigure the aircraft for airborne operations. Once the armoured force predicted that it would reach the area within 30 hours the first airborne lift would take off three hours later.

21st Army Group's Administrative Appreciation for Lucky Strike was circulated on 4 July.[23] In terms of logistics it was felt that the expected supply situation would be adequate if Phase II started before D+65. Priority of movement would need to be given to Truck Companies and medical units and it was thought that it might be necessary to pool motor transport resources and full advantage would need to be taken of the laying forward of fuel pipelines. The US advance would require the use of the road Flers-Argentan-Laigle. It was stressed that the Brittany ports would need to be captured and brought into operation to support any further advance beyond Phase II and the US forces would also need to use the railways earmarked for the British from Bayeux to Argentan.

The SHAEF study only considered Plan B for Phase II. Why is not clear, but this does suggest a preference for this option. SHAEF assessed that supplies would be adequate to support the operation and that motor transport would be sufficient for ground supply. It was also suggested that airlift would be required to supply the armoured force for five days from an airfield in France to a forward airstrip up with the advance. SHAEF also suggested that a pause would need to take place between reaching the Phase I line and the Phase II objective to allow for regrouping.

Neither SHAEF nor FUSAG – as 12th Army Group was then still called – had indicated a firm target date for the capture of the Phase II line. SHAEF considered that for Lucky Strike to succeed the forces advancing to the Orleans gap would need to have priority for supplies and that all other forces would therefore need to be maintained on a reduced scale. No road transport would be spared to support forces advancing into Brittany, although the early capture of the Brittany ports would still be important – capturing St Malo would release some transport as the corps in Brittany would then have much shorter lines of communications.

Meanwhile US Army officers attached to 21st Army Group were advocating that Lucky Strike should not be at the expense of the Brittany ports, and suggested Quiberon Bay as an important objective. On 4 July Moses, the Deputy Major General Administration, wrote to Colonel Bonesteel at G(Plans) arguing that not capturing the Brittany ports would affect the US build-up, and that sacrificing Brittany would also mean a delay in the US build-up and the advance west of the Seine:

> Any delay beyond about D plus 50 in the capture of QB, and capture of the Brest peninsula immediately thereafter, will result in the delay of the US build-up. It appears that from now on we must continually keep the administrative situation in mind, and as we approach the Phase I line the desired future operations should be considered in conjunction with thoughts on implementing Lucky Strike . . . We should not permit planning for Lucky Strike to interfere with a reasonably rapid capture of QB and other Brittany ports.[24]

On 4 July Browning submitted 'Operation Lucky Strike: Appreciation on SAS/SF Support' to 21st Army Group G(Plans). He gave the objectives as assisting the movement of the American armoured force and airborne force in Lucky Strike, and assisting the crossing of the Seine.

The paper identified that enemy lines of communications troops were currently concentrated in the areas Paris-Mantes-Evreux-Lisieux and Orleans-Chartres-Alençon. Browning argued that Resistance groups had had 'considerable success' around L'Aigle-Alençon-Lisieux, even infiltrating through enemy lines. SAS groups who were part of Operation Cain around Orleans had also been operating for over 14 days in the area north of Orleans. The Maquis were known to be active around Rambouillet, south-west of Versailles. In total there were 250 to 300 SAS Troops in the area and approximately 7,500 to 10,000 armed Maquis.[25]

Browning's paper identified the enemy lines of communications through the Paris-Orleans Gap as being very vulnerable as supplies and reinforcements would have to use the area passing east-west and north-south to the front. This was thought to be particularly likely as the deception of Operation Fortitude diminished and troops in the Pas de Calais might be routed via Paris. The area around Chartres, Orleans, Tours and Le Mans was open country and unsuitable for overt action by Maquis or SAS and most of the few woods were already occupied by enemy supply dumps. Browning also emphasised that the plan should not rely on the support that could be given by the Resistance or the SAS, rather that they could make an important contribution.

HQ Airborne Forces were already planning several operations for the SAS, Jedburgh parties and Resistance groups in Northern France. These included Operation Gain around Orleans, Operation Bulbasket in Poitiers, Operation Houndsworth in Burgundy, Operation Hardy near Dijon and Operation Hart north of Le Mans. Several proposals were explored for supporting Lucky Strike. One or two roadwatching parties could be landed along the proposed American advance to report on enemy activity. A Base Party could be established in the Dourdan area with a small number of SAS, Resistance and Jedburgh teams to provide reception, guides and information on enemy movements for the US armoured and airborne forces. Small parties could be landed to attack German lines of communications along the project route of advance with demolition stores and anti-tank mines. Jedburgh troops could be landed to organise French civilians and organise the repair and guarding of airfields, bridges and other installations. Local pioneer units could be formed on the spot and small parties might also be able to capture petrol and stores dumps and guard prisoners.

The allocation of aircraft for Operation Anvil in Southern France severely curtailed the ability of the Allies to plan large-scale airborne operations in north-west Europe. On 8 July Richardson signalled De Guingand and Browning to inform them that 412 aircraft had been allocated for Anvil, and therefore could not be included for planning purposes. The limiting factor with IX Troop Carrier Command was aircrew, however, as only 543 aircrews were available. HQ Airborne Troops continued to request information as to when the Anvil aircraft would return, stressing that it was essential to continue planning Lucky Strike. On 10 July Jock Whiteley at SHAEF informed HQ Airborne Troops that the Anvil aircraft were likely to return in 'dribs and drabs' from D+10 onwards and therefore were not likely to be operational for some time.

21st Army Group were also considering the crossing of the Seine as part of Lucky Strike. A letter dated 11 July from G(Plans) suggests that the operation would include five river crossings, and the Chief Engineer was asked to indicate suitable crossing locations. He suggested that with the available bridging two infantry divisions would take six days to cross while a corps of two infantry divisions and one armoured division – Canadian II Corps was mentioned – might take over 12 days. If the crossing was unopposed it might take up to 10 days to build up engineering stores and carry out reconnaissance. The most favourable crossing points were identified as Mézières, Rosny, Courcelles and Louviers. It was suggested that XXX Corps would cross at Mézières, VIII Corps at Rosny, XII Corps at Courcelles and I Corps at Louviers. II Canadian Corps, meanwhile, would cross as part of its existing plans for Operation Axehead.[26]

Planning for Lucky Strike also included Special Forces involvement. The plan for Operation Nelson was submitted by Browning to Richardson on 19 July. Nelson would see a Squadron of SAS troops with jeeps dropped by glider in ten to twenty scattered parties at the outset of Lucky Strike ahead of the American armoured advance to the Paris-Orleans Gap, with the object of harassing the enemy and gathering information. Browning saw them performing a similar role to the one that the SAS had played in North Africa, Italy and in Brittany and Normandy around the time of D-Day. The general concept was approved by 21st Army Group on 20 July but was rejected by 12th Army Group on 8 August, who stated that neither they nor the US Third Army wanted the operation to take place.[27] The Americans felt that the party would be too small to influence the situation and that they would be liable to be shot up by the American spearheads. They also felt that the French Resistance would be able to perform the task instead. However, 21st Army Group recommended that the sixty jeeps be provided on the basis that a similar operation might be required later. The possibility of fitting 3in rockets to jeeps, as used by Typhoon fighter bombers, was also discussed within 21st Army Group.

The drop zones for Nelson would be five to 10 miles either side of the enemy lines of communications area, along the route Laval-Le Mans-St Galais-Châteaudun-Dourdan in the north and along the route Laval-La Fleche-Chateau Renault-Blois-Etampes in the south. The parties would be heavily armed, with each Jeep carrying either a Bazooka or a PIAT, three Vickers 'K' guns and a Bren gun in reserve, and operate based on surprise and firepower, withdrawing to hideouts. It was planned that the parties would eventually join up and operate on the flanks of the advancing US armoured advance. Sufficient fuel would be carried to cover 600–700 miles and food and ammunition for three to four days.

Special Operations Executive were asked to comment on the plans and had some objections. Their policy had been to limit resistance activity in north and north-east France and Belgium to clandestine operations against the enemy lines of communications with the objective of maintaining a threat level and tying down guard troops away from the front. This would conflict with the intention to involve the resistance in the area in more active role in military operations. They also felt that there was a lack of suitable resistance groups from north of the Seine as far south as Mulen. There were concerns within SHAEF that there were misconceptions about the effect of SAS troops arriving behind enemy lines. There had been examples of premature risings among the French Resistance resulting in aggressive reactions by the Germans. Therefore SAS troops and Jedburgh teams would be required to control and guide them. The present arrangement only allowed each SAS Regiment to support signals from four bases in the field. Therefore it was suggested that it would be a waste to send a signal set accompanying an SAS party unless it had at least 60 men with it. SHAEF also felt that the ability of uniformed troops to operate behind enemy lines in France after D-Day was being overestimated.

The breakout towards Avranches during Operation Cobra was certainly in line with the first phase of Lucky Strike, but its further conduct once the US forces turned east diverged from the original plan. Although Patton would consider the operations to the south of the Falaise Pocket to be an 'American idea,' he had been briefed by Bradley on plans for Lucky Strike.[28] Montgomery specifically ordered Lucky Strike to be implemented in his directive M516 on 4 August. The Allied strategy was specified by Montgomery as to swing the right flank round towards Paris, and to force the enemy back against the Seine. A strong airborne force would then land in the Chartres area to block the Paris-Orleans Gap.[29] Montgomery ordered Bradley to include the proposed airborne operation in his planning. The campaign in Normandy, however, was dogged by Bradley's desire for independence, Patton's failure to adhere to the agreed strategy and Bradley's inability to order him to do so. Montgomery's directive M516 of 4 August had also ordered 12th Army Group to send one corps into Brittany to clear the peninsula and the rest of Third Army to direct itself towards Laval and Angers.[30]

Lucky Strike was still being considered by Allied headquarters into August, when the major dilemma was the depth of the sweep. Brereton's diary for 5 August records that FAAA was asked to review Lucky Strike B, described by Brereton as 'a wide sweeping movement around the southern flank of the German forces in Normandy'. Parks was sent to SHAEF Forward HQ to clarify the airborne phase of Lucky Strike, which Brereton named as Operation Transfigure, reflecting the connection between the two plans.[31]

Montgomery's next directive, M517, was published on 6 August.[32] He described the Allied intention as 'To destroy the enemy forces in that part of France contained in the following area: The R.Seine from the sea to Paris – thence southwards to Orleans – thence the R.Loire from Orleans westwards to the sea.' Montgomery's intention was to 'swing hard' on the southern flank and in towards Paris, with the Paris-Orleans Gap being closed ahead of the advance. The enemy would be driven up against the Seine, over which all bridges from Paris to the sea had been put out of action. 12th Army Group was ordered to establish a strong 'rear protection' around Rennes, Laval, Angers and Nantes. The Army Group was then to move to the Seine eastwards on a broad front, with its main weight on its southern flank. Montgomery ordered that the right flank should swing rapidly eastwards, and then north-eastwards towards Paris. The plan to drop an airborne force in the Chartres area was again emphasised, with the aim of blocking the escape of the enemy through the gap between Paris and Orleans. Montgomery ordered that the airborne forces would be dropped once 12th Army Group had crossed the general line of Le Mans-Alençon.

Directive M518 was published on 11 August.[33] Montgomery's intentions were unchanged from his previous directive five days before. He re-emphasised that the Allies' priority would be to close the gap behind the German forces so that they could be destroyed in northern France: 'It is definitely beginning to look as if the main battle with the German forces in France is going to be fought between the Seine and the Loire . . . This will suit us very well.'

12th Army Group was ordered to swing its right flank forward from Le Mans up to Alençon, and then towards a general line between Sees and Carroges. Montgomery again stressed that the Allies needed to be ready to implement an airborne operation in the Chartres area if it appeared likely that the Germans might escape from Normandy. 12th Army Group was ordered to continue to plan the airborne operation as referred to in directive M517 and that it might have to be put into action at short notice and therefore had to be 'on very simple lines'. What these 'simple lines' might have meant for the airborne personnel carrying them out is open to speculation.

No detailed planning was carried out for Lucky Strike at Airborne Corps level, below Browning and Walch taking part in planning syndicates. No drop zones were considered or selected, and there is no mention of Lucky Strike in 1st Airborne Division's War Diary.[34] Lucky Strike clearly did not have a profound effect on any personnel in the 1st Airborne Division. The operation does demonstrate, however, that the airborne forces were at the mercy of complex and at times unpredictable policy formulation before their use had even been decided upon.

Although it has been argued by historians that Lucky Strike was devised because of the battles in the beachhead it would be more accurate to describe it as an evolution of the general principles espoused by Montgomery and his staff before D-Day, rather than as a completely new conception.[35] Planning emanating from 21st Army Group before and shortly after D-Day – and accepted by SHAEF – suggests that Montgomery's strategy had always been to break out with the American forces towards Avranches and then complete a wide envelopment to the Seine.[36] If anything, the Lucky Strike concept was a more ambitious and daring proposal than how Allied strategy in Normandy transpired. Lucky Strike would have involved a much wider envelopment, trapping most German forces in Normandy against the Seine, rather than in a much smaller pocket around Falaise. It would also have included an airborne element, which the battles around the Falaise Pocket did not.

SHAEF never seem to have been keen on Lucky Strike, which was initially a 21st Army Group plan from before D-Day, and was, as a wide hook, far removed from a broad-front strategy. It has also been suggested that the SHAEF planners disliked Lucky Strike as potentially jeopardising a methodical move forward.[37]

Might Lucky Strike, if implemented, have delivered results? Certainly, it is interesting to compare the plan for Lucky Strike with what transpired in the Falaise Pocket. Although large numbers of

German forces were destroyed at Falaise it was a small encirclement compared to Lucky Strike and was not really planned in the true sense of the word. There were also debates around where and how to close the gap, with Patton and Bradley reluctant to attempt to close it at all. Lucky Strike, on the other hand, would potentially have created a large pocket from Normandy to the Seine.

OPERATION TRANSFIGURE

While Lucky Strike was a strategic concept that was discussed prior to D-Day, it included relatively little consideration of potential airborne operations. Operation Transfigure was the evolution of the Lucky Strike concept once the Normandy campaign had begun, but unlike Lucky Strike it was very much an airborne operation. Transfigure was, in essence, an evolution of the airborne ideas that had been discussed during the development of Lucky Strike.

2 August

On 2 August Montgomery wrote to his confidante Major General Frank Simpson, the Director of Military Operations at the War Office, to outline his general plan as the Allied armies were advancing out of the Normandy beachhead:

> The broad plan remains unchanged. I shall swing the right flank round, and up towards Paris. And while this is going on I shall try to hold the enemy to his ground in the Caen area. Then I hope to put down a large airborne force, including 52 Div, somewhere in the Chartres area and cut off the enemy escape through the gap between Paris and Orleans. The big idea would be to push the enemy up against the Seine – and get 'a cop.' However these things don't always work out quite as planned!! Although the present operations are absolutely as planned.[1]

3 August

Brigadier David Belchem, the Brigadier General Staff of Operations at 21st Army Group, wrote to HQ Airborne Troops on 3 August stating that 52nd Division was to prepare and train 'with speed' to be capable of landing in an area seized by airborne troops, particularly on airfields or specially-constructed landing strips. It would help to establish a firm base for further operations, securing facilities for air forces to

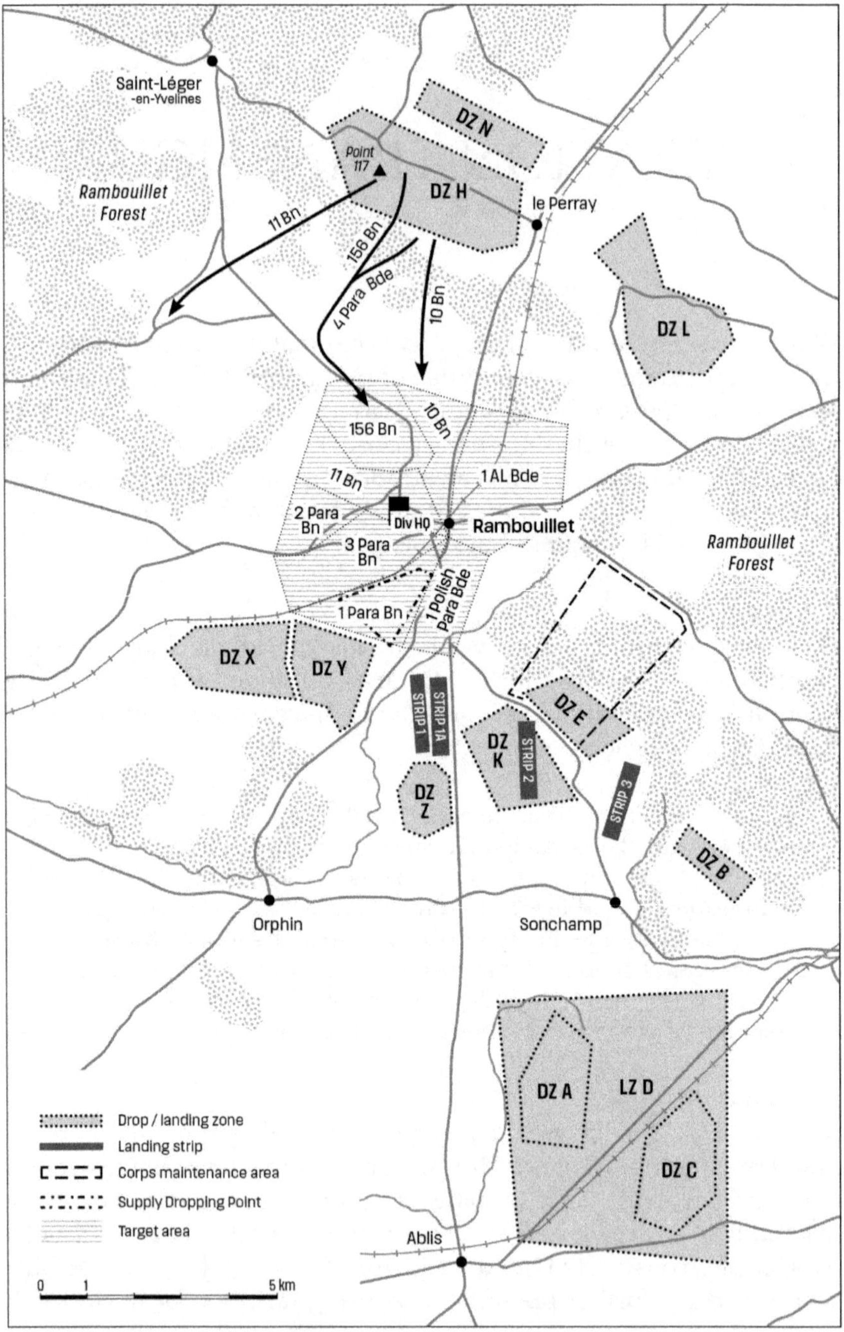

Map 2: Operation Transfigure (Sources: TNA WO 171/494, WO 171/366)

supply by air and form a striking force capable of operating from that firm base, for example to capture a sea or river bridgehead. 21st Army Group emphasised that training would have to be carried out with 'utmost speed' as the division might be required for operations in the 'immediate future'. Staff tables and maintenance requirements would also have to be studied and developed. Arrangements were being made for the division to move to the Buckinghamshire area to be close to its departure airfields.[2]

5 August

Transfigure – distinct from Lucky Strike – seems to have originated from a meeting between Montgomery, Bradley and Leigh Mallory on 5 August.[3] The meeting in an orchard near St-Lô was held to discuss the air supply of ground forces and plans for future airborne operations. The swift advance of US forces towards Brest and the unexpectedly rapid clearing of the Brittany peninsula had made the planning for Operations Hands Up, Swordhilt and Beneficiary redundant. Instead plans were considered for landing airborne troops behind enemy lines in the Chartres area to break up the German front by blocking the gap between Paris and Orleans, making it more difficult for German troops to retreat to the east. It was felt that the operation might be mounted by the middle of August. The AEAF Official History alludes to the difficulty of planning the use of transport aircraft, and particularly the difficulty of compromise between air supply of ground troops on one hand and the deployment of airborne forces on the other.

After the conference Leigh Mallory flew back to Britain to start the air planning, holding a staff conference at his headquarters on 6 August. He outlined the plan that he had discussed with Montgomery and Bradley and was asked by his staff whether there would be sufficient aircraft for the operation due to the diversion of resources to Anvil in the South of France. Leigh Mallory thought that there was adequate lift for one division.

Also on 5 August Brereton recorded in his diary that Montgomery had informed Browning that he wanted First Allied Airborne Army – which had been activated on 1 August – to review Lucky Strike B, which Brereton described as 'a wide sweeping movement around the southern flank of the German forces in Normandy'. His chief of staff Parks was sent to SHAEF Forward Headquarters to clarify the exact status of the airborne phase of the plan, which had been codenamed Transfigure.[4]

6 August

The US Air Force Historical Study suggests that SHAEF and FAAA agreed to Transfigure on 6 August, and that Eisenhower was strongly in favour of the plan, calling it 'the blow most likely to end the war in Europe'.[5] Browning and Walch flew to Normandy to visit Montgomery, and the next day returned to Britain and held a conference with Brereton at FAAA Headquarters at Sunninghill Park.[6]

While in France Browning and Walch left a paper with De Guingand with options for Operation Transfigure. In a nod to the roots of Transfigure Browning's paper was titled 'Lucky Strike'.[7] Browning's order of battle comprised 1st Airborne Division, 1st Polish Parachute Brigade, 52nd Division, 1st Battalion SAS and the 2nd Light Anti-Aircraft Battery. He also asked for the American 878th Airfield Construction Engineer Battalion, the Airborne Forward Delivery Airfield Group and to – rather belatedly – upgrade his headquarters to a full war establishment.

The objective was to 'block the Paris-Orleans Gap and/or operate against the southern flank of the German Army retreating North East across the Seine ferries'. Browning's paper predicted that it would take 2,000 sorties to lift 52nd Division and it was hoped that using four air strips receiving 36 aircraft per hour the division would be fully landed in 16 hours. To get the troop carrier aircraft configured for airborne operations they would have to be withdrawn from running air supply to the American ground forces at least 48 hours before the airborne landing. Browning also stipulated that the American armoured columns should be within 24 hours of the airborne assault area before latter are launched. In making this condition Browning was mindful of the risk of the airborne force being cut off, even though he would accept longer periods in future operations.

Browning concluded that the proposed operation was feasible 'provided routing is carefully organised and the highest priority is given by AEAF to the landing of the force as an air operation'. Browning also stressed the vulnerability of troop carrier aircraft to fighters and flak and predicted that even if the operation was carried out in daylight and the air formations were routed over enemy territory, losses of 25 per cent were likely.

Browning identified a suitable area for drop and landing zones around Chartres, Montenan, Rambouillet, Dourdan and Denouville. The terrain provided adequate protection against armour, space and cover for camouflaging armoured formations, and the proposed operational area controlled the exits through the Paris-Orleans Gap including the strategically important road centre at Chartres. Browning suggested that the airborne and armoured formations between them would also be able to operate against the other two main road centres at Dreux in the north and Etampes in the south. He also suggested that an 'absolute minimum' of seven days would be required for planning. After giving his paper to De Guingand Browning went on to meet with Bradley and then flew back to England.

Lieutenant Colonel Britten, a staff officer at 21st Army Group G(Plans), forwarded Browning's memo to Richardson with his own comments on 6 August.[8] He explained that although the operation had been ordered in Montgomery's latest directive, as he had not seen a copy of it he was 'a bit vague as to the real object'. Britten told Richardson that if the operation took place in seven or eight days it would need to use British airborne forces as the two US airborne divisions that had fought in Normandy were still reorganising, and as a result 21st Army Group would have to work with the US airborne divisions if airborne forces were needed later to help cross the Seine. He also foresaw that the planning process would be complicated by the fact that the still-forming First Allied Airborne Army would assume command of all British and American airborne forces, along with all troop carrier aircraft, and that HQ Airborne Troops and its constituent units would therefore come under what was at this point referred to as Combined Airborne HQ. As the proposed operational area was in the American sector Britten suggested that the operation would have to be planned with 12th Army Group, and that 21st Army Group's involvement would be on an administrative basis. A British staff increment would be sent to either 12th Army Group or First Army to assist with administrative matters. Britten understood that HQ Airborne Troops was short-handed, particularly as it had to send representatives to other headquarters with which it was working, and the Staff Duties section of 21st Army Group was asked to assist as the 'completion of HQ Airborne Corps . . . will be urgently required if this operation takes place'. Britten stressed that 'If this is so, we shall certainly have nothing to help us across the Seine, which seems to me to be an operation in which we are much more likely to need airborne help'.

On the same day Britten also wrote to De Guingand on behalf of Richardson, after he had visited the planning section of 12th Army Group.[9] Although the Americans had agreed to the planning procedure, Bradley's Assistant Chief of Staff for Operations, General Abram Kibler, and the planning staff at 12th Army Group were advising against Transfigure on several grounds. They wanted to keep the airborne troops for use during the crossing of the Seine and were also certain that their armoured units would be able to reach the Paris-Orleans Gap without airborne assistance. The Americans feared that the airborne drop would interrupt the use of troop carrier aircraft in the air supply role at a 'critical moment' and that an airborne operation east of Chartres would draw their armoured thrust off its axis by 'attracting it too far northwards'. They argued that the seaborne element of 1,393 vehicles – not including those of 52nd Division – would put too much strain on their already congested road network. Bradley's planners also argued that the proposed area for the drop around Rambouillet was too far south and would be on one of the main axes of their tank advance. They preferred for the drop to be moved to the area of Mantes-Gassicourt and St Germain and the northern outskirts of Rambouillet Forest. Their second choice was the area around Dreux, Houdan and Nogent 'as a compromise'. Interestingly, even though they had a lengthy list of objections the planning staff stated that they did not know the views of General Bradley or of his Chief of Staff.

When Browning returned to England he visited Brereton and they discussed Transfigure with Ridgway.[10] At this point Ridgway was still commanding the 82nd Division and would not take over command of XVIII Airborne Corps until late August, but he seems to have been regarded informally as Browning's opposite number in the meantime. After these discussions Brereton decided to submit a revised plan to SHAEF, designed to 'close the Paris-Orleans Gap and cut off the enemy's retreat'.

Later that day HQ Airborne Troops sent a warning order to 1st Airborne Division, 52nd Division and 38 Group for their commanders and planning teams to prepare to move to Moor Park the next day. However the move was later postponed for 24 hours until the evening of 8 August. 1st Airborne Division was also ordered to concentrate in its billet area and to be at two days' notice to move to transit camps. Leave was to continue.[11]

7 August

On 7 August Brereton flew to Normandy to consult with Bradley.[12] The two discussed the proposals for Transfigure and agreed that the operation should be prepared so that it could be mounted immediately.

Richardson wrote to de Guingand to inform him of the outcome of Browning's meeting with Bradley, having been updated by a liaison officer who had met Browning before he flew back to Britain.[13] Bradley was described as wanting the operation to take place, which was in stark contrast to the views that his staff had expressed the day before. Browning had asked for 1st Airborne Division, 52nd Division, the Polish Brigade, 1st SAS Battalion and 2nd Light Anti-Aircraft Battery, to which Bradley had added 82nd Airborne Division and 878th Airborne Aviation Engineer Battalion. Bradley had suggested 16 August as the earliest date that the operation could take place and 20 August as the probable date. He promised a minimum of three days' notice prior to D-Day. It was assumed that the new Combined Airborne Troops headquarters would want to plan the operation, especially as US units would be taking part. Richardson stressed that early action would need to be taken to get the Airborne Forward Airfield Delivery Group formed as without it 52nd Division could not be landed by air. Richardson assumed that the leading armoured forces would link up with the airborne troops within 24 hours. As it would take 48 hours to drop the complete airborne force Richardson suggested that it might be better to send an infantry division by road instead. He again emphasised that if the operation took place with the planned order of battle then 21st Army Group would potentially only have the 101st Airborne Division to take part in the Seine crossing, and then only if SHAEF agreed to allocate it to Montgomery.

A preliminary meeting to plan the operation was held in the Conference Tent in the G(Plans) field at 21st Army Group Main HQ at 1400 on 7 August.[14] It was attended by representatives from most of the staff branches at 21st Army Group.

1st Airborne Division's Outline Operation Order was issued on 7 August and stated that D-Day would not be before 16 August.[15] On 9 August a planning conference took place at Airborne Corps Headquarters at Moor Park, chaired by Walch and attended by Urquhart, his GSO1 MacKenzie and Major General Hakewill-Smith, the commander of the 52nd Division. The conference was also attended by representatives from the US 101st Airborne Division, IX Troop Carrier Command and 38 Group RAF. On the same day it was confirmed that the 1st Polish Independent Parachute Brigade would be placed under Urquhart's command for the operation, a development that took place prior to Market Garden. The Air Conference for Transfigure took place the next day on 10 August, attended by Browning, Urquhart, Taylor and Hakewill-Smith. Later the same day Urquhart held his preliminary divisional O Group at his headquarters at Fulbeck.

A common theme throughout airborne planning in the summer of 1944 was the inadequacy of the existing signals support. 21st Army Group staff had been discussing the signals implications of Transfigure as early as 7 August. As Airborne Forces HQ did not have a signals element it would have to be cobbled together from signals personnel who happened to be available – early on it was proposed that an Air

Support Signals Unit could be provided from those already in 21st Army Group, First Canadian Army and Second Army and the Phantom GHQ Liaison Regiment. All these personnel were already in France and would have to be sent back to the UK before Transfigure started.

Two different systems for ASSU were suggested. System A would have a control station with each airborne brigade or regiment, and with British and US ASSUs at Airborne Forces HQ, and at either First US Army or 12th Army Group. The exact system to be adopted, however, would have to be a US decision as it would be calling on support from the US Ninth Air Force. Eighteen signals personnel would need to be found from the combined resources of existing 21st Army Group Air Support Signals Units, GHQ Liaison Regiment and the ASSUs of First Canadian and Second British Armies.[16] It is not difficult to conclude that the signals picture was extremely haphazard.

8 August

A draft copy of the outline plan for Transfigure, unattributed but dated 8 August, contains some illuminating remarks noted in pencil.[17] The unknown author noted that the force was too small to capture the whole of the Paris-Orleans Gap, and 'Must do a part of the job (nearest Seine)'. While the original plan stated that airborne supply was not likely to be needed for the US armoured division, the commentator noted 'On the contrary, v. likely to be needed – unless Brittany is wound up by then'.

At an AEAF staff conference on 8 August Leigh Mallory explained that due to the possibility of mounting Transfigure, 'an all-out offensive against German fighter strength should be regarded as a necessary preliminary'. Leigh Mallory went to great lengths to allocate air support for the operation and his support was a major departure from his attitude to Wild Oats earlier in the campaign. Several days later on 12 August he travelled back to France to meet with Montgomery and Eisenhower, when the Supreme Commander pointed out that mounting Transfigure might mean diverting most of the fighter force from the battle area.[18]

On 8 August an Outline Plan for a 'Combined Airborne-Armoured' operation was published by Browning, prior to a conference at Airborne Corps HQ with Generals Ridgway and Taylor.[19] There would be two lifts on D-Day with the first lift consisting of the 101st Airborne Division, who would land in the area south of Sonchamp. Their objective would be to capture the St Arnault-en-Yvennes road centre and hold the road between Chartres, St-Arnault-en-Yvennes and Paris, as well as protecting landing strips for 52nd Division. Also in the first lift the Polish Parachute Brigade would land south-west of Rambouillet with the objective of securing the landing strips along the road between Rambouillet and Amblis. Airborne Corps Headquarters would land in the first lift along with unspecified SAS Troops and the Advance Party of the Airfield Control Unit. The second lift would land later on D-Day led by the 1st British Airborne Division south of Rambouillet. Their objective would be to capture the road centre in Rambouillet and dominate the roads running out of it while also holding the road between Chartres, Rambouillet and Paris. The glider element of the Polish Brigade would also land and join their Brigade while 878th US Airborne Aviation Engineer Battalion would land and build up to four airstrips between the Rambouillet to Ablis road. Once the airstrips had been constructed 52nd Division would be landed from D+1 onwards, concentrating west of Rambouillet around the Forest de Yvalents as a corps reserve.

It was hoped that the US Armoured Division leading the advance would aim for the road centre at Dourdan where they would link up first with the 101st at St Arnault-en-Yvennes. The operation would come under the overall command of US 12th Army Group. The British Airborne Corps Headquarters did not have the capacity to command anything other than airborne and airlanded formations and a US corps headquarters would have to take over control of the operation. It was stressed that the Armoured Division should arrive to link-up with the airborne divisions within 24 hours after the first airborne landings. At this early stage there was no indication of exact drop zones and landing zones, but these were planned to be in the general area of Rambouillet and Ablis. If the Airborne Corps Headquarters was not able to command the operation, it is not clear why it was taking part at all.

Originally 1st Airborne Division would be landed before 101st Airborne Division, but according to discussions between Colonel Richards at 38 Group and General Browning this was switched some time around 8 August.[20] It is not clear why this happened, but it may have been due to the operation happening in the American sector and under the overall command of 12th Army Group.

A loose minute found in the 38 Group files explored the 'Combined Airborne Armoured Operation "Lucky Strike"' on 8 August 1944.[21] The minute quoted heavily from the Airborne Troops Outline Plan and stated that:

It is desirable that the US Armoured Division directed to the Airborne area should seize control of the Dourdan Road centre, co-ordinate their operations intimately with the US Airborne Division at St Arnault en Yvennes and dominate the Dourdan road junction and the area to the south as far as and inclusive road Chartres-Etampes.

Two alternative air routes were suggested. The first would assemble over Salisbury and then pass over Vire, La Suze, Charsonville and Ymonville to the landing area, a total distance of 385 miles. The second would also assemble over Salisbury and pass over Vire but would then travel via Courtalain and Ymonville to the operational area, a total distance of 348 miles. These distances were at the limit of some of the glider and tug combinations – the radius of action of Albermarle–Horsa and C-47–Waco combinations was only 340 miles. Even then, if the aircraft were to fly in formation 40 miles would have to be deducted for forming up. The airborne forces were reaching the extent of their range from bases in England.

9 August

On 9 August it was decided that the seaborne tails of the British airborne units should be shipped to France as soon as possible.[22] It was also decided to form the AFDAG as soon as possible and that earmarked units currently in France would need to be shipped to Britain. REME and medical detachments had already been identified. It was decided that Koenig's Free French staff could be informed about the operation and the Special Forces advisers agreed that the area planned for Transfigure had potential for resistance operations. Sixty SAS jeep parties would be included in the operation to organise Resistance elements. Later the same day the proposed operation was allocated the codename Transfigure by 21st Army Group G(Plans) who signalled HQ Airborne Troops explaining that it referred to a 'possible airborne operation in the Chartres area in conjunction with advance East of 12th Army Group'.[23] However the code name was not forwarded to HQ Combined Airborne Forces until over a week later on 17 August.

Browning's movements around this time suggest just how gruelling his schedule was.[24] On 9 August he again flew to Normandy and back to meet with Montgomery and Bradley. The next day he met with Admiral Mountbatten – the Supreme Commander in South East Asia who was in Britain at the time – and General Crawford, the Director of Air at the War Office in London. Their meeting presumably concerned airborne forces in the Far East theatre, where Browning served as Mountbatten's chief of staff later in the war.[25] Later the same day Browning also met with General Koenig, the commander of the French Forces of the Interior. His involvement in planning operations in Britain and France and responsibility for wider policy and administration suggests that the dual role of his headquarters was simply too much and spread him and his staff too thin. This is particularly so when considered alongside the delicate inter-Allied relationships that Browning found himself working within. Another important consideration is that Browning had not attended Staff College, usually a prerequisite for higher command, and perhaps was not used to delegating tasks.

10 August

An administrative planning meeting for Transfigure was held on the morning of 10 August, chaired by Lieutenant Colonel Heard of 21st Army Group G(Staff Duties).[26] The main topic of discussion was the division of staff and administrative responsibilities as the operation included British and American units. The meeting was attended by representatives from G3 and G4 at 12th Army Group; G(Staff Duties), Q(Plans), Q(Movements), G(Plans), G(Air), Signals, Artillery, Engineers and G(Ops) from 21st Army Group and A and G Staff from HQ Airborne Troops. Heard explained that although the meeting was based on one specific operation similar conditions might arise at any time. While the strictly airborne assault phase of the operation might be short there might well be a lengthy period when airborne forces would function in a normal ground role, as had happened with the 6th Airborne Division in Normandy. This eventuality would drastically increase the logistical difficulties of supporting British forces in the American area.

Lieutenant Colonel Charles Mackenzie, who would later be Urquhart's chief staff officer at Arnhem, attended the meeting as GSO1 at HQ Airborne Troops and his notes for the discussions with 21st and 12th Army Groups on 10 August shed much light on the thinking at HQ Airborne Troops.[27] The units that would form part of the AFDAG still needed to be finalised, along with identifying which were in Britain and which were in France. The shipping of the airborne seaborne tail to France still needed to be arranged, along with concentration areas for it to gather. It was also suggested that the air route could be shortened considerably if the transport aircraft could fly north of Le Mans instead of south depending on the ground situation at the time. North of Le Mans the route would be via Vire-Alençon-Chartres, by the southern route it would be Vire-Le Mans-Chartres.

Securing firepower support for the lightly equipped airborne formations was a major concern, and HQ Airborne Troops were keen for artillery support from the American armoured divisions that would be relieving them. Airborne divisions carried much less artillery support and generally less powerful weapons than conventional infantry divisions. It was therefore even more important for airborne formations to secure artillery support as soon as possible from the ground formations which would be relieving them. HQ Airborne Troops also sought Forward Observation Officers from the Americans to call in artillery support and also requested information from 12th Army Group regarding air support. The US Ninth Air Force would be likely to provide tactical air support and HQ Airborne Troops requested two air support tentacles per division plus another tentacle at Corps HQ to monitor requests. This was later reduced to one per division.

Another complication caused by the attempts to establish the Airborne Corps as an operational formation was the issue of allocating airlift. HQ Airborne Troops requested information from 21st Army Group as to what units could be found in France to help form the AFDAG.[28] HQ Airborne Troops explained that they had been able to find sufficient REME detachments from 1st Airborne Division and 52nd Division, but this poses the question as to how those divisions would cope with a lower establishment, particularly as airborne and air-transportable divisions had a reduced scale of divisional troops in any case. HQ Airborne Troops also requested that units being provided for the AFDAG that were already on the continent should not be returned to Britain and should join the airborne force as part of the seaborne element.

On 10 August Brigadier McLean, the Chief of SHAEF's Plans Section, wrote to Richardson at 21st Army Group with orders for the planning of Transfigure to begin.[29] HQ Airborne Troops would plan the operation as the new HQ Combined Airborne Forces was not yet operational and HQ Airborne Troops was therefore still under the command of 21st Army Group. Clearly there were sensitivities over the change in airborne command, as McLean explained to Richardson:

> For these reasons and also because of the need for speed and difficulty of communicating with the new Combined HQ, we have dealt direct with General Browning . . . We don't want to tread on any toes over this, and so, if difficulties do arise over it, you could perhaps explain why, in this particular case, we have taken this course.

Planning for Special Forces involvement also continued and on 10 August 21st Army Group requested extra equipment for the SAS groups that were scheduled to take part in Transfigure.[30] This included 60 modified jeeps, 160 Vickers machine guns, 68 No.38 wireless sets and 60 Bazookas. Regarding the Bazookas it was emphasises that no suitable British equivalent existed for the Special Forces' role, the PIAT being seen as inferior.

On the same day De Guingand wrote to Browning to inform him that 12th Army Group had agreed that planning and executive action for Transfigure could begin at once. Responsibility for planning the operation would rest with 12th Army Group and HQ Airborne Troops, while 21st Army Group's role would be limited to providing the required British units. The airborne forces were to be at three days readiness from 15 August.[31]

Also on 10 August Oxborrow at 21st Army Group wrote to the Chief Signal Officer concerning air support communications. As Transfigure was going to be under US control decisions regarding the air support signals system would have to be made jointly with the US Army and the relevant Air Force. 21st Army Group suggested embedding air support tentacles with 1st Airborne Division and the Polish Brigade based on the units' own signals personnel, while Airborne Forces HQ could draw its air support signals from 21st Army Group's own ASSU. However it was suggested that Airborne Forces HQ could draw its signals from 1st Airborne Division instead. If 21st Army Group did have to provide an ASSU, it would have consisted of one Bedford QL Truck with a Canadian No.9 set which would be withdrawn from Second Army and shipped to the UK for conversion into an air-transportable control station.[32] It is hard to see how if HQ Airborne Troops had to borrow signals units from 1st Airborne Division it would not have impacted negatively on the latter. 21st Army Group, 12th Army Group and HQ Airborne Troops were also discussing the maintenance of British forces operating in the American sector including equipment, maps, prisoners of war, medical services, rations and civil affairs. A meeting took place on 10 August to discuss the division of responsibilities.[33]

The code word Transfigure was passed by Airborne Troops HQ to its subordinate units on the afternoon of 10 August.[34] The same day it was confirmed that the coordinating conference for Transfigure – although the signal referred to it as Lucky Strike – would be split into three separate conferences. The staff conference for the first and second lifts would take place at 0900 on 11 August at Eastcote. The conference for the third and subsequent lifts would take place at 1400 the same day, while the final command-level conference would be at Moor Park at 1700 on 12 August.[35] The two conferences on 11 August were to be attended by the GSO1s of divisions and no more than one other officer from each division, suggesting how many units were involved if space was so limited. Any subsequent points arising from the conferences were to be referred by the staff officers present to their commanders.

Commanders and staff officers would then attend the final conference the next day.[36]

Even while Operation Transfigure was being planned, senior planners were proposing alternatives. On 10 August Richardson wrote to de Guingand to suggest that '. . . 1st Airborne Division and Polish Parachute Brigade, and, if General Bradley agrees, 101 Airborne Division should be put at readiness to land in our own lines to give us the added strength which I feel may well be necessary to ensure decisive success in the forthcoming battle'.[37] It is hard to see Richardson's proposal as plausible, as airborne formations lacked mobility once on the ground and usually had to be provided with transport from other sources to enable them to keep up in mobile warfare. It would also not have been a good use of their training.

11 August
The coordinating conference for Transfigure took place at HQ Airborne Troops at Moor Park on 11 August.[38] The seaborne tails of 1st Airborne Division and the Polish Brigade would load on 13 August and arrive in France on 17 to 18 August, while that of 52nd Division would load on 16 August and arrive in France on 19 to 20 August. 52nd Division's involvement was still not certain – HQ Airborne Troops were under the impression that the division would take part despite De Guingand telling Browning otherwise. When this was pointed out Browning said that two plans would be developed, one with the division and another without. While HQ Airborne Troops had arranged for the seaborne element of 101st Airborne Division to load on 15 August and arrive from 17 to 18 August the 12th Army Group representatives at the meeting said – 'quite emphatically' – that no action should be taken regarding US formations or units at this stage due to the necessity for training replacements for 101st Division. It was stressed that this would have repercussions for the readiness of the whole operation and that if the operation did not take place the British airborne units would have administrative issues due to their seaborne tails having already sailed to France. It was therefore suggested that the seaborne elements should be divided into 'operationally essential' and 'non-operationally essential'. 12th Army Group would also not agree to allocate any specific artillery or forward observer units in advance to support the airborne troops.

The air support situation was described as 'not satisfactory'. Ninth Air Force were short of air support parties and General Bradley felt that two tentacles per division would be extravagant. HQ Airborne Troops suggested that the divisions could call for support directly from Ninth

Air Force, but this was vetoed by 12th Army Group. They requested that HQ Airborne Troops submit its air support requirements categorised as essential and non-essential. The meeting also heard that the air forces occasionally made substantial changes in the number of troop carrier aircraft available for airborne operations, which the 12th Army Group representatives agreed to discuss with SHAEF. 12th Army Group were clearly not enthusiastic about mounting the operation.

HQ Airborne Troops suggested that if the airborne force was relieved within three days it would not require the AFDAG or 878th Battalion, but if 52nd Division took part both units would be essential due to its need for airstrips. 12th Army Group insisted that 878th Battalion was needed to build airstrips to support the subsequent armoured advance. 12th Army Group were still doubtful as to whether they would be able to maintain the airborne force involved even without 52nd Division and would not make a definite decision about this until they knew the exact forces to be involved. Although General Koenig, the commander of the French Forces of the Interior, would be informed about the operation no information would be given to Resistance groups until six hours after the first troops had landed. HQ Airborne Troops were still keen to launch Operation Nelson, which had first been discussed during planning for Operation Lucky Strike, but it was stressed that if the SAS were to be used it must be strictly within the allotted Airborne Corps area. Browning also suggested that he would be willing to 'amend considerably' the interval between the dropping of the airborne troops and the arrival of ground forces – he had previously stipulated 24 hours as a maximum period. Browning changed his advice regarding the time that airborne troops could hold out before relief numerous times in the summer of 1944.

The air co-ordinating conference was held at Eastcote on 11 August, where It was decided to route the airborne lift via Vire, Alençon and Chartres.[39] Pathfinders would drop five minutes ahead of the main body. HQ Airborne Corps would need thirty gliders – their requirement for glider lift grew with every operation – which would come from 1st Airborne Division's allocation. It was also discussed whether the Corps headquarters should therefore land with 1st Airborne Division rather than the 101st. The air forces did not want to send fifteen gliders with the Airborne Forward Delivery Airfield Group with the second lift, but it was thought that Browning would insist on them being sent. Later the same day Browning held a conference with his divisional commanders and Major General Sosabowski of the Polish Brigade, probably to brief them on the air plan.

38 Group were informed that the SAS lift was to be put at the lowest priority and would only take place if enough Albermarles were available. If it was not possible to drop them on the evening of D-Day the SAS would be taken in with the second British glider lift on D+1 along with the Light Anti-Aircraft Battery.[40] The SAS was of a lower priority than the Corps headquarters, even though thirty gliders would almost be enough to carry an SAS Battalion.

The Operation Order for the SAS Brigade's involvement – code-named Kipling – was first issued on 11 August before an amended version was circulated on 13 August.[41] The only difference between the two orders was that the SAS troops had been moved from the first lift to the second. Major Verney, the SAS Brigade's GSO2, and a small clerical staff would join Airborne Forces HQ, landing in the first lift. The SAS would land in three groups – code-named Ponting, Mappin and Fortnum – each with twenty Jeeps. Ponting and Mappin would be under the command of Major Marsh of 1st SAS while Fortnum would be commanded by Major Farran of 2nd SAS.

The Jeeps would be flown in in Horsa gliders to a landing zone south of Sonchamp which should held by 101st Division. After assembling they would contact Corps HQ or Lieutenant Colonel Blair Mayne, who was commanding SAS Troops in the general area at part of Operation Gain, for further instructions. Mayne would also have the authority to amend their tasks as he saw fit.

Pointing troop was ordered to prepare to operate in the direction of Mantes, Drux, Nogent le Rotrou and Châteaudun. If a favourable situation arose the patrols were to attack convoys and lines of communications installations to create confusion in the rear of the German army. They would operate from the airborne area but would be prepared to rendezvous with SAS Operations Bunyan and Chaucer. Mappin troop were ordered to operate to the south and south-east of the airborne area. If conditions allowed they were to move towards Dommerville, Bellegarde and Chatillon Coligny to create confusion south of Paris, before linking up with Operations Kipling or Houndsworth. Fortnum troop were ordered to operate to the east of the airborne area, and to patrol out towards the area of Fontainbleau and Troyes to create confusion east of Paris, eventually linking up with Operations Hardy or Rupert.

The SAS were keen to establish Kipling before Transfigure began and six Jeeps and thirty men would be dropped in advance to form a forward base. On the first day the Jeep patrols would move north-west and try to link up with Airborne HQ as soon as possible, avoiding fighting *en route* but gathering information regarding enemy dispositions and movements, bridges, defences lines and the local resistance. No information about the operation would be given to any of the SAS bases operating in the area and they were to be informed about Transfigure by signal only once the operation had started. The party that would establish Kipling would carry out a reconnaissance towards the area of Operation Gain. Once SAS units had been briefed on Transfigure they were to be sealed into their marshalling camps at departure airfields.

Mappin and Fortnum were to be entirely self-supporting until they reached one of the existing SAS bases, carrying seven days of rations and motor transport spares. Ponting would be self-supporting for seven days but would be maintained by HQ Airborne Forces if operating from the airborne operational area. Any available space in gliders' payloads was to be made up of arms containers to give to the French Resistance. The SAS parties would use 22 and 38 sets for internal communications and each patrol would also take an MCR1 receiver – nicknamed the biscuit tin. One Jedburgh terminal would be taken by Fortnum while Lieutenant Colonel Mayne was believed to already have a Jedburgh terminal in France. Communication with HQ Airborne Forces would either be by radio or Jedburgh set.

An addendum to the SAS Brigade Operation Order was issued on 13 August. The first SAS group from 1st SAS would consist of thirty gliders, and the second group would be from 1st and 2nd SAS and would also consist of thirty gliders. Both groups would be lifted by 38 Group from Brize Norton and would land on LZ E. As an illustration of how time-consuming loading for an operation could be the SAS gliders would be available from 0900 on D-1, with loading to be completed that evening. The SAS would complete emplaning by 1720 on D-Day, ready for a 2100 landing. The SAS put in a rather impressive shopping list of equipment and weapons for their participation in Transfigure, including 1,000 Bazooka rockets, 200,000 rounds of carbine ammunition, 2,000 gallons of petrol, 200 gallons of oil, 660 smoke generators, 1,000 smoke grenades and 1,000 camouflage nets.

12 August

On 12 August HQ Airborne Troops circulated defence overprints of the area intended for Operation Transfigure. Indicative of the evolution of Transfigure, the overprints were labelled 'Lucky Strike'.[42]

A flurry of telephone calls took place on 12 and 13 August between 21st Army Group, HQ Airborne Troops and 12th Army Group as the various staffs hurried to finalise plans.[43] Late on 12 August Lieutenant Colonel Britten called Mackenzie at HQ Airborne Troops and told him that if the operation were to begin on or after 17 August that 1st Airborne Division and the Polish Parachute Brigade would need to move to airfields the next day. Britten stressed that the move had been ordered by De Guingand. Mackenzie replied that the airborne headquarters were having difficulties with the War Office failing to produce adequate transport to move the airborne formations to their airfields, which required four General Transport Companies. The seaborne elements were preparing to move to France and would be taking a substantial proportion of the division's transport with them. Colonel Poole at Q(Plans) was asked to press the War Office to provide transport.

Mackenzie was satisfied that if transport could be found by midday on 13 August the operation could take place by 17 August. However, if the area of the operation changed it might be 19 August before HQ Airborne Troops could lay on the operation. Mackenzie did not however want his estimate of timescales quoted as they had not been discussed with Browning or Walch.

There was a difference of opinion at this point over whether 52nd Division was to take part. Britten pointed out that De Guingand had ordered that the division was not to take part and that HQ Airborne Troops should plan for their absence as maintenance difficulties would probably make it impossible to use them in any case.

Mackenzie and Britten also discussed bringing HQ Airborne Troops up to establishment with the support units that it needed to function as a front-line corps. During a conference the previous day the airborne HQ had requested three pioneer companies and one pioneer platoon. After some discussion this was reduced to one pioneer company plus one platoon on Colonel Poole's guarantee that they could handle 800 tons of stores a day. Even at this late stage it was not possible to confirm the administrative units for the Airborne Corps as Poole was attending an admin planning conference at HQ Airborne Troops and would return with the result of that conference the next day. It is remarkable that five days before a corps was about to take off for an operation that it had virtually no corps troops allocated.

The most acute shortage was in crews rather than aircraft. The same day 38 Group reported that it had 339 aircraft available but only 303 crews. This was made up of eighty-three Albermarles at Brize Norton but only sixty-one crews, seventy-one Stirlings at Fairford but only sixty-two crews, forty-eight Stirlings at Harwell but sixty-one crews, sixty-nine Stirlings at Keevil but only sixty-four crews and sixty-eight Halifaxes at Tarrant Rushton with only fifty-five crews.

The first part of the air plan was circulated on 12 August. The 1st Parachute Brigade would land on DZ Y while the first lift gliders would land on LZ X. The 4th Parachute Brigade would land on DZ H, the 1st Airlanding Brigade on LZ N and the second lift divisional gliders on LZ L. The Polish Parachute brigade would land on DZ K and DZ Y with its gliders landing on LZ E. HQ Airborne Troops was keen to land 878th Battalion as early as possible, and on 16 August Browning signalled that his plan was to land them early. The battalion would then construct one landing strip, into which the AFDAG and what he called 'main Corps HQ' would land. Once the air strip had been constructed supplies would be landed there rather than dropped in divisional supply drop areas.[44]

The flight plan for Transfigure was compiled by IX Troop Carrier Command, 38 Group and 46 Group. Some of 38 Group's early planning documents for Transfigure were marked Lucky Strike, highlighting again that Transfigure was an evolution of the earlier operation and that much of the planning was reused.[45] Serials would be separated by six minutes for parachute aircraft and seven minutes for glider combinations. The airborne columns would gather over Banbury in the north and Salisbury in the south before crossing the French coast at Vire, then flying over Fyé and Bonneval to the landing area around Rambouillet.

The first lift for 1st Airborne Division would take off from Brize Norton, Fairford, Harwell, Keevil and Tarrant Rushton and would land the Divisional HQ, Reconnaissance Regiment, Anti-Tank Artillery, 1st Parachute Brigade and one Battery of the Light Regiment Artillery. It would take off at civil twilight at 0620 on D-1 and begin landing at 0850, completing landing by 1000. 1st Airborne Division's parachute lift would comprise 160 aircraft from 38 and 46 Groups taking off from Fairford, Blakehill Farm, Down Ampney, Broadwell and Keevil. They would begin landing at 0815 and return to base by 1058. The first glider lift would be made up of 210 aircraft from 38 Group, carrying the same number of gliders. They would take off from Harwell, Brize Norton, Keevil, Fairford and Tarrant Rushton, begin landing at 0945 and return to base by 1211.

The second lift would take off from Greenham Common, Welford, Aldermaston, Broadwell, Down Ampney, Blakehill Farm and Tarrant Rushton and would land the 4th Parachute Brigade, the rest of the Light Regiment and the 1st Airlanding Brigade. The Polish Brigade would land on Drop Zone K and Landing Zone E and would take off from Broadwell, Down Ampney and Blakehill Farm in the first lift, and Barkston Heath and Folkingham in the second lift. The second lift would take off at 1145 hours after civil twilight, begin dropping at 1415 and complete by 1540. This would include sixty aircraft carrying SAS troops, six Hamilcars carrying elements of 878th Battalion, elements of the AFDAG and a first resupply mission. It was also suggested that if the aircraft flew in two streams then the times are cut down by half. It would be carried by 235 aircraft from 52nd Troop Carrier Wing from Barkston Heath, Folkingham, Saltby and Spanhoe who would begin dropping at 1930 and return to base by 2231. 1st Airborne Division's second glider lift, the Polish Brigade gliders, 878th Battalion and the AFDAG would be carried by 53rd Troop Carrier Wing and 46 Group, with a combination of single-tow and double-tow gliders. They would begin landing at 1915 and return to base by 2243. The SAS glider lift would be carried by thirty aircraft from 38 Group taking off from Brize Norton. The SAS would begin landing at 2100 and would return to base by 2301. This would depend on enough Albermarles being left over from the first lift.

101st Division's first lift would include 432 aircraft from 52nd Troop Carrier Wing taking off from North Witham, Greenham Common, Aldermaston and Welford. They would begin dropping at 0815 and return to base by 1122. The 101st Division's first glider lift would comprise 450 tug aircraft from 53rd Troop Carrier Wing towing 900 gliders in a double-tow arrangement, taking off from Chilbolton, Ramsbury, Greenham Common, Membury, Aldermaston and Welford. They would begin landing at 0945 and be back at base by 1343.

HQ Airborne Troops would land on D+2 in gliders carried by eighteen C-47s and another eighteen C-47s carrying airborne signals. It is noticeable throughout the airborne operations in question that the Airborne Corps glider allocation grew for every operation. It is also interesting that Browning's headquarters would land on D+2 – one wonders whether this would have been worthwhile. The AFDAG would be landed in sixty-nine C-47s. Prior to the opening of a landing strip in the 101st Division area the US element of AFDAG would be landed on the first strip, and would then move over to a strip in the 101st Division area once it had been built.

13 August
On 13 August 21st Army Group G(Plans) wrote to other branches in the Army Group regarding movements preparing for Transfigure. What is perhaps most telling is that executive action would not take place until the orders had been passed by 12th Army Group. Eisenhower had also decreed that no aircraft being used for supplying the American forces

would be withdrawn to prepare for Transfigure 'until the last possible moment'.[46] It is not difficult to see the contradiction in Eisenhower wanting imaginative airborne plans, but not being prepared to take decisions that might upset his subordinates - Bradley and Patton - that would make them possible.

Britten wrote to Richardson asking for decisions on several key points in the planning of Operation Transfigure.[47] On whether 52nd Division was to take part, Britten wrote 'I think maintenance alone will prevent it', with which Richardson agreed. The order of battle was still causing problems, particularly the increase in units for the AFDAG agreed at the administrative conference at HQ Airborne Troops the previous day. Britten described the situation as a 'melting pot'. Britten also asked for clarification over the geographical area in which the operation would take place and argued that '. . . a change in area at this stage, though operationally desirable, may add to the time before which the operation cannot take place'.

Despite these concerns Richardson called Colonel Hyberg at 12th Army Group to tell him that 21st Army Group agreed that Transfigure might be more effective if moved further north with the objective of cutting the road from Dreu to Versailles, and suggested that 12th Army Group should instruct Airborne Troops to examine this. On the same day Lieutenant Colonel Britten spoke to McKenzie at HQ Airborne Troops. Britten pointed out that 12th Army Group might ask for Transfigure to be moved further north. Britten also informed McKenzie that although Eisenhower had authorised executive action on the American involvement in Transfigure, no action should be taken regarding American formations and units until orders to do so were received from 12th Army Group. Britten also stressed that Eisenhower had ordered that no transport aircraft were to be removed from air supply 'until the last possible moment'. In reply McKenzie stated that Airborne Troops were having problems through 'fluctuating availability' of aircraft from 46 Group.

Montgomery and Bradley met on 13 August and discussed plans for Transfigure.[48] Later the same day De Guingand sent a personal message to Browning informing him that Montgomery and Bradley had decided that 1st Airborne Division, 101st Division and the Polish Brigade were to be ready immediately. It had also been decided that 'owing to Twelfth Army Group's need of air supply' there would be no freezing of transport aircraft to prepare for the operation. Effectively, the demand for air supply vetoed the likelihood of airborne operations taking place. 52nd Division would be stood down for the present and their seaborne echelon would not move across the Channel.[49]

However, HQ Airborne Troops still informed units that they should move to their take-off airfields and be ready to take off from 17 August at the earliest, that they would be given a minimum of 48 hours' notice of take-off, and hopefully three days' notice. Corps HQ would move to Harwell airfield on 15 August.[50]

Also on 13 August 21st Army Group's Q(Plans) signalled that Eisenhower had instructed that plans for Transfigure should be implemented and that the airborne force would be at three days' notice for the operation commencing 16 August. The earliest date for the operation to start was given as 19 August.[51]

Transfigure was discussed at the Chief of Staff conference at 21st Army Group Main HQ on the evening of 13 August.[52] It was confirmed that 52nd Division would not take part in the operation and that its seaborne element would not move to France. The airborne forces were to go to three days' notice from 16 August and the G(Plans) staff were to ascertain what notice 38 and 46 Groups and IX Troop Carrier Command would need to switch from carrying out air supply for the Americans to airborne operations.

Assembling the seaborne tail in France would be a complicated affair. It would consist of both British and American elements and would need to move through both British and American-controlled areas once in France. On 13 August 12th Army Group allocated an area south-west of Bayeux, close to the village of Les Petits Carreaux, for the British seaborne elements to assemble. 1st Airborne Division's seaborne tail left for Normandy on 13 August.[53] It would remain in France until after Market Garden and would have a frustrating time waiting for its parent units to arrive.

Meanwhile preparations continued for embarkation. Glider units would move into their transit camps on 15 August, followed by parachute units on 16 August. Advance parties who would land with the pathfinders were to be in their camps by 14 August. However, later the same day another message arrived from HQ Airborne Troops informing units that they were to be ready to take off on 17 August. Thus the date of D-Day had changed twice in one day.

1st Airborne Division Operation Instruction No.6 was issued on 13 August along with an Intelligence Planning Summary. However, the next day Directive No.1 was received from Browning at HQ Airborne Troops – the day after Urquhart had issued his own Operation Instruction. The Division would land near Rambouillet and seize and hold the town and strategic points around it, particularly the road running between Chartres, Rambouillet and Paris. The divisional area was to be divided into three zones comprising of main defensive positions, false front positions and a standing patrol line. Urquhart's orders envisaged the battle being fought on the main defensive positions, but with the enemy being delayed on the false front line. The division would land in two lifts separated by a minimum of two hours. The first lift would see 1st Parachute Brigade, Urquhart's tactical headquarters and the 7th King's Own Scottish Borderers landing, along with some divisional troops. The second lift several hours later would bring in the rest of the division and Sosabowski's Polish Brigade.

1st Parachute Brigade would land on DZ Y, secure the town of Rambouillet, silence flak and then occupy and defend the area around the road between Rambouillet, Chartres and Bechereau. The King's Own Scottish Borderers would land on LZ X to provide protection for the divisional troops landing along with them, wait for the second lift, and then re-join the rest of the Airlanding Brigade. 4th Parachute Brigade would land on DZ H and occupy the road from Rambouillet to St Leger-en-Yveline. 1st Airlanding Brigade would land on LZs N and L, occupy the road from Rambouillet in the direction of Paris, Cernay-le-Ville and Claire Fontaine. The Polish Brigade would land on DZ K and LZ E and then provide local defence of airstrips within the divisional perimeter and occupy the road between Rambouillet, Sonchamp, Ablis and Orphin. The division's Royal Engineers were ordered to construct minefields and obstructions on defensive positions. Meanwhile the Reconnaissance Squadron would send out standing patrols on all roads leading out of Rambouillet and establish communication with the US 101st Airborne Division who would be landing at La Huniere. Divisional Headquarters would be established in a park – appropriately the Jardin à l'anglais – south-west of Rambouillet. Advance parties would move to the transit camps on 14 August followed by the glider lifts the next day. The parachute troops would go to the airfields on 16 August while the gliders would be loaded the same day.

Planning Intelligence Summary No.1 outlined an uncertain picture, no doubt due to the difficulty of obtaining information as the battle situation in France was in a near-constant state of flux. Intelligence suggested that there were no fixed enemy defences in the Rambouillet area and that there were no permanent garrisons of troops. The main threat to the airborne troops was thought to be flak, the Germans having significant anti-aircraft weapons in the Rambouillet area as it was a transit area for troops moving towards the front in Normandy. Although the fluid state of the front line, especially in the American sector, made it impossible to define a precise order of battle for the enemy it was estimated that two Panzer, thirteen infantry and two parachute divisions had been virtually destroyed in the fighting in

Normandy although the remnants were still fighting in battlegroups. This was an early indication of the ability of the Germans to form ad-hoc battlegroups even after airborne landings had taken place.

The airborne forces were provided with remarkably detailed local intelligence during the planning of Transfigure that was far superior to information provided for most other planned operations. Rambouillet had an estimated population of 7,250 people. The area was part of the 'market garden' of Paris and consisted mainly of agricultural land. The town was a key road junction as the main road from Chartres to Paris passed through Rambouillet. The French Resistance in the area was estimated to be comparatively small because of severe German oppression. The Intelligence Summary also included an extremely detailed list of amenities such as hotels, garages, contractors and schools as well as an annotated sketch map of the town centre. More Intelligence information was provided in a supplement the next evening. It identified that German divisions were escaping through the Falaise Gap towards the east and that the airborne forces should expect to have to fight the remnants of these units if they continued withdrawing towards Paris. Air reconnaissance sorties flown over the area had identified anti-aircraft guns, power lines and other features. This information shows the benefit of aerial reconnaissance which was possible partly due to overwhelming Allied air superiority, and of having plenty of time to plan airborne operations. Airborne forces are at their most vulnerable while they are dropping and assembling on the drop zones and intelligence on obstacles and enemy defences would no doubt have been extremely useful. Photographic reconnaissance sorties were however much more difficult to order for operations that were taking place at shorter notice.

Browning issued his Directive No.2 on 13 August.[54] Considering how busy Browning was meeting with other senior commanders on both sides of the Channel and planning operations it suggests a picture of a commander micro-managing tactical aspects to a remarkable level. The directive describes the country as close and thickly wooded and ordered that roads and tracks should be denied to the enemy. Browning predicted that the enemy would be likely to withdraw across country, possibly in small parties through woods, and stressed that it would be fatal to attempt to be strong everywhere and that main roads, tracks and dominating features overlooking them should be held in strength. Smaller tracks, paths and woods were to be held by snipers who should work in pairs with one killing and the other observing. They would have to be patient, stay concealed and still for extended periods with sufficient ammunition and food to remain on their own for a considerable amount of time. Browning asked divisional commanders to 'work out' their sniper organisation so that it could be put into effect immediately after landing. Browning also stressed the importance of communications, 'Without good communications no battle can be fought – much less won.' Overall, the directive strikes a slightly bizarre note for a Lieutenant General serving as a corps commander to send to his divisional commanders, and was mostly content that should have been part of more technical summaries. It is not unusual for commanders who are out of their depth to obsess over minutiae to the detriment of the bigger picture.

On 13 August Parks flew to France to meet with Bradley.[55] He reported to Brereton that Bradley had changed his mind from his meeting with Brereton on 7 August and now agreed with the decision not to use the airborne forces in what Brereton's diary described as 'small harassing operations such as requested by General Montgomery'. Bradley, who seems to have frequently changed his mind during the campaign, favoured what was described as a 'long hook', but was aware that that operation might not be possible for at least two weeks. Brereton suggested that airborne forces could help to close the noose in a 'short hook', but Bradley replied that if the airborne forces could not be dropped within five days it would be too late. It was therefore agreed to plan an operation to block the Germans from using pontoon bridges over the Seine by using airborne troops to cut off the German withdrawal on the roads leading north-east from Falaise and Argentan.

On 13 August Troop Carrier Combined Command Post (TCCP) asked RAF Central Flying Control for refuelling facilities at airfields to enable the quickest possible turnaround, particularly on the afternoon of D-Day between the first and second lifts. It asked for facilities at Hurn, Holmsley, Beaulieu, Stoney Cross, Ibsley, Thorney Island, Tangmere, Ford, Merston, Westhampnett and Tarrant Rushton, all airfields along the south coast that would reduce the distance required to be flown by the troop carriers. The increasing size of proposed airborne operations, as well as the changing locations of where they might take place on the continent, meant that the air force planners were also increasingly looking at using different airfields. For Transfigure 38 Group considered using advanced landing grounds in Normandy including A-5 at Chippelle, A-6 at Beuzeville-la-Bastille, A-10A at Carentan, A-15 at Maupertus and B-14 at Amblie.[56]

The plan for maintaining Operation Transfigure was published on 13 August.[57] The document was extremely detailed and illustrates the administrative legwork that was required to make airborne operations possible. HQ Airborne Troops would be responsible for maintaining the British and Polish formations taking part, assisted by the War Office Dispatch Organisation. After being maintained by air resupply for a minimum of three days the airborne forces would be supplied by 12th Army Group once a junction had been made. 21st Army Group would supply all equipment of British origin while 12th Army Group would maintain 101st Airborne Division and 878th Battalion throughout. On D+1 the British airborne formations would be resupplied by 210 aircraft and the US formations by 140 C-47s, while on D+2 the British would be resupplied by 140 aircraft and the Americans by the same number. This would be repeated each subsequent day as required and further drops would be held ready for emergencies. A resupply by road would be prepared and would move up by column with 12th Army Group with 21st Army Group liaising regarding British supplies. The British seaborne elements were already in France and once the operation had taken place would move up and come under the command of 12th Army Group. It would be commanded by Brigadier Russell of the 157th Infantry Brigade if the 52nd Division took part, or by Major Coke, the second in command of the 7th King's Own Scottish Borderers, if it did not. Up to and including the night of D+2 and D+3 divisions would collect their own supplies into their divisional transport area from their own Supply Dropping Points, and after D+3 they would be collected and held in a Corps Forward Maintenance Centre.

The maintenance plan highlighted that the Airborne Corps did not have sufficient corps troops to be able to command the operation effectively. The units required to land by air included a HQ Forward Maintenance Centre, a Royal Engineers Stores Detachment, 261 Field Park Company Royal Engineers (which would be borrowed from 1st Airborne Division), a Pioneer Company, 165 Company Royal Army Service Corps (borrowed from 52nd Division whether it took part or not), a US hospital, a signals section and one REME Detachment (from 52nd Division). These would be followed up by other corps troops by road including one Defence Issues Depot, a General Duties Platoon Royal Army Service Corps, a Casualty Clearing Station, two Field Dressing Stations, two Field Transfusion Units, two Field Surgical Units, medical stores personnel, one REME Light Aid Detachment and one REME Detachment Workshop.

HQ Airborne Troops also asked for other personnel including thirty-two tradesmen, a cook, two provost sections, a postal unit, two US Truck Companies and a US Army surgical team. It also requested more transport. That these units would have to be found at such short notice before the start of an operation indicates that HQ Airborne Troops was not set up to operate as a corps command in the field. This is particularly so when compared to the corps that had already been fighting in Normandy for several months and had their own organic corps troops, who they had exercised with before D-Day and had been able to build a relationship with.

21st Army Group had accepted responsibility for finding the units and personnel for establishing a Forward Maintenance Centre for the Airborne Corps. As the operation would be taking place on the US lines of communications it was agreed that British troops would be supplied with American rations but that 21st Army Group would arrange for tea to be provided to swap for the coffee. 21st Army Group would also arrange for a bread issue. The first road convoy would consist of two days' ammunition for all formations, 100 miles worth of POL and two days' compo rations for the whole force. It would also bring 3,000 Lee-Enfield rifles and 450,000 rounds for the French Resistance. Divisional medical units were to be prepared to retain casualties for up to 72 hours. After that they would be evacuated by air via airstrips, returning to Britain in the aircraft that would land 52nd Division. The AFDAG would establish medical services in the corps area to oversee air evacuation. Another notable gap in HQ Airborne Troops establishment was the lack of a corps REME workshop. Instead divisional workshops would have to undertake major repairs that they would normally pass back to corps units.

Until D+3 prisoners of war were to be retained by divisions, and as soon as contact was made with ground forces they were to be sent back to the Forward Maintenance Centre from where Third US Army would collect them. First-line reinforcements were to be left in camps in England and would be flown in by air if required.

One aspect rarely considered in analysing airborne operations is the countermeasures for preventing airsickness. For Transfigure troops were ordered to eat their last meal at least four hours before embarking, with a snack and a cup of tea two hours later. They were warned to only eat little and often whilst in the air rather than large meals. Each man was to take a dose of Hyoseine, a motion-sickness medicine, an hour before boarding and would have to be seen taking it. The dose could be repeated in six hours if necessary. Overcrowding was to be avoided on aircraft and troops were warned that 'fresh air is most important'. They were told to be sick into vomit bags which were issued on a scale of three each. They were even instructed to fold them after use and to throw them out of the aircraft on the leeward side.

The Maintenance Plan also includes a detailed list of stores that had been requested as part of Operation Transfigure. The Royal Engineers had asked for various plant and machinery including 12 tons of timber, 17 tons of corrugated sheeting, 13,400 water purification kits, 546 assault boats, 6.3 tons of tools, 10,425lbs of trench shelters, almost a ton of paint, 10,500lbs of pick axes, 18,000lbs of shovels and 136 tons of mines. Rations would run to 32,000 compo rations, 1,423 two-man ration packs, 2,000 water sterilisation kits, 18 gallons of methylated spirits, 135 bottles of ale, 128 bottles of stout and seven bottles each of brandy and whisky. These would weight a staggering 72,274 tons. Also requested were 74 tons of fruit, custard, cocoa, Horlicks, canned milk, salmon, sardines, tea, sugar, and hexamine tablets. Fuel would include 940 tons of burning kerosene, 5.5 tons of petrol for cookers and 15,282 gallons of petrol, oil and lubricants. In terms of medical supplies over three days the British airborne formations would receive 1,750 stretchers, 5,250 blankets, 1,750 groundsheets and 690 pairs of pyjamas. One parachute resupply for 52nd Division alone would include 600 stretchers, 1,800 blankets, 600 ground sheets, 200 pairs of pyjamas, 360 candles and 90 boxes of matches. 1st Airborne Division and the Polish Brigade would also receive 20 airborne shelters – a small tent – 425 sleeping bags and 84 Thomas splints between them.

The first ordnance resupply or 'brick' for Transfigure would arrive with the first road convoy with two more ready if required. Each resupply would consist of 40 radios of various types, 4,000 batteries, 5 torches and 20 telephones. There would also be a resupply of weapons made up of 75 Stens, 5 Vickers, 50 Brens, 30 PIATs, 25 2in mortars, 25 3in mortars and 60 Lee-Enfield rifles. Other equipment would include 12 mine detectors, 10 folding bicycles, 100,000 sandbags, 350 pairs of boots, 200 helmets, 250 sets of battledress, 50 Dennison Smocks, 1,000 blankets and 700 pairs of socks. There would be a small number of vehicles including four jeeps, four trailers and 16 motorcycles, and there would also be replacement artillery pieces in the form of one 75mm pack howitzer and two 6-pounder anti-tank guns.

The resupply would be carried by two Quartermaster Truck Companies and the priority of movement would be in order medical, engineer, quartermaster, signal, ordnance and then chemical. Two trucks would carry 1,000 smoke grenades, 1,000 gas masks and 1,000 tubes of anti-gas ointment. The engineer equipment would be loaded onto 18 trucks, including 5,000 anti-tank mines, 72 barbed wire stakes, over 2,000 pickets and 5kg of nails. Medical supplies sufficient for a ten-day resupply would fit into one truck. The Ordnance equipment would be carried by no less than 52 trucks including 164 tons of ammunition, from small arms up to 75mm howitzer. The Quartermaster Truck Company itself would require 18 trucks, partly to carry its own rations, and the signals equipment would be carried on five trucks.

14 August

On 14 August Leigh Mallory flew to meet with Bradley in France. Bradley seems to have grown even less keen on Transfigure and felt that it might not now be required due to swift advance of 12th Army Group and the light opposition that they were facing. Bradley also argued that diverting transport aircraft from the supply of ground troops and fighter aircraft from tactical support for several days would be problematic. Despite Bradley's lack of enthusiasm Leigh Mallory flew back to Britain and later the same day a conference took place at AEAF to plan the air transport and fighter cover for Transfigure. Even as the meeting was taking place Air Commodore Kingston Mcloughry, the Chief Planner of Air Operations and chair of the meeting, explained that it was now doubtful whether Transfigure would take place. This warning proved well founded. On the morning of 15 June it was reported that the American advanced troops had reached Chartres and were believed to be advancing towards Versailles on the outskirts of Paris and had therefore overrun the planned dropping zones for Transfigure.[58]

Despite Bradley's misgivings and the high degree of cross purposes between the Allied commanders, Eisenhower authorised the launching of Transfigure on 14 August. The Airborne force would be on three days' notice from 16 August, with 19 August the earliest date for launching the operation.[59]

1st Airborne Division's brigades issued their Operation Orders for Transfigure on 14 August. 1st Parachute Brigade's objective was to capture Rambouillet itself.[60] Brigadier Lathbury's plan for 1st Parachute Brigade entailed using two of his battalions to take up covering positions on the outskirts before sending his third battalion in to take the town. The brigade would land on DZ Y. The 3rd Battalion would drop first at 0820. After initially taking up a position astride a junction on the road from Le Buissonnet to Rambouillet, when the town was reported clear the battalion would then take up a defensive position facing west, around the railway running south-west. The 2nd Battalion would drop next at 0826. The battalion would move round to the south and east of Rambouillet and take up a defensive position facing east and north-east, with one company covering the road from Rambouillet to Cernay la Ville. The rest of the battalion would establish a roadblock on a road junction nearby. When Rambouillet was reported clear the battalion would assume a defensive position covering the town from the north, around the railway running north-east out of Rambouillet. The 1st Battalion would drop at 0832 and remain at their rendezvous on the drop zone until ordered forward by Lathbury to clear Rambouillet. When Rambouillet was reported clear the battalion would be ordered to take up a defensive position covering Rambouillet from the south and east. The brigade used code-words for each battalion's route that would be re-used in Market Garden – Leopard, Lion and Tiger. Relief by US forces was expected on D+3. As the approach march was to be short each man was to carry as much as possible, including two sandbags. Intelligence suggested that no enemy had been reported in the Rambouillet area, but with the caveat that columns with mobile flak may be moving through.

4th Parachute Brigade's war diary for the period covering the planning of Operation Transfigure sheds light on the activity required in a parachute brigade headquarters during the planning of an airborne operation.[61] At 1700 on 10 August Brigadier Hackett attended a conference at 1st Airborne Division Headquarters on the seaborne scale of transport and then held his own brigade conference the next day. The brigade's seaborne tail left under the command of Major Eyles, the Deputy Assistant Adjutant and Quartermaster General on the evening of 13 August and the next day maps drawn from the Topographical Depot at Newbury were delivered to units by 2100. The Divisional O Group took place at 1000 on 14 August attended by Hackett, his Brigade Major Charles Dawson and the Intelligence Officer Captain George Blundell and straight after at 1100 the Divisional Intelligence Conference was attended by Blundell. At 1400 that afternoon Hackett met with his unit commanding officers at his headquarters to brief them on Transfigure – described as Transfiguration in the brigade war diary – before a full Brigade O Group at 1900. The Brigade Operation Orders were distributed to units the next day on 15 August and later the same day the Brigade's glider and advance party group left for their transit camps at the airfields. Even as they were arriving at their transit camps, however, Transfigure was postponed for 24 hours. The operation was postponed again for another 24 hours the next day, until it was cancelled altogether in the afternoon of 17 August and the Brigade went to five days' notice for operations. The brigade's advance party group returned from the transit camps on 18 and 19 August. On 20 August the planned exercise codenamed Transfigured was postponed, and then cancelled the next day. Whether Transfigured was connected to Transfigure or was being used ironically is unclear. After a week of frenetic activity the brigade personnel were given leave periods of 48 hours each between 22 and 28 August.

Although only the advance party assembled at their transit camps the staff had been working non-stop between 10 August and 17 August, including attending conferences at divisional headquarters some distance away. The brigade's battalions and other units under its command would have been carrying out preparations in their barracks which would have prevented the carrying out of other training. It is not hard to see that although the rank-and-file personnel of the division would have known little of the strategic background staff officers and commanders would have grown increasingly frustrated as the summer wore on.

Operation Instruction No.1 for Transfigure was issued on 14 August 1944.[62] The general plan was for the US First Army and 21st Army Group to advance towards the Seine from the sea to just north of Paris, while the US Third Army with five or six armoured divisions and some motorised infantry divisions would advance rapidly on the right flank to prevent the enemy escaping south of the Seine through the Paris-Orleans Gap. There was no known defence system in the area apart from some mobile flak, and enemy units were expected to be moving through the area across the Germans' lines of communications eastwards. 2nd Airlanding Light Anti-Aircraft Battery would be responsible for the anti-aircraft defence of the first airstrip constructed and the defence of other strips would be arranged as they were built. HQ Airborne Troops had no corps artillery under its command, unlike a conventional corps headquarters which normally had an Army Group Royal Artillery attached. It was hoped that it might be possible to provide Forward Observation Officers from the US Armoured Force once contact had been made. Neither did HQ Airborne Troops have any organic engineering units of its own. It would only have under command either a British Field Company or a US Engineer Battalion, suggesting that whichever unit came under its command it would be at short notice. 878th Battalion would be responsible for constructing landing strips under the orders of the Commander of Royal Engineers of HQ Airborne Troops. It was hoped to complete four strips as soon as possible and afterwards as many as US Third Army might need. Mines were only to be laid by engineers, and no bridges or access roads were to be demolished without permission from HQ Airborne Troops.

The airborne forces would be able to call on air support through two US support parties with 101st Division and one with HQ Airborne Troops, while 1st Airborne Division would be provided with two

76 radio sets for its own use. Calls for air support could be made from brigades and divisions direct to US Third Army, while HQ Airborne Troops would monitor calls made by divisions 'so as to carry out any co-ordination of priorities'.

Arrangement was made for liaison with the French Resistance and civilian population and one liaison officer from the French Forces of the Interior would be attached to each division and to the Polish Brigade. Lieutenant Colonel Broad and Commandant Millet of the FFI would function as liaison for the Gauloise mission between HQ Airborne Troops with the Resistance and civilian population. French volunteers would be used to assist the force but not on active service. A large sector in the woods south-east of Rambouillet was earmarked for a Corps Maintenance Area. The GHQ Liaison Regiment – Phantom – would provide a patrol for corps headquarters and for each division to maintain direct communication with 12th and 21st Army Groups. Lieutenant Colonel H.O. Wright would act as liaison officer for the Airborne Corps at US Third Army. Corps headquarters would land on LZ D and set-up initially in the wood at La Garenne, later moving to St Arnoult-en-Yvennes.

The AFDAG was scheduled to land after D-Day to facilitate the landing and organisation of reinforcements and supplies and the evacuation of wounded at temporary airstrips. It would consist of a Forward Maintenance Centre headquarters and a signal section, an Airborne Control Section of each airfield, a Detachment of a Field Park Company Royal Engineers, an Airborne Light Composite Company Royal Army Service Corps a Defence Issue Details, a General Duties Platoon RASC, a US Airborne Hospital, two Field Dressing Stations, two Field Transfusion Units, two Field Surgical Units, a Medical Stores Detachment, two stores sections Ordnance Detachment, a Royal Electrical and Mechanical Engineers Workshop detachment, a Type B Light Aid Detachment and a Pioneer company and section.

Browning issued separate directives to Urquhart and Taylor, commanding 1st Airborne and 101st Airborne Divisions respectively. Urquhart's primary task was to capture Rambouillet, with a secondary task of using the Polish Brigade to protect airstrips north of the road between Orphin and Sonchamp. Urquhart was ordered to make every effort to hold one brigade in reserve that he was permitted to commit at his own discretion but was to inform Browning as it may be necessary to bring this brigade into corps reserve. Taylor was ordered to capture St Arnoult-en-Yvelines. His secondary task was to establish a Regimental Combat Team with anti-tank guns around Sonchamp to cover the open country to the west and protect the routes to the airstrips. Taylor's third task was to dominate the road between Chartres, Dourdan and Paris.

On 14 August the SAS were ordered to move to transit camps at their take-off airfields the next day.[63] Units were to make their own arrangements for transport and concentration. At 1940 on 17 August the SAS Brigade were informed that Transfigure would not be taking place that night, but that gliders were to remain loaded for the time being.

15 August

Parks circulated FAAA's Outline Plan for Operation Transfigure on 15 August, his covering letter stating that it was by command of Lieutenant General Brereton and was to be considered a general directive from FAAA HQ.[64] FAAA's outline plan was identical to previous versions of the same document, but asked ANXF to notify the relevant sea and harbour defences of the proposed route and schedule, presumably to prevent friendly fire from anti-aircraft units. 12th Army Group were asked to do the same with friendly ground forces. As the Allies now held a sizeable portion of territory in Normandy troop carrier aircraft would be able to make use of advanced landing grounds for emergencies and refuelling. Six were identified at Mauperus, Colleville, Querqueville, Binniville, Rennes and Courtils.

In the evening of 15 August Bradley – even though he was clearly not in favour of the operation – was still working on the assumption that Transfigure would take place. At 1940 he signalled 21st Army Group requesting that a Special Forces detachment and a Jedburgh team should be attached to 101st Airborne Division for Transfigure.[65] However, a message signed by Bradley and sent to 21st Army Group Tac HQ and to SHAEF at 2130 on 15 August confirmed that Bradley did not want to launch Transfigure on 17 August. In the same message Bradley confirmed that he would advise them 36 hours in advance of the operation if it were needed, and within three days if it were not required at all.

Maintaining what amounted to a British corps in the US Army Group's sector would require a considerable logistical organisation. On 15 August Poole at 21st Army Group forwarded a maintenance plan to Colonel Barringer at 12th Army Group.[66] After landing the airborne forces would be resupplied by air for three days, organised by HQ Airborne Troops. After the US armoured units had made contact they would then receive supplies by road convoy organised by 12th Army Group. There would however be emergency maintenance by air as and when necessary. 101st Division and 878th Battalion would be maintained direct by 12th Army Group even though they were under the operational command of HQ Airborne Troops. HQ Airborne Troops would develop a Field Maintenance Centre for all British troops under their command to which 12th Army Group would deliver supplies. The situation was further complicated by the fact that although some supplies and equipment were common to all Allied formations, some were nationality-specific.

Assembling the AFDAG would be a considerable undertaking particularly as it did not in reality exist as a formation and units earmarked for it were scattered all over Britain and France. The HQ of the Field Maintenance Centre would move by air from Britain along with a Pioneer Company and a US field hospital. However the majority of sub-units were already in France and these would have to move by road through 12th Army Group's area. These included one Defence Issue Details, one Casualty Clearing Station, two Field Dressing Stations, two Field Transfusion Units, two Field Surgical Units, a Medical Stores detachment, a Type B REME Light Aid Detachment, a REME workshop detachment, two Provost sections, a Pioneer Company and a postal unit detachment. US units required by road would include two Truck Companies and a surgical team.

21st Army Group would arrange for all British stores to be transported to a 12th Army Group lines of communications transhipment point, which it was hoped would be as close to a British Rear Maintenance Area as possible. Transfer of stores and personnel from the British Rear Maintenance Area would be the responsibility of 12th Army Group, who would supply all rations to British and US troops. Two days' worth of rations would be included in the first road convoy. 21st Army Group would also arrange for the 'normal British tea scale' to be provided to British troops and rations delivered by air for British troops would be 'normal British rations'. 12th Army Group would be responsible for the supply of Petrol, Oil and Lubricants to all units and would arrange for 100 miles of petrol for every British vehicle to be supplied to the Field Maintenance Centre as soon as possible. Divisional medical units would be prepared to retain casualties in their care for up to 72 hours and the AFDAG would establish Casualty Air Evacuation Centres at airstrips as soon as possible. After contact has been made responsibility for medical evacuation would then pass to 12th Army Group. The REME Light Aid Detachment would accompany units on a light scale with personnel carrying only hand tools and spares. Third or fourth line repairs would be carried out by the divisional workshops but as no corps workshops would be available – as would be the case with a normal corps establishment – divisional workshops would also carry out major repairs. The divisional commander of REME was asked to inform the Deputy Director of Mechanical Engineering at HQ Airborne Troops 'if vehicle casualty list is approaching limits beyond capacity'. Units were ordered to only cannibalise parts to keep vehicles running if ordered by a commanding officer or REME officer. As soon as airstrips were available one was to be earmarked for the use of the British and one for the US. Divisions would have to retain Prisoners of War until D+3. As soon as contact was made with ground forces it was hoped that prisoners would be sent back to the Field Maintenance Centre from where they would be passed on to Third US Army.

It is quite clear from planning documents for Operation Transfigure that HQ Airborne Troops was not fit for front-line service. Unlike front line corps such as those fighting in Normandy it did not have any organic support units attached. As a result it was proposed to assemble an ad-hoc group of support units that were available for various reasons including some that had been attached to Beach Groups to support the initial landings in Normandy, and had been part of Brigades that had been disbanded. Beach Groups, however, had trained together in this role for months before D-Day. Although it was no doubt sensible to find these units from those that were spare or had fulfilled their initial tasking, the short notice with which they were identified suggests just how unprepared HQ Airborne Troops was to function as a corps in the field. The corps headquarters that were in action in Normandy had had months, in some cases years, to exercise with their organic support formations. Beach Groups had been assembled in a similar fashion and had trained and exercised for their specific role. It is hard to escape the conclusion that the headquarters was not established to go into action.

Even though American troops had reached the target area on 15 August, 1st Airborne Division moved into their transit camps two days before the planned take-off date and Urquhart's Tactical HQ moved to Browning's headquarters at Moor Park.[67] The same day the SAS Brigade was informed that its part in Transfigure would-be code-named Operation Dodo.[68]

Despite these steps the odds were turning decisively against Transfigure. Brereton recorded in his diary that SHAEF had decided to withhold the operation and use all troop carrier aircraft to transport supplies, principally to move forward 2,000 tons of supplies to Le Mans.[69]

16 August

On 16 August Urquhart was informed that take-off for the operation had been postponed by 24 hours. He later attended a conference at Browning's headquarters and visited his troops in their transit camps.[70]

The air plan for Transfigure was published on 16 August.[71] The airborne columns would gather over Banbury and Salisbury and cross the English Channel over Christchurch in Dorset and the French coast at Vire before flying over Fyé and Bonneval to the landing area around Rambouillet. The first lift on the morning of D-Day would be made up of 432 aircraft carrying the parachute elements of 101st Division, 450 aircraft double-towing 900 gliders from 101st Division, 160 aircraft carrying the first parachute lift of 1st Airborne Division and 210 gliders from 1st Airborne Division. The second lift on the afternoon of D-Day would carry the balance of 1st Airborne Division's parachute troops in 125 aircraft, the balance of its gliders in 175 loads, all of the Polish Parachute Brigade in 110 aircraft and 176 gliders, the American portion of the 878th Aviation Engineer Battalion in 144 gliders, airfield control parties in 16 gliders, the British portion of 878th Battalion in 10 gliders, 60 gliders carrying SAS Troops and the first resupplies for both the American and British divisions. The third lift on the morning of D+1 would carry British anti-aircraft artillery in 30 gliders and a second resupply for both divisions. HQ Airborne Troops had also submitted a list of locations that it had identified for pre-briefed tactical air support missions which included Ablis, St Arnoult-en-Yvelines and Sonchamp.[72]

Arrangements for mounting Transfigure were continuing in Britain. Anti-Aircraft Command arranged for searchlights to be visible from 0530 to 0625 and again from 2215 to 2359 at critical points on the airborne route in Britain, presumably as a navigation aid. Other searchlights within 20 miles would be blacked out.[73] On the same day AEAF received a request from ANXF to include a detachment of forty-eight men from 30 Assault Unit Royal Marines and Royal Navy personnel in the 1st Airborne Division's lift. After landing, the naval and marines' personnel would proceed independently to Paris to prevent the destruction of 'certain enemy equipment' and obtain intelligence data. It is not known how the naval personnel were to be landed, whether they were parachute or glider trained or what the enemy equipment was.[74]

Even though Brereton had recorded in his diary the previous day that SHAEF had decided against Transfigure, Eisenhower signalled 21st Army Group at 2320 on 16 August informing them that transport aircraft were standing by loaded ready for Transfigure.[75] They were to remain loaded unless a firm demand was received for air supply or Transfigure was cancelled. In an indication of the priority that airborne operations were receiving, Eisenhower stated that 'we appreciate that demands for air supply lift will have priority over Transfigure'.

17 August

The air support plan for Transfigure was circulated by AEAF on 17 August 1944. Distribution was withheld in view of the cancellation of the operation, but it was thought that the plans would be useful as air support for any future airborne operation will probably follow the same general principles.[76] Even in this document it was suggested that the situation was changing rapidly in France and that the document was circulated as much for future operation as for Transfigure.

Air support would be delivered by elements of AEAF, Eighth Air Force and Bomber Command and would be supervised by AEAF Advance HQ. It would include fighter-bombers supporting the airborne formations, fighter escorts from the UK to the drop zones, attacks on enemy night-fighter airfields, close air support to ground operations once the airborne force had landed and air-sea rescue service and diversionary air operations. It would also include photographic reconnaissance and the neutralisation of enemy flak positions along the route and around the drop zones. Given the relatively wide latitude under which the strategic bombers operated it is not surprising that their brief for Transfigure was comparatively open. Eighth Air Force were 'requested' to attack all known enemy airfields and landing strips within a radius 100 miles from Paris, as well as diversionary bomber operations in an area east and north-east of the French capital. Bomber Command were similarly requested to carry out diversionary operations in the area generally north of Paris. The Allied ground forces were requested to ensure that friendly anti-aircraft fire would be prohibited, and barrage balloons would be close hauled.

Preparations for evacuating the wounded also continued. On 17 August Airborne Troops signalled that US casualties would be evacuated by IX Troop Carrier Command to Ramsbury or Membury, while British casualties would be evacuated by 46 Group or IX Troop Carrier Command to Blakehill Farm, Broadwell or Down Ampney.[77]

1st Airborne Division issued a more detailed Planning Intelligence Summary No.2 on 17 August.[78] US forces were believed to be on the line of Argentan-Laigle-Dreux-Chartres and there were thought to be tanks in the Foret de Rambouillet. However, the garrison of Rambouillet had increased to 400 men, intelligence that had been provided by one man who had cycled through the town. Convoys were passing through the town, covered by flak trucks at the roadside. There were also reports of small numbers of tanks being dug in near crossroads outside the town. The Intelligence Summary also identified the potential problems of liberating civilians, stating that 'in the early stages all civilians must be kept off the streets and we must avoid creating our own refugee problem'. Despite the apparent strengthening of the German garrison, the Intelligence Summary painted an optimistic picture, and suggested that the airborne troops might not need to fight at all: 'If there is no fighting and no Germans it may not be necessary for troops to enter the town at all. In such an event the entire population may be found in the streets, everyone with a bottle of wine for the troops . . .'

No sooner had this optimist picture been painted however than Transfigure was cancelled. At 1755 HQ Airborne Troops signalled the units under its command to inform them.[79] This signal was preceded by a similar signal from 21st Army Group.[80] The cancellation was almost certainly because Patton's troops had already reached Rambouillet the previous day.[81] Brereton recorded that Transfigure had been cancelled because the US Third Army's advance eastwards was only nine miles from Paris, and that 'General Patton's swift advance had made the airborne operation un-necessary'.[82]

It is important to consider what the cancellation of an airborne operation actually meant for the units that were due to carry it out. Many units had moved to marshalling camps close to their airfields from which they were due to take off. Aircraft and gliders had to be unloaded, work that occupied the airborne troops and the air force personnel. All troops had to be briefed and were given a 24-hour leave pass. The division was placed at five days' notice and was to remain in transit camps.[83]

The cancellation of Transfigure seems to have brought morale issues within 1st Airborne Division to a head. On the same day that the operation was cancelled – Lieutenant General Browning wrote to all members of the Division:[84]

> I most fully understand the irritation and disappointment which all ranks feel at the postponement of the planned airborne operations for cutting off the retreat of the German 7th Army in the Paris-Orleans Gap.
>
> I know this is more acutely felt perhaps by the 1st British Airborne Division, who have been alerted already more than once before, and still have to operate against the enemy in France. I want all ranks to know that the Supreme Commander and C-in-C of the Allied Armies realise full well the potential power they have at their disposal in this Airborne Force. They realise further the annihilation of the German Army is of infinite greater importance than driving it back by slow degrees all the way through Europe.
>
> Hard though these periods of waiting are, we must appreciate that we may be used for the decisive plan only, and not frittered away on an operation which the Supreme Commander does not consider as vital, and which can be achieved by other and less important means.

A great deal of hard work is entailed in planning, moving and loading for operations, and when disappointment follows we are apt to criticise the direction of affairs. Commanders operating large armies cannot afford to miss possible opportunities. This means that we have to plan numerous operations in time, and the cancellation or postponement of an operation is extremely irritating and depressing to us.

I have always tried to take you into my confidence as far as I am able, so I will say this:

1. The German Army must be smashed, and we constitute one of the instruments which will finally accomplish just that thing
2. We shall be kept for the decisive blow
3. We may have further plans and operations to prepare and then have them cancelled.
4. That we shall be used decisively is certain
5. And finally, if you are as irritated and impatient as I am, I am very sorry for the Germans when we do go.

Whether this was Browning's job – he was not the divisional commander – is open to conjecture, particularly given his tendency to be overbearing with Urquhart. Was Browning still attempting to lead the division that he had previously commanded?

1st British Airborne Division's seaborne element had already sailed to France and as of 19 August was camped in Normandy, north-west of Le Tronquay. The preparations for Transfigure had been so rapid that on 17 August HQ Airborne Troops asked 21st Army Group where the seaborne element was, but also asked that it should remain in France under the latter's command. The presence of the seaborne tail in France, although a necessity, would be an ongoing problem for the next month.

Although the airborne units had been told that Transfigure had been cancelled the RAF were under the impression that it had only been postponed. At 1018 on 17 August TCCP signalled RAF Groups and stations that it had been postponed for 24 hours, and that the earliest take off would be 19 August. The final cancellation was passed from TCCP to Groups and airfields at 1930 on 17 August 1944. Stations were ordered not to unload gliders.[85]

Transfigure also brought to light problems distributing reconnaissance photographs for briefings before airborne operations. On 17 August the Commander Glider Pilots, Colonel Chatterton, reported that some of his crews at US airfields were short of briefing photographs. It was discovered that the required photographs were being held back at TCCP with no intention of distributing them as it was thought that the operation would not take place and that the photos were not of sufficient value to warrant issuing them. None of the intended recipients had been informed of this and it was argued that while US aircrews might feel able to dispense with the photographs, that British glider pilots might still want them. As a result 38 Group agreed to supply all requirements for both its own crews and 46 Group's, as well as glider crews on their stations and 9th Troop Carrier Command stations where landing zones and drop zones were to be used by both British and US aircraft.[86] This suggests that there were still teething problems with standardising procedures.

19 August

Even though it had been cancelled Transfigure had a significant effect on the future development of airborne operations. As of 19 August 1st Airborne Division's seaborne element remained concentrated in Normandy south-west of Bayeux.[87]

The problem or air support communications would continue to tax the airborne planners. Although IX Troop Carrier Command aircraft had the ability to communicate with fighter-bombers in the air and would be able to call in air strikes, 38 and 46 Groups did not have this means of communication, which would presumably have placed them at greater risk of flak than their American counterparts. In an earlier memo on 20 August Wing Commander Musgrave of 38 Group's Operation Staff had commented on the lack of flexibility in the air plan. 'Presume that first class communications network has been evolved. Directive on who is controlling what. Whole plan has become so inflexible, doubt if a rapid alteration could be made within timings of phases.'[88]

Transfigure showed how Allied airborne command and decision-making was becoming increasingly confused, a problem that was only exacerbated by the emergence of the First Allied Airborne Army. Having bowed to pressure from Washington to form the new command, Eisenhower was unable to take a firm line with his subordinates, particularly Bradley and Patton, meaning that airborne planning and the context on the ground in the 12th Army Group sector were not joined up.

As the airborne troops were briefed on Transfigure and assembled at airfields before it was cancelled, it features in post-war recollections. Major John Waddy commanded a company of the 156th Battalion of the Parachute Regiment, and was therefore privy to more information than many other members of the 1st Airborne Division: 'Another one we got very close to doing was in the Rambouillet area, and this was to land the whole of the Airborne Corps in the forest area south-west of Paris to hold that area to allow Patton to swing south of Paris.'[89]

Peter Wilkinson was an officer in the 1st Airlanding Anti-Tank Battery:

> I remember one operation that actually comes to mind was one on Rambouillet where General De Gaulle had his headquarters, I remember the name quite well. We were going to land in the area of Rambouillet in advance of the troops coming up. But as you know the advance through North Europe once they had broken out of the bridgehead was really quite quick and easy because the Germans withdrew and Paris fell with relative ease, so nothing really was required. Until, of course, it came to September.[90]

Harry Gibbons was a glider pilot:

> We were transferred to Aldermaston and we were going to be towed by the Americans . . . and the object of the exercise, we were told, was to close what was known as the Falaise Gap . . . we were briefed an all the rest of it. But the front was so fluid that by the time we would have taken off it had moved on and it was cancelled.[91]

OPERATION AXEHEAD

Well before D-Day Allied planners had begun to think about the crossing of the River Seine. Planning for the crossing – codenamed Axehead – is one example of Allied long-term planning for beyond D+90. Although 21st Army Group's plans have often been used to justify criticism of Montgomery's performance – the phase lines used at his briefings before D-Day have become infamous – this kind of long-term forecasting was to give the logistical staff a basis on which to carry out their own planning. One of the chief concerns prior to D-Day was the long-term logistical picture, and as a result the capture of the Seine ports such as Le Havre was clearly going to be a medium-term target.

Knowing that North-west Europe had some formidable water obstacles, the Allies had given considerable thought to river crossings before the Overlord plan had been produced. A British Army Technical Report on river crossings had been published in October 1942. As early as 11 October 1943 the then Chief of Staff of 21st Army Group wrote to Second Army ordering a study of the problem of an assault crossing of a tidal estuary, and an exercise with an infantry brigade headquarters and an infantry battalion over the River Ouse at Goole with 7 Army Troops Royal Engineers. It was hoped that this exercise would help the Army Group develop a Technical Doctrine. Four days later, however, this order was cancelled as not enough bridging material was available. Instead of an exercise Second Army was requested to carry out an indoor exercise with the Commander Royal Engineers Kent Troops who was 'fully acquainted with the technical aspects'.[1] 43rd Wessex Division also spent considerable time in Kent practising river crossings.

Although 21st Army Group's doctrine on the subject was published on 28 January 1944, in April 1944 the Assistant Commandant of the School of Infantry at Barnard Castle wrote to 21st Army Group explaining that 'no one seemed to have any views on the subject'.[2] The 21st Army Group doctrine did however give detailed thought to the assault crossing of tidal estuaries.[3] A tidal estuary is vulnerable to fast tidal currents and the distance than any assault might take place from the river mouth would affect the types of boats or craft that could be used. An estuary might also be more vulnerable to wind and rough water and would be likely to have mudflats at low tide. The doctrine suggested that early reconnaissance should be made of crossing places, as well as aerial reconnaissance at high and low tide. Weather reports would also need to be obtained. Crossing places had to be chosen with vehicles in mind and with suitable assembly areas close to the banks.

The doctrine suggested that it was unlikely that an assault crossing of a tidal estuary could be carried out with less than 10 days preparation after troops had arrived on the near bank. It suggested a static organisation on the near bank headed by a Beach Master, similar to a Beach Group during amphibious operations. They would have to control a large number of units, provide boat crews and construct bridges. They would need to be an additional organisation and not made up of divisional units. These Beach Groups would be mostly Royal Engineers and would be commanded by a Chief Engineer. It was suggested that a divisional assault crossing would require eight Class 18 rafts and four Class 40 rafts, and that a platoon of thirty DUKW amphibious trucks would be needed to carry across stores and ammunition. Crossing a tidal estuary would be a major engineering task and it was thought that congestion on the riverbank was likely, and that bridging would not be able to start until 12 hours after the initial assault. A division would require one Class 9 Bridge and one Class 40 Bridge, with at least 24 hours needed to build a Class 9 and 48 hours for a Class 40. The ability of artillery to support the assault crossing was also important – if the surrounding country was flat indirect fire would be difficult to observe and an Air Observation Post would be required. Counter-battery fire would be critical to preventing enemy artillery targeting traffic congestion on the approaches to the river. Daylight and close air support would aid the crossing considerably. A Bank Control Group would consist of three Field Companies, a Workshop Field Park Company, and an Infantry or Pioneer Battalion Headquarters with three companies, as well as mechanical, signals, provosts, REME and medical detachments. In terms of vehicles it would have a platoon of DUKWs and fourteen Alligator tracked amphibious vehicles. Nine Royal Engineer Field Companies were to be trained in the operation of boats and rafts – two companies as boat carriers, four for vehicle rafting, two for tank rafting and one to man spare raft sites. The Infantry and Pioneer Companies would be responsible for making

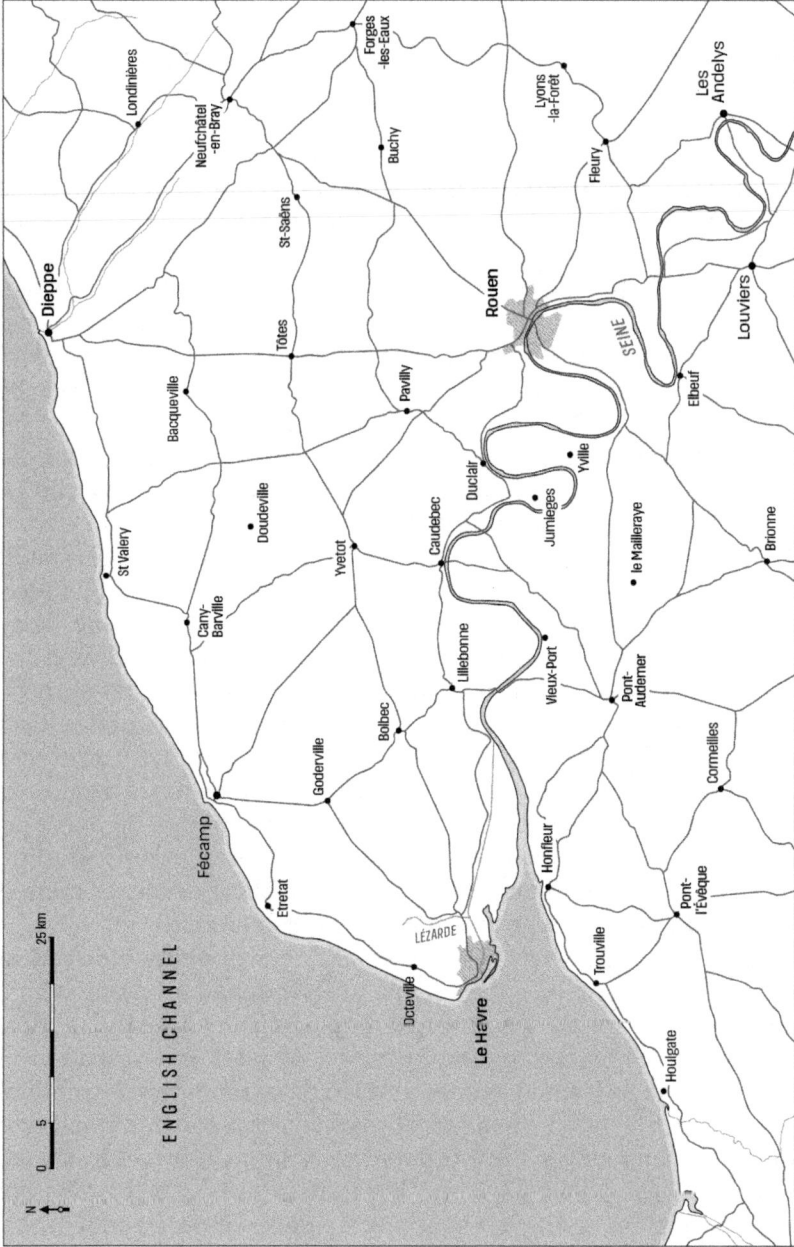

Map 3: Operation Axehead. (Sources: TNA WO 205/662, WO 205/672, AIR 37/621)

and maintaining vehicle tracks on both sides of the river. Although the Allies had tracked amphibious vehicles such as the Landing Vehicle Tracked their use was not straightforward.[4] On 26 August the First Canadian Army requested the use of a platoon of LVTs, presumably for the Seine crossing, but 21st Army Group advised against their use as they would have to be moved by transporters and would not be ready in time.

As D-Day approached planning for river crossings intensified. On 1 March 1944 a 21st Army Group Report by De Guingand covered the role of the First Canadian Army in Operation Overlord. The Canadians were scheduled to land after British Second Army and to then assume responsibility for the left-hand flank of the bridgehead. The Canadian Army was also given responsibility for developing an outline plan for the crossing of the River Seine, code-named Operation Axehead. De Guingand stressed that although a detailed plan would not be possible prior to the D-Day landings he asked Crerar, the commander of Canadian First Army, and his staff to study the problems that the Seine crossing would entail. In the interests of security this would be undertaken by a small planning cell at his headquarters.[5]

The Canadians were asked to consider the use of a seaborne assault as part of the Seine crossing equivalent to a Naval Assault Force, presumably to land on the Normandy coast north of the Seine. They were also asked to consider the use of an airborne division with the appropriate airlift and the use of DD swimming tanks for crossing the river. De Guingand told Crerar to assume that at the time of Axehead his Army would consist of three infantry divisions and two armoured divisions, some of which may be British. Specially trained engineers would also be available from 21st Army Group troops. Crerar was asked to liaise with the other relevant arms and headquarters including Allied Naval Expeditionary Forces, 84 Group RAF, 79th Armoured Division and General Browning at HQ Airborne Troops.

The next day on 2 March 1944 Brigadier Brian Kimmins, who was at the time De Guingand's deputy, wrote to First Canadian Army with a training directive for an 'Assault Crossing of a Tidal Estuary', almost certainly with the Seine crossing in mind.[6] At least one formation of engineers was to be trained as specialists in the assault crossing of tidal estuaries, which would be a different challenge to a conventional river crossing. The Canadians were ordered to hold an exercise in March 1944 on the Ouse at Goole and another exercise was to be held before the end of April involving the specially trained engineers, an infantry brigade headquarters in a brigade assault and a battalion group to carry out its part of the plan.

On 7 March a conference was held at 21st Army Group Headquarters at St Pauls School in London to produce a staff study on Operation Axehead. The conference agreed that a seaborne assault would not be feasible but that airborne forces could play a key role. The study identified opportunities to drop them north of the River Seine to delay the arrival of enemy reserves, or in the vicinity of Fécamp to assist with the seaborne landings. The staff study concluded that the most suitable task for the airborne component would be assisting with the river crossing.

On 18 March De Guingand approved the Axehead paper produced as a result of the staff study. He agreed that a seaborne landing would not be suitable and that the best use of airborne forces would be to support the river crossing, and also suggested the possibility of carrying out Axehead further eastwards down the Seine. A copy of the paper was sent to First Canadian Army as the formation earmarked to carry out the operation and another copy was also forwarded to SHAEF. The paper was later adopted as a Joint Appreciation.[7]

The object was the capture of Rouen and Le Havre at about D+90 to secure the use of the port of Le Havre. The appreciation highlighted the importance of providing sufficient bridging to support the crossing of the Seine and that in the initial stages the forces reaching the east bank of the river would have to rely on ferries. Between Rouen and Le Havre the Seine cuts a steep valley into limestone hills. It also meanders significantly – from Rouen to Le Havre as the crow flies is 25 miles, but by river the distance is 58 miles. The hills and banks were mainly wooded and there were no bridges in this section, but numerous ferries operating from concrete or granite slipways. The tidal range and bore would affect bridging and the approaches to the river from the south were well wooded, especially south of Caudebec where the Forest de Rotonne ran down to the bank. The north side of the river was also wooded, and intersected by tributaries.

Although a seaborne assault had been rejected the appreciation still considered the suitability of the coast for assault landings. The coast from Le Havre north to Ault was a line of chalk cliffs at least 200ft high in most places, which were considered unscalable. In a small number of places there were isolated beaches where rivers and streams ran to the sea, but out of thirty-five of these beaches only four were over 1,000 yards wide, with nine over 800 yards. They beaches were often backed by towns or villages. Apart from St Addresse and Fécamp all beaches of more than 800 yards were north of Fécamp, which itself had a beach of 700 yards. The beach at St Addresse immediately north of the Le Havre breakwater had a steep gradient, making it suitable for the rapid disembarkation from small landing craft, but its exit capacities were relatively small. The likelihood of a seaborne landing seemed remote, but the opportunities for using airborne forces were more promising. As the inland country was mainly arable and generally suitable for airfields and good going for armoured vehicles it was thought that there would be no difficulty in finding drop zones and landing zones for the airborne operations.

The Germans were thought to only have isolated small detachments of troops at ferry sites, with no organised defence line. The coastal defences were much more formidable and the batteries of the Le Havre defences were able to fire downriver as far as Quillebeuf. Gaps in the cliffs were defended by guns, wire, obstacles and mines and coastal ports such as Dieppe, Fécamp and Le Havre had all-round defence systems inland. The area from Le Havre to Fécamp was garrisoned by a division of two regiments while the area between Fécamp and the Somme was held by two divisions, each of two regiments. As a major port Le Have was very strongly defended with defences stretching landward on a line from Harfleur to Octeville. The harbour was thought to be defended by a boom and was probably mined. The River Lezarde was flooded 2,000 yards inland from Harfleur. The port and town along with airfields at Octeville were defended by a heavy concentration of artillery, including a number of anti-aircraft guns deployed in an anti-shipping role.

The seaborne assault force for any amphibious landing would have to be withdrawn into reserve from the forces engaged in Operation Neptune, and marshalled either on the Continent or in the UK to re-equip for an assault landing. It was thought unlikely that it would be possible to withdraw a complete division to the UK without affecting the main build-up in Normandy, and that vehicles would have to be left behind. The naval assault force would consist of one Landing Ship Headquarters, nine Landing Ship Infantry (Large), 126 Landing Craft Assault, 18 Landing Craft Assault (Hedgerow), 18 Landing Craft Support (Medium), four Landing Craft Headquarters, 39 Landing Craft Infantry (Large), 33 Landing Ship Tank, 110 Landing Craft Tank, seven Landing Craft Flak, eight Landing Craft Gun (Large), eight Landing Craft Tank (High Explosive) and nine Landing Craft Tank (Rocket).

The Appreciation also considered carrying out a diversionary seaborne landing to distract German reserves. The north Normandy coast was ideal for defence, as potential landing beaches were few and widely separated, making it difficult to establish a continuous beachhead. In terms of air cover the shorter distance of the coast between Fécamp and Le Treport put any landing within closer range of air bases in south-east England. As the diversionary landing had to aid in the eventual objective of capturing Le Havre it would need to take place within striking distance of the town. Fécamp was the recommended target, with Yport and Etretat other possibilities. Any diversionary seaborne landing would have had to be carefully planned and take place before the assault crossing of the river, which would mean the loss of the element of surprise for any airborne landings.

The strong defences at Le Havre meant that it could not be captured directly either from the sea or the Seine. It was thought that the coastal defences could be neutralised by bombardment from the sea or air and by artillery firing from the area north-east of Trouville. Given the importance of the port to the Allied logistical plans damage to the docks and other facilities would have to be avoided, which also mitigated against a frontal assault on the town. The only beach in Le Havre, at St Addresse, was also heavily defended and blocked.

A crossing of the Seine above Rouen was undesirable given that the overall objective of Axehead was to capture Le Havre. Bridging anywhere below Rouen would be a formidable task given the width of the river and current – the appreciation included the phrase 'the less water gap the better' – and would probably take six or seven days. An assault below Vieux Port was not considered practicable as the river was wide, the approaches were marshy and the tidal range was large, all of which would complicate rafting and bridging. The tidal bore was known to run as far up river as Milleraye. Below Caudebec it was described as 'probably a nuisance, not a menace.' Above Caudebec crossing sites were limited by steep wooded slopes running down to the river, marshy area and in places high or near vertical banks. The only suitable sites for an assault crossing were identified as being at Duclair, Yville-sur-Seine, Jumièges and La Mailleraye. Several of these sites were, however, overlooked from the far bank.

The Appreciation also considered the possibility of using Landing Craft Mechanised – LCM – during the operation. It was thought that they could be moved overland on tank transporters or 4-ton trailers, and might be ideal for ferrying soft-skinned and light armoured vehicles. The Appreciation also considered the feasibility of using DD tanks during the river crossing as well as Alligator tracked amphibious vehicles, designated Buffaloes by British forces.

The Appreciation suggested that an airborne force employed during Axehead could be dropped either immediately north of the Seine to assist in the assault crossing, further north to delay the approach of enemy reserves or to support the seaborne diversionary landing around Fécamp. It was thought that out of these the first option as the most suitable. This suggestion bears strong similarities with the role that the 6th Airborne Division would play during the Rhine Crossing in March 1945.

It was impossible to forecast the naval bombardment support that would be available, apart from LCL(L) and LCT(R) landing craft in the naval assault force for any seaborne landing. The number of ships available would depend on the losses incurred during the D-Day landings, the number of ships required to escort convoys and other naval requirements. However for planning purposes the appreciation assumed for a force of six cruisers, six to eight destroyers and one monitor.

The estimation of the enemy situation for Axehead assumed that most of the German mobile divisions were likely to have been drawn away from the Canadian Army front to counter the threat to the Loire and Brittany ports. The German strategy was likely to be a defensive one, and it was suggested that they would attempt to hold a line between Houlgate, Dives and Argentan with mainly infantry divisions. The enemy would find it difficult to reinforce their front but would withdraw to the east as slowly as possible and try to contain the Allies as far possible west, at least until the Allies could threaten Paris and the Seine. The Seine would be a natural barrier for the Germans to withdraw towards, reinforced with mines, demolitions and other water obstacles. It was an ideal water obstacle but its winding course would also make it hard to hold economically, and the Germans would have to hold it stubbornly as any breakthrough between Paris and the coast would threaten to envelop their forces further south. It was predicted that when the Allies eventually crossed the Seine the Germans would probably mount a larger counterattack earlier than they would during the D-Day landings.

First Canadian Army's Appreciation and Outline Plan for Axehead was published on 12 April 1944. The plan assumed that by D+90 the Canadian Army would have landed in its entirety, comprising two corps of at least three infantry divisions and two armoured divisions and that the army would be in contact with the enemy on a front stretching from Houlgate to Argentan. An airborne division and one armoured regiment of DD tanks would be available for Axehead but any seaborne assault would require the assembling of an ad-hoc naval force from ships and craft that had taken part in the landings on D-Day. Understandably, forecasts regarding enemy forces and reserves were difficult prior to D-Day with the prospect of 90 days of fighting before the assault crossing, but it was hoped that by the time the Allies were approaching the Seine German reserves would be few and far between.

Crerar's plan stated that if British Second Army was not able to reach the Seine alongside the Canadians then Axehead would be impractical as Crerar's army would be too exposed to German attack from the direction of Paris. This statement was underlined in pencil and questioned by an unknown author commenting on the plan, who wrote 'can't possibly say this authoritatively now. Depends on enemy reactions' in the margin. Crerar also argued that it was 'quite essential' that the crossing points between Louviers and Rouen should be seized and firmly held before the assault crossing, presumably so that the assault forces would not have to fight to capture the near bank prior to their crossing.

The topography of the country between Le Havre and Rouen shaped Allied planning. Crerar's staff agreed with the 21st Army Group appreciation that crossing above Rouen would be undesirable, but also that it would be difficult due to the tidal nature of the river.

The Chief Engineer at First Canadian Army had considered the potential of three crossing sites at Jumièges, La Mailleraye and Caudebec and felt that assault crossings would be difficult, but possible, in each of these locations. La Mailleraye and Caudebec would be affected by the tidal bore, and due to a lack of information bridging would not be possible at either location. The approach roads at Jumièges and Caudebec were completely exposed and at all sites a significant amount of work would be required to assemble rafts and pre-load trucks with supplies ready to be ferried across, to reduce the amount of time under enemy fire. The Chief Engineer estimated that using Class 18 and Class 40 rafts a total of 2,900 tons could be ferried across the river in the first 24 hours. Storm boats could also be used but due to the nature of the riverbanks DUKWs were not considered suitable. LCMs were also considered unsuitable due to the time required to prepare routes and launch the craft.

At the time that the Canadian report was published a separate staff study was considering the possibility of a diversionary seaborne landing around Fécamp, Yport and Etretat. Crerar was strongly opposed to any seaborne assault, arguing that it would require excessive resources in terms of training, support and specialist troops that would have to be diverted from other operations. He therefore discounted the possibility of any coastal 'left hook' in the Axehead plan.

Crerar outlined a number of potential options for implementing Operation Axehead. 'Course A' included an assault crossing around Jumièges, La Mailleraye and Caudebec, with the objective of capturing a bridgehead around Duclair, Yvetot and Lillebonne. Bridging and ferrying would aim to support a corps for a period of seven to 14 days. Once a bridgehead had been established the assault forces would advance to the north-west and west, clearing the far riverbank and then capturing Le Havre. Crerar was opposed to this course of action as he thought that the build-up and maintenance of the assault force by bridging and ferrying would be impossible. He was also cautious of any advance from the far bank of the Seine if there was the threat of a counter-attack from the east that would threaten his flank.

'Course B' would involve an assault crossing in the same area and capturing a bridgehead in an equivalent area. A prerequisite for 'Course B' would be that British Second Army should hold the west bank of the Seine between Rouen and Louviers to protect the Canadians' right flank. After crossing the Seine the Canadians would advance north and then capture Le Havre. Crerar proposed to adopt 'Course B', which would take part in four phases. Phase one would be an assault crossing along the front of Jumièges, La Mailleraye and Caudebec and the capture of a bridgehead at Duclair, Yvetot and Lillebonne. The assault would be assisted by an airborne division, DD tanks and LVT vehicles. Phase two would see the capture of Rouen itself and subsequent crossing points at Elbeuf. Phase three would then see the extension of the bridgehead to include the line St Victor, Doudeville, Bolbec, St Valery and the outskirts of Le Havre. Finally, Phase four involved the capture of Le Havre, the clearance of the coast between Le Havre and Dieppe and the securing of lines of communications between Rouen and the coast.

Crerar's covering letter of the same date, addressed to Montgomery, stated that the airborne tasks outlined in his appreciation had been approved by Browning. Crerar also disagreed with Montgomery's staff's predictions that the Germans would prioritise the defence of the Brittany ports, and argued instead that the enemy would strongly defend the Channel ports such as Le Havre. His covering letter emphasised his concern of a potential German counter-attack during the operation.

Crerar's plan for the implementation of Axehead was much more cautious than previous iterations. Compared to the assault crossing and seaborne landings, the potential airborne operations had barely been considered. Potential tasks or drop zones had not been suggested nor identified, and it is not evident from contemporary documents how far from the river the airborne division might have been landed, or how a junction with the assault forces could have been affected.

Meanwhile the Allied air forces were also thinking about the implications of a Seine crossing on their operations. On 30 March

Leigh Mallory's Senior Air Staff Officer, Air Vice Marshal Philip Wigglesworth, wrote to Air Marshal Sir Arthur Coningham at Second Tactical Air Force to request a plan for tactical air support for an 'Operation to capture the ports of Le Havre and Rouen', explaining that 'Concurrently with the planning for Operation Neptune, it is necessary to study the subsequent problem of capturing the ports of Le Havre and Rouen'.[8] Coningham was asked to contribute towards a Joint Appreciation and given the estimate that the operation was likely to take place on or about D+90. The instruction from AEAF gives the impression that Second Tactical Air Force would be leading the combined air planning, stating that 'it is appropriate that the Joint Appreciation be compiled by your headquarters in collaboration with a representative appointed by ANCXF and HQ 21st Army Group'.

Montgomery had delegated to Crerar the responsibility for studying the problem of the capture of Le Havre and Rouen. As a result AEAF suggested that the commander of 84 Group, Air Vice Marshal Leslie Brown, would be the most appropriate air headquarters to work with Crerar. Second Tactical Air Force were authorised to correspond directly with Commander F.N. Craven, the Naval Staff Officer at 21st Army Group, HQ First Canadian Army, HQ Airborne Troops and the Troop Carrier Command Operations Staff at AEAF.

It was predicted that by the time the operation began both Second Tactical Air Force and the Ninth US Air Force would be operating from the Continent, minus their light and medium bombers. The air support available would depend on other air commitments at the time. This was especially true for the Strategic Bomber forces which were under only loose control of SHAEF. AEAF told Coningham's planners to assume that sufficient troop carrier aircraft would be available to lift one airborne division. The operation could have been mounted either from Britain or the continent, and both scenarios were to be planned for. At the time of writing it was clearly not possible to predict what the status of the Luftwaffe was likely to be. It was, however, thought likely that the enemy would not be able to offer any effective fighter opposition, but that bombers could not be discounted.

On 1 April Group Captain T.P. Gleave of AEAF Air Plans circulated the Air Appreciation for Operation Axehead. The object was:

> To provide air cover and support within the sources available for the protection and assistance of the First Canadian Army in effecting the capture of Rouen and Le Havre at about Neptune D+90, with the object of securing the use of the port of Le Havre.[9]

84 Group was designated to provide tactical air support to the Canadian Army and would move to the continent after 83 Group, which would support the British Second Army, were fully established in Normandy. For planning purposes it was assumed that as the Canadians would be implementing Axehead that 84 Group would be providing tactical air support during the operation.

The first ten airfields constructed in Normandy would be occupied by units of 83 Group and therefore the arrival of 84 Group in theatre would be dependent on the availability of shipping and the rate at which additional airfields could be made available. The aim was for 84 Group to have eighteen fighter squadrons, eight fighter-bomber squadrons and three reconnaissance squadrons beginning to arrive on or around D+17 and to be fully established on the Continent by D+40. However, it was stressed that the rate of build-up of 84 Group would be contingent on the bridgehead being extended enough to permit the construction of airfields. This would clearly be made more difficult if 83 Group was not able to vacate its initial airfields in the sector that the Canadian Army and 84 Group were due to take over. The situation was further complicated by the assessment that the area north-west of Rouen and Argentan and between the Seine and the Dives was generally unfavourable for constructing airfields.

It was thought that a river assault could be maintained, provided that adequate bridging was provided, but in the initial stages it would be necessary to rely on ferries. A seaborne assault would by necessity have to initially be maintained by sea. Coastal shipping would be provided along with at least one Beach Group, at the expense of the beaches in the Neptune area. Given the Allied need for port facilities it was stressed that damage to the docks and other facilities should be avoided as far as possible. A landing on the north Normandy coast, however, was thought to be more feasible, and one suggestion was a diversionary landing on the coast to help to distract enemy reserves. A seaborne landing between Fécamp and Le Treport would be within closer range of air bases in southern England than the Normandy landing beaches were and thus would be afforded good air cover.

The airborne operation would aid the overall plan by either landing north of the Seine to assist in the crossing of the river, dropping north of the Seine to delay the approach of enemy reserves or by being dropped around Fécamp to assist in the capture of a beachhead if a seaborne landing took place. It was thought that the suitability of these tasks for an airborne force were in descending order.

As D-Day approached planning for Axehead became more detailed and was devolved further down. On 3 May Crerar's chief of staff,

Brigadier Churchill Mann, ordered II Canadian Corps to initiate a staff study to consider its implementation. The intention was to enable the corps commander to develop and outline plan, but also to consider Montgomery's views of Crerar's appreciation. The study assumed that British Second Army would hold the riverbank on the right flank of the Canadians. The study was to include Browning and Major General Sir Percy Hobart of 79th Armoured Division. Crerar wrote to Guy Simonds, the commander of II Canadian Corps, several days later on 8 May. Forwarding a copy of his outline appreciation of Axehead, Crerar ordered Simonds to assume that his corps would be carrying out the operation and would have under their command an additional infantry division, an armoured brigade and a regiment of DD tanks, as well as an airborne division which would come under Simonds' command upon landing. Simonds was ordered to cross the Seine at Duclair and Caudebec and to establish a bridgehead on the line of Duclair, Barentin, Yvetot and Lillebonne. Simmonds was also ordered to plan for the eventual capture of Le Havre, Rouen and Dieppe.

Crerar's letter to Simonds gave significant attention to the role of airborne forces. Crerar explained that his policy for the use of the airborne division was that it should be landed so that it could quickly seize the high ground that dominated the area between Duclair and Mailleraye and the high ground as far west as St Wandrille-Rancon. Crerar also stated that 'if possible' the airborne division should seize the crossings at Duclair and Caudebec. Simonds was given permission to correspond with Browning directly and with Major General Hobart regarding the use of DD tanks.

Crerar had developed a policy for deploying airborne forces without reference to Browning or to Urquhart, and then presented Simonds with a *fait accompli*. While Simonds was ordered to liaise with Hobart – an operational divisional commander – regarding the use of DD tanks, in contrast he was ordered to discuss airborne operations with Browning, at this point still an administrative commander, thus sidelining Urquhart, the officer who would have had to have carried out the operation and would have come under Simonds' command. Not for the last time Urquhart was being cut out of airborne planning.

Planning for Axehead advanced as far as the ordering of briefing models in several scales. Crerar informed Simonds that a 1:25,000 model of the area had been prepared and that 1:5000 models would be available soon. Subsequently, on 19 May Crerar wrote to SHAEF's G3 section requesting 12 sectional briefing models of three foot by five foot at 1:5000 scale to be made of the intended area for Axehead. The models were to cover the line of the Seine from Caudebec to Duclair.

A paper considering the logistical implications of Axehead was published on 26 May by 21st Army Group Q (plans). It would be necessary to establish a forward maintenance area for each corps by pre-dumping 15,000 to 20,000 tons of stores including 5,000 tons of Engineer stores for the river crossing. It would take an estimated 20 days to move the required stores up to the front from the rear maintenance areas in close to the Normandy beaches.

On 3 June 1944 – months after Crerar had started work on his plans – Browning issued a memorandum entitled 'Employment of an Airborne Division during Axehead'.[10] The memorandum was distributed to Canadian First Army, II Canadian Corps and 38 Group but was not cascaded to 1st Airborne Division. Browning outlined two options for airborne tasks operations connected to Axehead. The first option would assist with the crossing of II Canadian Corps by occupying the high ground around Ste Marguerite-sur-Duclair, Pt 127 and St Paer. The airborne division would drop several miles north of the Duclair bend in the Seine around Croix Marie Blacqueville and march advance south to their objectives, linking up with the assault forces crossing the river. This would put the airborne troops down behind the enemy's gun area, but it could have entailed them having to fight through German artillery positions. The second option would see the airborne troops dropping around Valliquerville, Louvetot and Yvetot. They would then march south to capture high ground north and north-east of Caudebec to deny its use to the enemy and to assist the Canadians crossing the river by holding a position around Epinay-sur-Duclair and Ste Marguerite-sur-Duclair. They would form the left flank of the bridgehead until relieved. Browning suggested that the second option would be a more viable operation 'from an airborne point of view'.

Although Browning estimated that Axehead would be ordered for D+60 – unlike the earlier assumption of D+90 – he also stressed that as it was impossible to say when exactly the operation would take place it would be impossible to predict whether it would be a no-moon period or not if the operation was to take place at night. As the transport aircraft could not drop the airborne forces at night in a no-moon period the air plan could not be decided until it was known if the operation would be taking place by day or night, or until enemy dispositions were better understood.

The problem of moon periods and the difficulty of predicting the situation months ahead of an operation point are two of the most problematic issues for planning airborne operations with anything more than short notice. As has been seen during the planning for Wild Oats the naval and air forces had firm, virtually immovable policies regarding transport aircraft flying by day and by night. These in turn restricted the periods in which airborne operations could take place as no-moon periods were out of the question.

In his plan for Axehead Browning also made a rather intriguing statement, that although quite sensible for the operation in question, would be increasingly ignored in airborne planning as the summer wore on, 'Airborne troops once landed or dropped are comparatively immobile owing to lack of transport, and 3 miles is the maximum for an approach march prior to battle'. How Browning could say this several days prior to D-Day yet ignore his own conditions several months later is perhaps indicative of his flexible approach to doctrine and getting his command into action.

Planning for Axehead took place almost exclusively within 21st Army Group and First Canadian Army. It was not until 8 June 1944 that a copy of the plan was sent to SHAEF after Major General Harold Bull, the head of SHAEF's G3 section, wrote to 21st Army Group's G(Plans) section to request a copy. Despite the pre-D-Day prediction that the Allied armies would reach the Seine around D+90 21st Army Group were at pains to ensure that Axehead could be implemented more flexibly if required, possibly if there was an unexpected enemy collapse in Normandy. On 24 May a 21st Army Group memo outlined a forecast of future airborne operations for planning purposes. It proposed a time bracket between D+60 and D+100 for Axehead but stated explicitly that the operation may well be ordered before D+90.[11]

Despite the significant amount of planning that took place at Army Group, Army and Corps level for Axehead, the planning does not seem to have involved 1st Airborne Division – the unit that would have been required to carry out a significant and risky part of the operation. The war diary of the divisional headquarters makes no mention of the operation at all.[12] This suggests that if the operation had been ordered the division would have been planning the operation at very short notice, even though the nature of the Seine crossing would probably have required a longer notice period than other operations. The need to have sufficient engineering and bridging materials in place would probably have given the airborne planners more time to prepare. A draft memo by 21st Army Group's G(Plans) branch that considered the possibility of driving towards the Seine at the expense of securing ports in the Bay of Biscay first estimated that before Axehead could take place 15 to 20 days of preparation would be required to dump ammunition and other stores prior to the assault crossing.

SHAEF's response to Axehead was dominated by logistics, and the implications for Allied strategy. On 6 June – D-Day – Colonel

N.N. Vlissing, the Deputy Chief of SHAEF G-4's Movements 3 & 4 Staff, sent an analysis of Axehead's likely impact on US forces to the Deputy Assistant Chief of Staff of G-4 Movements and Transport.[13] Previous studies had estimated that for the British forces to operate north of the Seine they would require at least 3,000 tons per day to be moved by rail from the beach maintenance area to a railhead around L'Aigle or Lisieux. This would require a significant reduction in the quantity of supplies that could be moved forward to US forces, who would operate from a railhead at Le Mans. The capacity of the line from the US beaches to Le Mans was estimated as being the equivalent of thirty-two Truck Companies by D+65 and thirty-seven Truck Companies during the period D+80 to D+90. As this number of Truck Companies would be required to move 43,800 tons of reserve stores to Chartres, if the capacity of the line were given over to the British at D+60 the anticipated phase line for the US forces at D+90 would have to be set 'considerably further back'.

Vlissing also argued that as Axehead would require the British forces to maintain their predicted phase lines south of the Seine this would need to be cleared with SHAEF G-3. If the British were to operate part of their forces north of the Seine, it might, in his opinion, make it difficult for the remaining British forces south of the Seine to maintain a phase line sufficiently eastwards to cover the construction of a railway line south from Caen to Le Mans, the American railhead. Several points emerge from Vlissing's concerns. Firstly, that the US planners were clearly fixed upon the infamous phase lines and secondly that he was clearly saw part of 21st Army Group's role as covering 12th Army Group's lines of communications from Caen to Le Mans.

On 15 June Lieutenant Colonel Gompertz of SHAEF G4's Mov 3 section replied to Vlissing.[14] He had consulted with 21st Army Group's Movements and Transport staff, SHAEF G-3 Plans and SHAEF's Logistics Plans Staff. He reminded Vlissing that Axehead was a 21st Army Group operation and that SHAEF had nothing to do with the planning. He saw Axehead itself as an amendment of the D+90 phase line to take Allied forces over the Seine south of Rouen instead of being on the south bank of the river.

21st Army Group had decided to establish the Lines of Communication railhead for Axehead at Bernay. Bernay was in advance of the D+60 line that therefore no stores could be dumped there before D+60, and probably not before D+70 at the earliest. Gompertz therefore estimated that Axehead would not be able to take place until D+85. 21st Army Group had however reminded him – Gompertz states that this was 'at great pains' – that Axehead could be launched immediately once sufficient stores had been dumped at Bernay regardless of the date. SHAEF's G3 planners had confirmed to Gompertz that they planned for British forces south of the Seine to be able to maintain a phase line sufficiently far east to cover the construction of the US rail line from Caen to Le Mans. SHAEF G3 foresaw Axehead as a continuation of the existing Allied strategy without cancelling the 'normal' Canadian advance to the Seine.

21st Army Group's Movements staff responsible for railways in the British sector were 'firmly of the opinion' that they would need to construct or repair railway lines between Conches and Bernay and Bernay and Rouen to maintain the Canadian forces that would carry out Axehead. This would require only one railway crossing of the Seine at Rouen, but as Axehead would inevitably require the construction of further railway lines north of the Seine, Gompertz strongly objected to any new construction that would slow down the building that was already planned. He concluded his letter by stating – accurately – that 'The whole of Axehead at the moment is somewhat in the air' .

On 14 June De Guingand wrote to Montgomery regarding potential future roles for 1st Airborne Division. De Guingand mentioned that a regiment from 79th Armoured Division would be allocated to the Canadian Army for Axehead; no mention was made of an airborne involvement in the operation.[15] For the time being at least Axehead remained a concept.

A paper produced on 6 July on Lucky Strike suggested that any separate crossings as part of Lucky Strike would not be planned until it was clear that that operation would be possible. The British and Canadians thought that it would be best to cross the Seine on a convex bend in the river, which would limit opposition and would enable artillery to give support from the near bank. There were five potential locations, at Vieux Pont, Yville, Moulineaux, Elbeuf and Louviers. It was predicted that the Germans would react strongly. One limiting factor in the number of crossing operations might be the availability of bridging equipment, particularly as the tidal part of the Seine would require specialist engineers. The crossing would also have to consider the tidal bore, a strong wave caused by spring tides, between 5 and 9 August and 2 and 7 September. This would necessitate breaking bridges into rafts which would slow down the rate of reinforcement across the river.[16]

For Axehead First Canadian Army had recommended the crossing at Yville west of Rouen as it had a much wider frontage and a slower current than other sites. Elbeuf, Pont de l'Arche and Louviers were also suggested but had narrower frontages, a faster current and in some cases would require tracked vehicles. Engineer resources would be required on the scale of two brigades assaulting each with one battalion leading. sixteen stormboats making ten trips per hour each would be used as ferries along with four Class 9 rafts each making four crossings per hour. If DD tanks were not used two Class 40 rafts would be provided, making three trips per hour each. A Class 4 bridge would take two to five days to build, depending on the tactical situation and the arrival of 400 to 600 tons of equipment. If a crossing took place at Elbeuf LVTs could be used.

Airborne troops could be used to support crossings at either Yville, Elbeuf or Louviers. They would be dropped north or east of the river to prevent the movement of enemy reserves or to infiltrate south and south-west, mopping up opposition on the high ground overlooking the crossing sites. Airborne formations could be supplied by air with between 240 and 360 tons per day. This would be difficult however if the US armoured force in the Paris-Orleans Gap required supply by air at the same time.

The administrative situation would lead to a pause as soon as a bridgehead had been secured. It was thought that each bridgehead would be able to sustain three brigades each on a scale of 250 tons of supplies per day, which could be ferried across by DUKW, Terrapin amphibious vehicles, LVT-2 or 4 or M29 Weasel amphibious vehicles, of which the DUKW would be the most suitable. The Terrapin had inadequate hold space and the LVT would need to be transported to the crossing site. The Weasel carried only half a ton of stores.

It was thought that amphibious vehicles would be the best way of getting the maximum number of infantry troops and support weapons across early. It would not be possible to use DD tanks during the assault crossing as the crossing sites would require preparation to enable them to reach the river. Instead they would be used as part of the follow-up force. One hundred and ninety-one DD tanks were available, sufficient to support one brigade. They would have to be withdrawn for training, which would leave none free for other operations. Another option would be to split regiments into independent squadrons to support the assaults.

Air support targets were likely to be enemy reserve formations north of the Seine and defences overlooking the river. The area inside convex bends would be 'drenched' prior to crossings but care would be taken to avoid cratering the approaches to the river. Air support would require coordination with airborne forces. The idea of developing air strips near the shoulders of river bends was considered, which could be protected by airborne forces.

The paper concluded that crossings should take place as close to the Channel ports as possible, and that engineer resources would limit the crossings to three locations with only one below Rouen. These should take place, it was suggested, at Yville, Louviers and if possible Elbeuf.

Setting a target date for Axehead, and any resultant planning, obviously relied on Allied progress during the Battle of Normandy, and uncertainty over the likely date for Axehead led to much correspondence between staffs. On 15 July Colonel Oliver Poole of 21st Army Group's Q(Plans) wrote to the G(Plans) section requesting a provisional date for the operation to enable planning. On 21 July Lieutenant Colonel G.V. Bullen of 21st Army Group's G(Plans) section replied to Poole's letter. He stated that it was unlikely that the operation would take place before D+90 but that under certain circumstances it could take place before. Bullen felt that if events went 'exceptionally well' the Allies might reach the Seine near its mouth by D+65 to 70. He suggested D+65 as a sensible provisional date but that he did not feel that future events were sufficiently predictable to ask De Guingand to approve this. An anonymous handwritten note affixed to Bullen's letter stated, 'C/S will not fix a Y day for Axehead. The odds are against Axehead – but no final decision has been made.'

On 14 August De Guingand wrote to Crerar telling him that it was now unlikely that Axehead would take place and that he should therefore assume that there would be no crossing of the Seine north-west of Rouen.[17] That was not the end for Axehead, however. HQ Airborne Troops' war diary records that a planning instruction was issued on 20 August for an 'Airborne Operation to assist 21st Army Group in crossing the R Seine'. The next day on 21 August Browning held a conference with Brereton and the following day he visited 21st Army Group before returning to England.[18]

The Planning Instruction issued by HQ Airborne Troops sheds light on how the airborne element Axehead might have been implemented.[19] It stressed that airborne troops would not be used if the ground troops could cross the river without their assistance, and that planning for an airborne operation to assist in the Seine crossing was a contingency in case the ground forces needed assistance. By late August the Germans were disorganised and withdrawing towards and across the Seine, and were expected to establish defensive positions on the east bank. The Allies were in pursuit and hoped to establish a bridgehead soon after reaching the Seine while the enemy was still disorganised. It was hoped that making an immediate crossing would allow the Allies to dispense with the need for a ten-day wait for bridging and artillery to be brought up for a set-piece crossing. Although the Planning

Instruction stated that detailed terrain information had been issued to 1st Airborne Division, including possible LZs and DZs, there is no evidence of this in the Division's war diary.

The operation would be carried out by 1st Airborne Division with the Polish Brigade under command, and if necessary reinforced by 52nd Division and Airborne Corps HQ who could be landed in a second phase. The force would be commanded by Urquhart until Browning arrived, in contrast to earlier plans where Urquhart would have come under the command of the ground forces corps commander. Airlift would be provided by 38 and 46 Groups and the US IX Troop Carrier Command and the transport force would be commanded by Hollinghurst.

Detailed planning was to be carried out by 1st Airborne Division in conjunction with 38 Group. Planning teams from both would visit Second Army, under whose command the ground operations would take place. This reflects a departure from the earlier planning for Axehead which had envisaged the operation being carried out by the Canadians. Demands for support including for tactical air support and artillery, signals and administrative assistance were to be submitted to Second Army, but the planning instruction also stipulated that any requests were to be copied to HQ Airborne Troops. This 'copied in' status suggest that HQ Airborne Troops was rather superfluous. The target date for all preparations to be completed was 25 August. Axehead did not in the event take place.

The proposed plans for Operation Axehead bear a remarkable resemblance to the Rhine Crossing in March 1945 – the assault crossing of a formidable river obstacle, against a far bank defended by the enemy and with the use of an airborne division on the far side. The plan to drop the airborne division on the far side of a single water obstacle simultaneously with an assault crossing of the Seine certainly seems, at first glance, more realistic and less risky than Operation Market Garden.

There were significant differences of opinion within 21st Army Group regarding Axehead. Montgomery had been pressing for a more ambitious operation including a seaborne assault on the Channel coast while Crerar was anxious about an assault crossing being exposed to a German counter-attack in the southern flank. The relationship between Montgomery and Crerar was a difficult one and this may have affected the likelihood of Axehead taking place, or at least it being under Canadian command. Crerar being asked to plan Axehead was likely a pragmatic choice, as Dempsey was occupied planning D-Day. How the operation might have been implemented within these differences,

Generals Bradley, Marshall and Arnold meeting in France, 12 June 1944. (USNA 111-SC-2064)

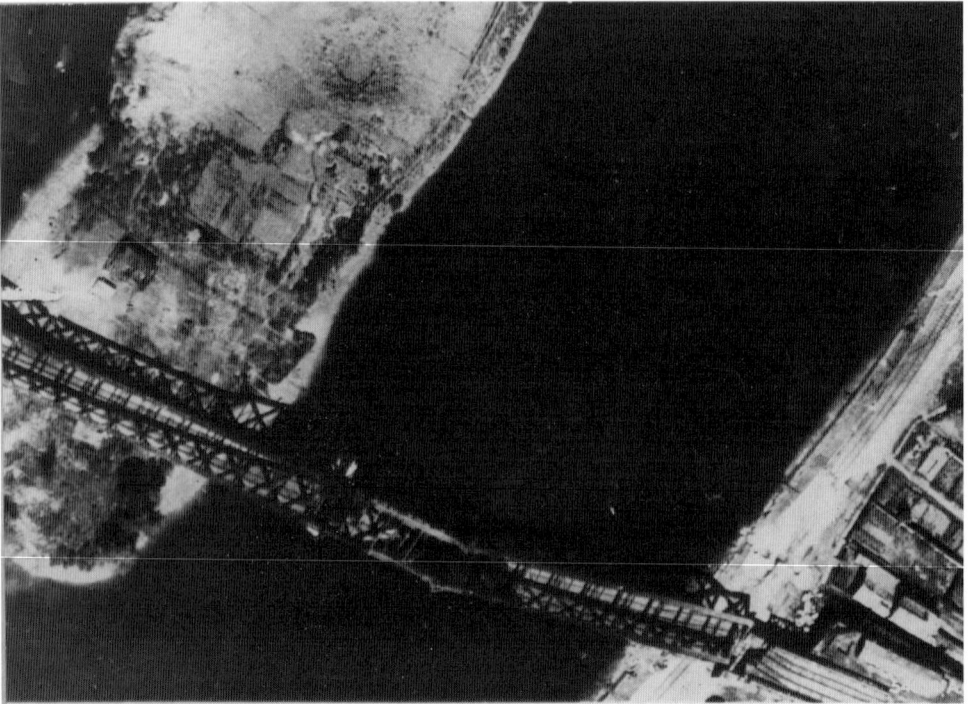

Bomb damage to Rouen–Sotteville Bridge over the River Seine. (USNA 342-FH-3A18269-54839AC)

The bridge at Mantes-Gassicourt was a key choke point for German forces fleeing the Paris-Orleans Gap. It was bombed on 21 August by B-26 Marauders. (USNA 342-FH-53378AC)

US Ninth Air Force bombing in Rouen, trapping German forces attempting to cross the Seine. (USNA 342-FH-3A19136-116475AC)

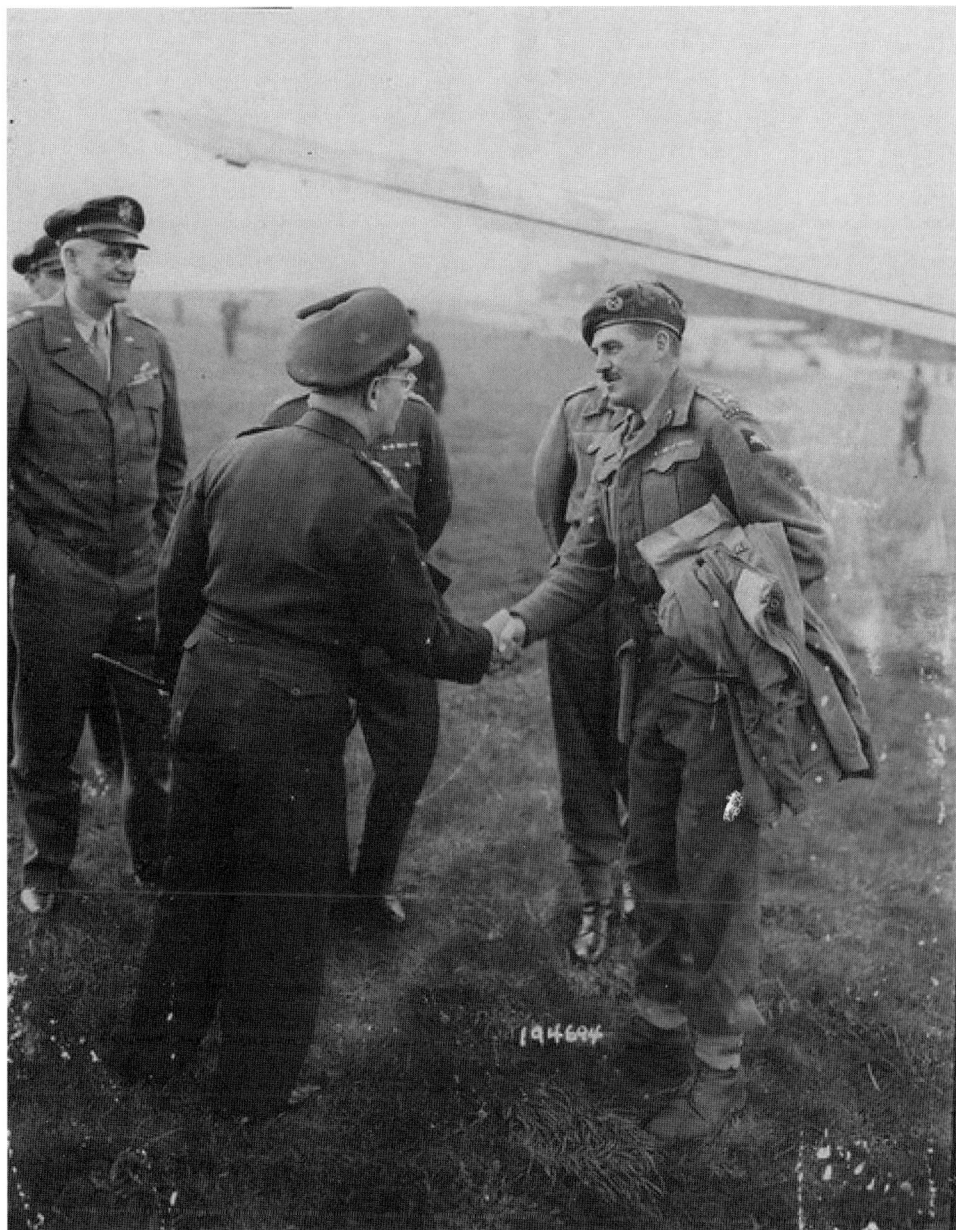

Lieutenant General Brereton greeting Major General Urquhart on his return from Arnhem.
(USNA III-SC 194694)

Nijmegen and the bridge over the River Waal. (USNA 111-SC-194568)

Allied airborne troops landing during Operation Market Garden. (USNA111-SC-354702)

Brigadier General James B. Newman, Jr. explains how an airborne bulldozer is used to build and repair airstrips in liberated France. (USNA 342-FH-3A17269-53187AC)

with 1st Airborne Division being brought into the plan at short notice and with the airborne component being advised by Browning, is a matter of conjecture.

The time and effort devoted to preparing Operation Axehead shows that the Allies – and particularly 21st Army Group and Montgomery – were thinking beyond the target of reaching the Seine by D+90, and to a much larger extent than has previously been thought. Airborne planning within 21st Army Group was clearly dominated by Browning, with 1st Airborne Division having very little involvement at all. Although the absence of Axehead in the divisional headquarters war diary belies the notion that Urquhart and his staff had to plan every operation proposed for them between D-Day and Arnhem it does beg the question, not for the first or the last time, what expertise was Browning actually bringing to the table?

OPERATION BOXER

Some of the operations considered during the North-west Europe campaign were only fleeting and had little to no effect on the airborne troops who would have taken part. Among these was Operation Boxer, a concept for an operation to clear V-Weapon sites inland from Boulogne.

Warren, the author of the US Air Force Official History, suggested that the idea for Boxer rests with First Allied Airborne Army, who proposed an operation to land an airborne force 30 miles inland from Boulogne to 'take the port and harass the German retreat in the face of the Canadian First Army'.[1]

Brereton's diary entry for 19 August stated that preparations for Boxer had been completed and that the operation would see the airborne army landing 'behind Boulogne'.[2] He outlined four objectives for the operation – to capture Boulogne, operate in a south or south-easterly direction against the right flank of the enemy, attack the flying bomb launching sites and create a diversion in the Boulogne area that would hopefully draw off enemy forces from the main front.

Montgomery's Directive M519 was published on 20 August.[3] Montgomery stressed to all commanders 'the need for speed in getting on with the business' and also said 'there is no time to relax, or to sit back and congratulate ourselves. I call on all commanders for a great effort. Let us finish off the business in record time.' Montgomery described his intention as 'to complete the destruction of the enemy forces in north-west France. Then to advance northwards, with a view to the eventual destruction of all enemy forces in north-east France.' Second British Army was ordered to advance with all speed to the Seine and cross the river at selected places. The Army was then ordered to advance to the Somme and pass between Amiens and the English Channel, after which it would be prepared to move northwards into the Pas de Calais. Operations in the Pas de Calais would be combined with airborne operations, with 'air landings being made ahead of the advancing army'.

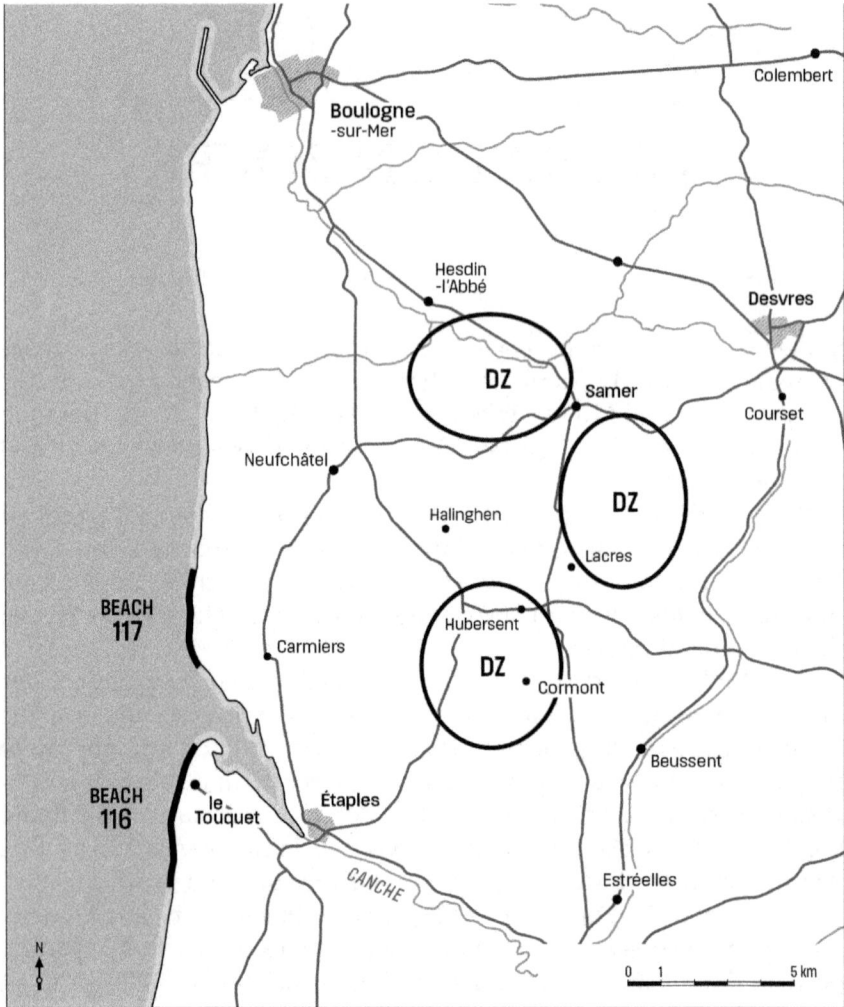

Map 4: Operation Boxer. (Source: TNA WO 219/4980)

An undated document found in the First Allied Airborne Army files, possibly for a planning conference on 21 August, posed no less than seventeen different questions that FAAA felt needed to be answered, demonstrating the complexity of planning airborne operations.[4] These focused very much on the air side of operations including the risk of friendly fire from attacks on flak positions. The document suggested that if the airborne troops were to be landed by day then the drop should not take place in a 'hot' spot as it would take time – estimated at up to an hour – for the airborne force to rendezvous and assemble into a fighting unit. It also considered the extent of aircraft losses that FAAA would be willing to accept. FAAA was keen to secure support from heavy bombers and fighter-bombers to attack flak defences and to clarify the extent to which fighter-bombers could operate at the same time as the troop carrier aircraft. A further set of notes in the FAAA files titled 'Things to bring up at planning conference this afternoon' was printed on 21 August 1944. These asked whether a dummy para-drop could be carried out in daylight and whether Maquis personnel could be dropped in the first lift.

On 22 August 38 Group produced an outline flight plan and routes for an 'Airborne Operation in the Boulogne and Cap Gris Nez' area.[5] The object was 'to drop and land three airborne divisions plus supporting elements in the Boulogne area'. They would be landed in daylight and two alternative air routes were suggested. Route A would see the airborne columns gathering over Bordon in Hampshire and then crossing the Channel at Selsey Bill. Two Eureka navigation beacons would be placed on ships in the Channel and the airborne force would cross the French coast north of Le Touquet. Route B would see the airborne force crossing the North Sea at Clacton and North Foreland before crossing the French coast west of Sangatte. Both routes avoided special defence areas on the south coast between Eastbourne and Deal and between Reigate and Romford – these areas were presumably aimed at defending London against V-Weapons. The 38 Group planners preferred the southern route if the drop zones were to be south of Boulogne and the northern route if they were to be further north. In terms of ground defences the area was thought to be heavily defended. The best entry points on the coast were thought to be between Boulogne and Le Touquet, another point in favour of the southern route. Focus on the point of entry across the coast became increasingly important as the Allied planners considered airborne operations in the Pas de Calais region and the low countries, which had strong flak defences built up during the preceding years of the Allied bomber offensive.

It was assumed that all aircraft would fly two lifts on the first day. As the turn-around on returning to base was six hours and the round trip was three hours, both lifts could be completed in a 12-hour window. To ensure accuracy the last landing had to be half an hour before twilight at 2030. If the first landings took place at 0943 this would allow three hours of daylight for bombing of ground defences. The first units of the morning lift would take off at 0745, release over the landing zones from 0945 and return to base by 1215. The second lift would then take off by 1830, drop from 1930 and return to base by 2200. Before a final decision could be made 38 Group were keen to obtain defence overprints that would show not only anti-aircraft concentrations but also intelligence on small arms and other defences in the area. Already the air force planners were becoming increasingly concerned with the possibility of losses to flak.

On 23 August a further document was published by FAAA entitled 'general notes on present operations'. The objective of the operation was given as 'the absolute neutralisation of enemy heavy, light and small arms flak'. The airborne landings would be preceded by a carpet of bombing on an area approximately eight miles by eight miles square. An area three miles north and south of the dropping area would be targeted by heavy and medium bombers prior to the drop. Fighter bombers would then cover the area to neutralise any flak that might have survived. The bombing would have to finish by 1000 so that the transport aircraft would have enough time to make another landing before nightfall, but even then the glider tugs would have to return to the UK in darkness. The US 82nd and 101st and British 1st Airborne Division's parachute troops would land in the first drop and roughly two-thirds of the British glider lift would then come in soon after, with the rest due to land at about 2000. The remainder of the airborne forces would then land as soon as landing strips could be constructed. Aerial photographs and map traces attached to the document suggest that the operation would have taken place just inland on the stretch of coast between Boulogne and Etaples.

The next day on 24 August FAAA published a detailed appreciation of the situation for the operation. The object was described as 'To secure a bridgehead in the Pas de Calais by airborne action in order to execute any of the following subsequent operations, as may be ordered by C-in-C 21st Army Group'. The airborne force would operate in a south or south-eastern direction against the right flank and rear of the enemy, attack the area from which flying bombs were being launched and draw off enemy forces from the main front by creating a diversion in the Boulogne area.

The enemy forces in the Pas de Calais were thought to be mainly static coastal garrison troops of unknown strength. There were a small number of field divisions, including the 47th Infantry Division around Boulogne, Calais and St Omer as well as three Ost Battalions. There were not believed to be any mobile or armoured divisions in the area. It was estimated that the 712th Infantry Division from the Bruges area could arrive by D+1, and that the 245th Infantry Division could arrive from the vicinity of Dieppe in 36 hours. Further reinforcements could arrive from the Low Countries or Scandinavia. In terms of flak defences there was a thick belt of both heavy and light flak at a depth of six miles stretched along the coast between Gravelines and Buiron, and the coastal belt was backed up by concentrations of flak further inland. Further south towards Le Touquet the intensify of flak decreased, but increased again further south. Despite the thick flak defences – described by FAAA as 'dangerously intense'– it was deduced that the Le Touquet gap would be the most suitable approach. The depth of the flak would require the maximum possible bomber, fighter-bomber and fighter support to neutralise. The airmen were clearly focused firmly on flak.

The coastal defences had been developed to guard against a seaborne invasion. They included an intense belt of minefields stretches along the entire coast and inland for a depth of about four miles, with pillboxes and strongpoints both on the beach and inland covering the minefields. Inland there was a further string of strongpoints and pillboxes and there were strong artillery units and mobile troops are set in depth throughout the area. The FAAA appreciation suggested that the airborne forces would have to land behind these defences and then work back towards the beaches. Lightly equipped, they would only be capable of clearing lanes through the minefields. Engineer units with heavier engineering equipment coming over the beaches would then expand and clear the remainder.

Although it was estimated that the enemy would not be able to mount any determined air opposition, fighter cover and escort would be provided to protect troop carrier aircraft. Fighter cover would then be maintained throughout D-Day and afterwards as necessary. It was pointed out that preliminary bombing would risk losing the element of surprise, and in consequence diversionary missions would also have to be flown elsewhere.

Immediately following the end of the heavy bombing fighter-bombers flying on the flank and beneath the troop carrier formations would attack any flak batteries, guns or troops firing on troop carrier aircraft. This, it was hoped, would maintain the neutralisation accomplished by bomber aircraft and deny the enemy time to recover after the initial bombing. The fighter and fighter-bomber effort would then continue until last light. After the initial drop ground attacks would be restricted to zones flanking the Drop Zone and Landing Zone areas and to the immediate beach area. These were within a larger area approximately 10 miles by 10 miles which would be neutralised by heavy bombing. In addition a strip three to five miles deep north and south of the DZs and LZs would be bombed. An additional five to seven miles east of the easternmost limit of the DZ and LZ areas would be neutralised to enable troop carrier formations to turn about. The total area bombed would be approximately 18 by 18 miles. This would have been a significant air support effort.

The air lift for Operation Boxer would need a total of 1,191 parachute aircraft, 1,944 Waco gliders, 526 Horsas and 38 Hamilcars. An additional 144 Wacos and 10 Hamilcars would be needed to drop two Airborne Engineer Battalions. As of 5 September it was estimated that there would be a total of 1,694 aircraft available – 1,242 American and 452 British – along with over 3,000 gliders. The real limitation on air operations was the number of crews available, with only 1,690 gliders crews ready, and to use all gliders available it would be necessary to fly without co-pilots. Therefore it would be necessary to drop all parachute troops of the three divisions and approximately 75 per cent of the British gliders in one lift and the glider infantry of the US Divisions and the balance of the British gliders in the second.

US XVIII Airborne Corps asked for a large number of additional formations for Operation Boxer. These consisted of no less than two tank battalions, a cavalry reconnaissance squadron, two self-propelled field artillery battalions, two conventional field artillery battalions, a special amphibious engineer brigade, a light pontoon company, an anti-aircraft battalion, a mortar battalion, a quartermaster truck group, two grave registration platoons, a destination hospital, an ambulance company and a clearing company. The size and extent of these additional forces demonstrates not only how lightly supported the airborne divisions were in terms of logistics and heavier weapons but also that the two airborne corps were simply not established with the same kind of organic formations as a conventional corps.

The planned area for Operation Boxer was roughly 10 miles south-east of Boulogne. Possible Drop Zones and Landing Zones were suggested along the general line of the road between Estreelles and Cormont; close to Mont Fleury, Halinghen and Hubersent; along the road between Hubersent, Lacres and La Verte Voie. However, it was also noted that all these zones were heavily obstructed by poles. Alternative dropping areas were identified around Courset and Doudeauville. It was felt that the whole force could be landed around the objective but that the main glider lift would have to be postponed until the second lift to allow time for the parachutists to clear the pole obstructions.

Two beaches were earmarked for seaborne landings, Beach 116 south of Le Touquet and Beach 117 north of the Canche Estuary, south-west of Camiers. Engineers with tractors and matting material would land on the beaches to construct exits. Airborne forces would not be able to attack heavily-fortified areas unless they were reinforced with heavy artillery, and initially they would only be able to capture the high ground, hold it, and clear lanes to the beaches. Their lack of transport meant that the airborne forces would be less mobile than ordinary infantry since they were compelled to carry all their weapons by hand and carry out any reconnaissance on foot. That this had to be stressed at all is evidence that perhaps not all involved in airborne planning were aware of this limitation. The planning document also stressed that the Germans were well aware of the limitations of the Allied airborne forces, argued that if the airborne drop was not supported by a seaborne landing then the purpose of the operation would be nullified as the Germans would conclude that the airborne drop could be defeated in detail.

On 25 August SHAEF allocated a code name – Boxer – to the operation. However, as swiftly as it was christened Operation Boxer was rejected. Warren has suggested that although the plan was approved by SHAEF on 24 August it was turned down by 21st Army Group the next day. It was felt that the operation would not be decisive and would be away from the main line of Montgomery's advance – at this point his eyes were clearly fixed firmly to the east and towards the Rhine. The coastal flak belt was also raised as an issue.[6] Brereton's diary entry for 26 August does not shed any more details, stating simply 'Operation Boxer is cancelled'.[7]

Unfortunately it is not clear who at 21st Army Group rejected Boxer as Montgomery himself was still thinking about an airborne operation along the lines of Boxer even after it had been rejected. M520, his last directive as Allies land forces commander on 26 August – the day after Boxer had been rejected – gave the destruction of enemy forces in the Pas de Calais as an objective for 21st Army Group.[8] Montgomery explained that the enemy had now been driven north of the Seine and that the Allies had liberated Paris. The enemy forces were stretched and disorganised and were 'in no fit condition to stand and fight us'. 21st Army Group's immediate tasks were to advance northwards and destroy enemy forces in north-east France and Belgium, to secure the Pas de Calais area and airfields in Belgium and to secure Antwerp as a base. Montgomery also referenced the flying bombs that were landing on England at the time of writing, suggesting that the elimination of their launching sites was playing a part in his thinking:

Speed of action and of movement is now vital. I cannot emphasise this too strongly; what we have to do must be done quickly. Every officer and man must understand that by a stupendous effort now we shall not only hasten the end of the war; we shall also bring quick relief to our families and friends in England by over-running the flying bomb launching sites in the Pas de Calais.

Montgomery's intention in M520 was given as 'to destroy all enemy forces in the Pas de Calais and Flanders, and to capture Antwerp'. To aid the Canadian Army Montgomery allocated the First Allied Airborne Army to co-operate with it in the Pas de Calais area. He ordered that the airborne forces should be dropped 'well ahead of the advancing columns' and suggested that in the conditions at the time of writing they would be able to operate on their own for a week to 10 days – a longer period than he would specify for Market Garden. Planning for this airborne operation would take place at Main HQ 21st Army Group.

Montgomery assessed that the Germans did not have sufficient troops to hold any strong positions now, and that

> The proper tactics now are for strong armoured and mobile columns to by-pass enemy centres of resistance and to push boldly ahead, creating alarm and despondency in rear areas. Enemy centres of resistance thus by-passed should be dealt with by infantry columns coming on later. I rely on commanders of every rank and grade to 'drive' ahead with the utmost energy; any tendency to be 'sticky' or cautious must be stamped on ruthlessly.

It is intriguing that the inter-Army Group boundary between 21st Army Group and 12th Army Group had been pulled further south, particularly as Montgomery's earlier directive had identified Antwerp as the boundary. 21st Army Group was being pulled further south by the Americans and hence having to spread itself too thinly, and in turn affecting its ability to concentrate its forces.

It is certainly intriguing that Montgomery seems to have hoped to implement Boxer even after it had been rejected by his own staff. He was perhaps hoping that the operational picture would become more favourable, but it illustrates just how confused the airborne planning mechanisms had become. Montgomery was also clearly more isolated from his staff than he had been in the past.

There is no evidence that planning for Operation Boxer ever went any further down the command chain than the First Allied Airborne Army. It was not studied by any of the airborne divisions who would have been employed and the seaborne element does not seem to have been planned beyond the airborne headquarters. Boxer was only seriously studied from an air perspective – the planning documents produced by the Airborne Army are overwhelmingly air-focused, unsurprising perhaps given that FAAA was dominated by officers from an air background.

From its first mention on 21 August until its rejection on 25 August Operation Boxer only existed as a concept for less than five days. And, not for the first time, even after its supposed cancellation Montgomery held onto the prospect of eventually carrying it out.

Part III – The Low Countries

OPERATION LINNET

After Boxer came one of the most controversial of all airborne plans, which would very almost fracture the Allied airborne command structure. Fortunately, Operation Linnet is also one of the best-documented plans, meaning that it can be examined in some detail.

Operation Linnet arose at a time when tensions within the Allied high command were barely contained.[1] These were particularly troublesome for airborne planning, and given that they required the co-operation of so many forces and headquarters, there was little room for disagreement. Tedder, who had apparently proposed Operation Boxer, avoided co-ordinating with Montgomery for example, whose 21st Army Group would have had to carry it out.

25 August

On 24 August Browning and Walch went to see Brereton at Sunninghill Park and the next day Browning flew to France and back.[2] It is not known who he visited but the US Air Force Official History suggests that Linnet was agreed on by Montgomery and Brereton on the same day.[3] Although Brereton visited HQ 21st Army Group in France he met with De Guingand rather Montgomery himself. Even at this early stage of planning Brereton's thoughts were on a landing in the Aachen-Maastricht Gap:

> General de Guingand wished us to drop in the Doullens area, about 25 miles north of Amiens. I refused this mission because it is of a tactical nature and the linkup with ground forces would occur within 48 hours. I suggested that in view of the speed of the advance of the ground forces we discard all planning except a landing in the Aachen-Maastricht Gap, which would not have to be closely coordinated with the advancing armies. The armies are moving so swiftly we can't keep up with them unless we are released from all air resupply operation.[4]

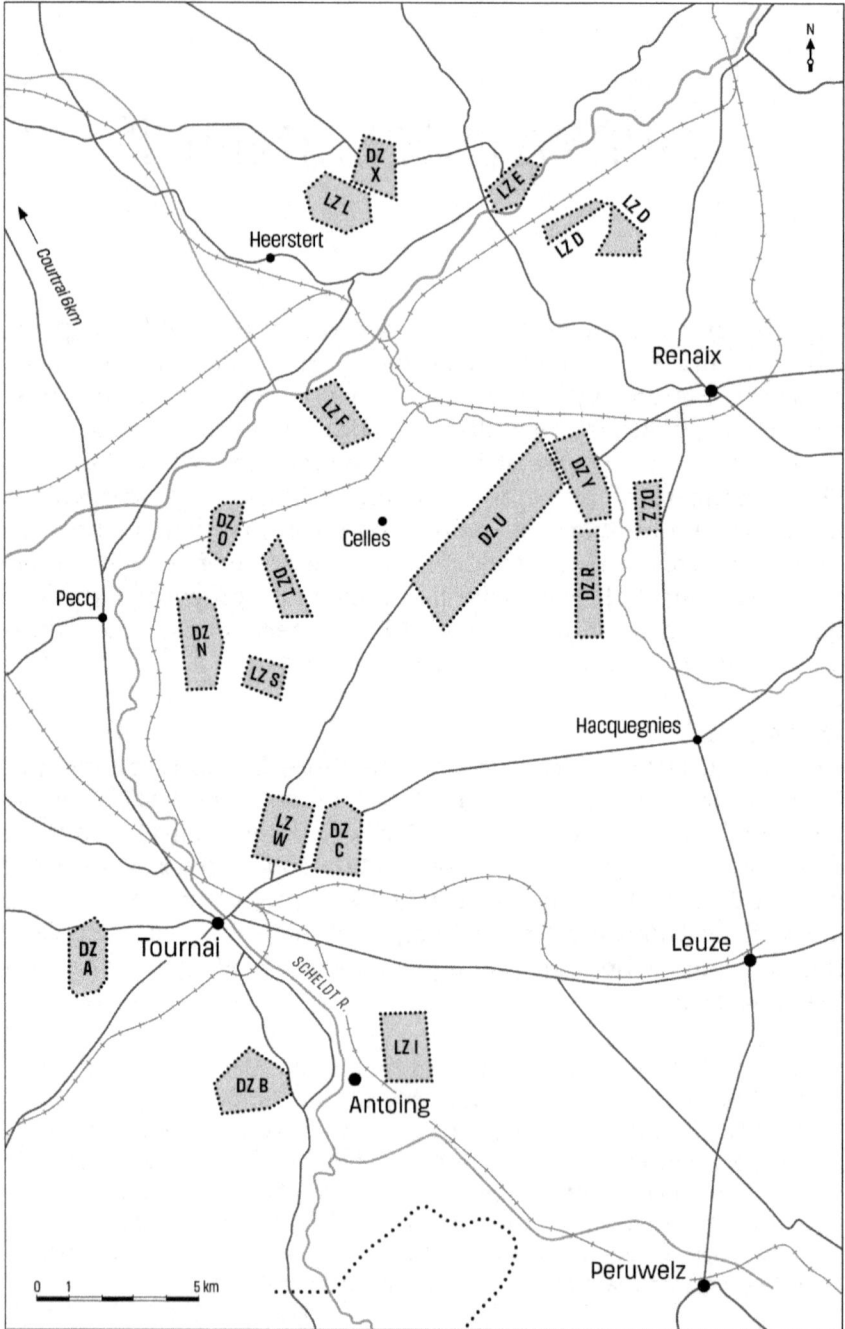

Map 5: Drop Zones and Landing Zones for Operation Linnet I. (Sources: TNA WO 205/866, WO 219/605)

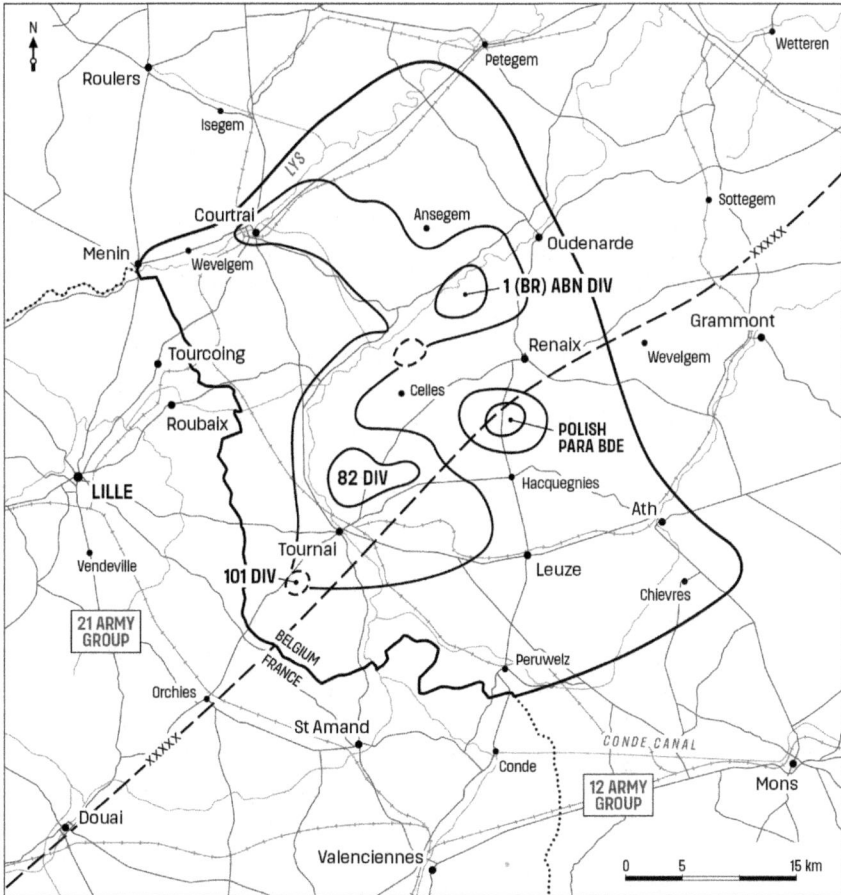

Map 6: The operational area for Operation Linnet I. (Source: TNA WO 208/93)

Montgomery and Brereton agreed an operation in the Lille-Douai-Arras area. This would take place directly ahead of the advance of British Second Army and would have the objective of cutting off the German line of retreat. The operation was christened Linnet. On 26 August First Allied Airborne Army identified Tournai as the target, and initial instructions were issued the next day. SHAEF and 21st Army Group agreed on 3 September as the target date and the US 82nd and 101st Airborne Divisions, the British 1st Airborne Division and the Polish Parachute Brigade were slated to take part.

On 25 August Oxborrow, 21st Army Group's BGS(Air), produced a paper entitled 'Appreciation of air support control requirements for an airborne operation in an area 80 miles beyond R Seine'.[5] The force would be 'picked up' by one of the armies in 21st Army Group. Air support would be provided either by 83 Group for Second Army or 84 Group for First Canadian Army, or from a 'small decentralised force' in south-east England. It was suggested that as air support tentacles with airborne forces only had short-range radio sets, air support would be better controlled from the Force HQ. It was also felt that a corps-level headquarters would be better placed to 'sift' air support and reconnaissance requests. Some elements of fighter control would be included in the Force HQ to enable pilots to be briefed in the air, to prevent friendly fire mistakes and to allow for reconnaissance to be passed direct from the air. The Force HQ could make use of its existing low power radio links to divisional and brigade headquarters, and high power links to communicate with Army headquarters and other headquarters in the UK.

On the same day 21st Army Group G(Plans) circulated 'Linnet' as the code word for 'possible airborne operation in Northern France'.[6]

26 August

The US Air Force Official History suggests that Tournai was picked as a target by FAAA on 26 August, and that SHAEF and 21st Army Group approved 3 September as the target date.[7]

A loose minute drafted by Squadron Leader D.R.L. Wallace of 38 Group on 26 August gives some idea of the challenge facing the air forces in laying on the airlift for Linnet.[8] Wallace estimated that 1st Airborne Division would require 12 pathfinder aircraft, 525 Horsas and 28 Hamilcars. 38 Group had available 150 Stirlings, 60 Albermarles and 40 Halifaxes. Ninety-three gliders would be required in a third lift on D+1 to carry in SAS Troops and the Airlanding Light Anti-Aircraft Battery. Wallace estimated that area bombing would take place between 0640 and 0730, with the first parachute drop beginning at 0730. The first glider lift would land at 1045, and the second glider lift at 1845. He had made allowances for aircraft casualties of 12.5 per cent in each lift.

27 August

On 27 August Browning was designated to command the airborne element of Operation Linnet.[9] The mission was to 'Seize a firm base in the vicinity of Tournai, Belgium, secure and hold bridgehead over the Euscat river at Tournai and control the principal road nets leading northeast through Tournai, Lille and Courtrai.' The target date was 3 September. In the meantime he was asked to begin detailed planning in accordance with conversations that he had already had with Brereton and his planners at FAAA. Browning was authorised to liaise directly with 21st Army Group, US 82nd and 101st Airborne Divisions, 878th Battalion, IX Troop Carrier Command and 38 and 46 Groups if they were allocated to the operation by the RAF. He was ordered to 'give consideration to the immediate seizure of a paved airdrome in the area of the operation in order to facilitate supply'.

The same day Brigadier-General David Schlatter, the Deputy Chief of Staff for Operations at Ninth Air Force, sent a lengthy memo to Stearley, the Assistant Chief of Staff G3 at FAAA.[10] Schlatter noted that Allied forces were at the time of writing occupying a line roughly on the Somme with the coast between the mouth of the Somme and Dieppe in Allied hands. Therefore there would be no German flak along that section of coastline. Schlatter proposed to route the airborne columns to cross the French coast between the mouth of the Seine and Dieppe. The exact target area had not been defined but was believed to be around Lille, Tournai and Courtrai. Schlatter described Target area 1 as east of Tournai, area 2 as north and north-east of Tournai around a bend in the Euscat and area 3 would be east and south-east of Courtrai. Schlatter assumed that all Allied air forces would be available to support the operation. He thought that Air Defence of Great Britain would provide escort cover as far as Amiens at which point Eighth Air Force fighters would take over and cover the landings themselves and the return to base. He recommended that Second Tactical Air Force and Ninth Air Force be used to attack flak along the routes. Schlatter envisaged bombers attacking 'centres of resistance' such as flak concentrations and road and rail bridges to delay the arrival of enemy reinforcements but also suggested a more detailed study into potential bomber targets. Although an airborne route had been proposed crossing the coast between Dunkirk and Ostend, Schlatter thought that flak would make it costly to the troop carrier aircraft, flying low and with no self-sealing fuel tanks or armour. Another route had been considered crossing the coast over Holland, to which he applied the same concerns. Air force officers were determined to avoid losses, with minimal concern for the effect that this might have on the operation once on the ground.

28 August

Montgomery's directive M522, published on 28 August, outlined a decision to drop airborne forces in the Tournai area. The boundary between the Canadian Army and Second Army was altered to run from Ypres to the Dutch frontier and then to the Scheldt, and that between 21st Army Group and 12th Army Group would run from Mantes to Douai, Tournai, Brussels, Louvain and Diest. Montgomery described the role of the airborne force in Linnet as

> To be landed west of a line joining Renaix and Leuze, and to the east side
> of the bend in the Euscat between Tournai and Escanapples . . . The role
> of these forces will be to operate offensively from the area secured, and
> to attack and destroy all enemy bodies attempting to escape eastwards
> from the coastal belt within their radius of operations. Tournai itself will
> be securely held.[11]

Linnet was scheduled to take place on 3 September. The Airborne
Corps would be under the operational command of 21st Army Group
and would be in radio contact with Montgomery's, Dempsey's and
Bradley's Tac HQs respectively. The issue of control of the Airborne
Corps was left fluid in Montgomery's directive: 'I will decide later
whether command of the Airborne Corps should pass to Second Army
when that Army approaches Tournai area, or whether the Airborne
forces should remain directly under 21st Army Group.'

The Corps Commander's conference to commence planning for
Linnet took place at 1600 on 28 August. It was chaired by Browning and
attended by Hollinghurst of 38 Group, Crawford from the War Office,
Ridgway of XVIII Airborne Corps, Urquhart of 1st Airborne Division,
Taylor of 101st Airborne Division, Gavin of 82nd Airborne Division,
Major General Bud Miley of 17th Division, Williams of XI Troop Carrier
Command, Cutler and Goldsmith from FAAA, Richardson from 21st
Army Group, Walch from 1st Airborne Corps, Brigadier Burns of 52nd
Division, Colonel George Chatterton the commander of the Glider
Pilot Regiment, Lieutenant Colonel Stevens who was the liaison officer
with the Polish Parachute Brigade), and representatives from TCCP
Eastcote and Phantom. Intriguingly the Polish Brigade commander
Major General Sosabowski seems to have been overlooked, hinting at
a growing discord between him and Browning that would come to a
head later.

Browning summarised the object of the operation as 'to seize a firm
base in the vicinity of Tournai and secure and hold bridgehead over
the Euscat river at Tournai and to control principal road nets leading
NE through Tournai, Lille and Courtrai'. The provisional target date
was 3 September. The target area was to be on one of the Germans
main lines of communications, but there were not thought to be any
lines of communications troops in any strength nearby. It was thought
that the only troops likely to be encountered would be either remnants
of the German Army retreating from Normandy towards Germany or
reinforcements from Germany.

The Tournai area was dominated by three pieces of high ground.
The Euscat Canal was a formidable obstacle, but less so up to Courtrai.

Tournai was also identified as a major road centre, with a main road leading to Brussels and with other important roads running south-west and south-east.

The strategy for Linnet would see 21st Army Group driving up the North Sea coast with its left flank on the sea. 12th Army Group would advance on the right, but would also have a secondary role of turning east into Germany through 'gaps'. Bradley's Army Group might in the future be ordered to encircle the withdrawing German Army. Browning also stressed to the conference that the airborne force might be out of touch with Second Army 'for a week or more'. Browning had requested that no Belgian Resistance personnel would be armed or encouraged to operate within the airborne operational area. A map trace was issued showing commanders which bridges over the Euscat were to be demolished, and the order of priority, but the extent of bridge demolitions would be decided by Montgomery. Airborne Corps Headquarters would have radio links with the Airborne Base in the UK, Second Army, 21st Army Group and Third US Army. The US airborne divisions would have direct links with Com Z and XVIII Airborne Corps.

The conference also discussed the need for additional administrative units for the airborne forces to function for a prolonged period on the ground. 21st Army Group would obtain British requirements, and would submit US requirements to 12th Army Group who had already been ordered by SHAEF to comply. In the second phase of the plan the airborne force would need to build airstrips, as there was only limited recourse for parachute resupplies. If the supply situation became serious the airborne forces would have to capture the most suitable airfield in the area to allow supplies to be flown in. At the time of the conference the air plan was still in progress.

The final route had not been decided but it was expected that it cross the coast between Ostend and Dunkirk. The Air Conference was to take place at AEAF the next afternoon (29 August), but Browning argued that a decision would be needed in the morning and Goldsmith of FAAA undertook to try to move the conference. It was expected that the air support plan would be produced the next day and that it would include the support of heavy bombers, tactical air forces, and dummy para drops. Browning stressed to divisional commanders that they should not expect bombing as close support and that their bomb lines would need to be in in advance of their front lines. Major General Taylor asked for fighter sweeps at pre-arranged times which could be called down onto selected targets. Richardson pointed out that close air support could not be provided quickly as the tactical air forces were operating from airfields 100 miles away. Instead, general interdiction lines were discussed south and west of Lille.

Williams warned that to fly the required number of aircraft from the northern area the troop carrier forces would need four extra bases, and Browning pointed out that unless 82nd Division could fly from the northern airfields it would not be able to take part on D-Day. FAAA undertook to ask for permission to use Botterford, Fulbeck, Woolfox Lodge and Langor airfields. If these airfields could not be obtained troops would have to be flown on D+1 from airfields in the Exeter area. Browning stated that if decisions had to be made as to which divisions would take off from the northern airfields priority would be given to 82nd Division. Richardson at 21st Army Group had checked with SHAEF and 52nd Division was available for the operation. Browning planned to fly the division in as soon as airstrips were available.

Resupply would initially be by parachute drops into divisional areas until airstrips had either been constructed or captured sufficient to receive a daily tonnage of 1,250 tons. The existing Airborne Corps troops would only be able to handle 700 tons, however, and the relieving ground troops would have two days' worth of supplies for the airborne force pre-loaded. The airborne divisions were to retain their own casualties – presumably as the Airborne Corps did not have the usual corps medical troops, and a Casualty Clearing Station would have to be found and brought in later. As HQ Airborne Troops had not been established as an operation headquarters a number of ad-hoc attachments were requested at short notice. The Commander of Royal Engineers requested Major Hancock, an Aviation Engineer from 12th Army Group, and engineer representatives from the US airborne divisions. The US Airborne Divisions were also asked to provide liaison officers and a Phantom detachment would also be required for Corps HQ and each division, as well as civil affairs detachments. Walch stated that Belgians with local knowledge would be attached to each division, and would arrive in transit camps on 1 September. Both US Airborne Divisions were to open offices at Airborne Corps HQ at Moor Park the next day on 29 August.

A preliminary meeting was held at FAAA to discuss Operation Linnet on 28 August.[12] The target area would be the triangle Lille-Courtrai-Tournai with a target date of 3, 4 or 5 September. The Deputy Supreme Allied Commander, Tedder, had ruled that all available air forces in Britain could be called upon to support the operation. It was thought that enemy fighters would not be able to cause effective interference and that there would be adequate fighter escorts available. It was decided to select a route that was as free of flak as possible.

There were two alternative routes, the first crossing the friendly zone of France then over the front line area to the landing area, involving a considerable period flying over hostile territory. The second option was much shorter and would cross hostile coast around Dunkirk, and then fly a short distance over enemy territory to landing area. It was unanimously agreed to use the second route. It is interesting that the route was selected on air factors alone without consideration of the battle on the ground. It was tentatively agreed that Eighth Air Force and Bomber Command would be responsible for eliminating flak along the route, particularly the coastal area. Eighth Air Force fighters would carry out armed reconnaissance by day and night. Diversionary bombing could take place around the coastal defences in the vicinity of Boulogne, as well as the laying of smokescreens. It was agreed however not to lay smoke around the drop zones. The dropping of dummy paratroopers would be left to Browning to decide. It was also felt that the detailed allocation of air support tasks was 'not worth discussing' until the required air support operations had been decided.

On 28 August SHAEF signalled AEAF to request that either 876th or 878th Airborne Engineer Aviation Battalions be released by Ninth Air Force to take part in 'a large airborne operation in the near future'.[13]

Although the Allies had taken hundreds of thousands of photographs of occupied Europe in the run-up to D-Day and afterwards there is little evidence in planning papers of how this photographic intelligence was used to support airborne operations. While the assault troops who landed in Normandy were issued with detailed defence maps that identified barbed wire, trenches and individual machine guns, this level of intelligence was rarely possible once operations became more mobile. The defence overprints used for Linnet were based on photographs taken on 29 August and were issued by SHAEF. There were numerous defences around Courtrai while Wevelgem airfield nearby was defended by fifteen anti-aircraft guns, several searchlights and machine gun positions. The town itself had fire trenches overlooking and bisecting the railway along with anti-tank walls. There were also machine gun positions and anti-tank walls at both ends of the bridges in the town. Seveghem nearby was defended by six anti-aircraft guns and there was a defended position or 'hedgehog' on a wooded feature on high ground north of St Anne, consisting of four machine guns in concrete emplacements and communication trenches. Oudenarde was undefended, but the River Euscal south-west of the town was heavily flooded along its banks. Most of the main roads in the area had had trenches dug along their verges. Tournai was lightly defended, with a number of fire trenches along with anti-airlanding obstacles on the drill ground to the west of the town. There were many anti-aircraft guns and searchlights in Lille. South-west of Courtrai the bridges over the Euscat at Trieu-Dalsart and Helchin had been blown, along with the canal bridge at Petit Lanoy. The Euscat south-east of Courtrai had been heavily flooded. Overall the fixed defences in the area were relatively light, and it was not prepared for defence. There were however many flak guns, a legacy of the Allied bomber offensive. Only Courtrai had prepared defences around its bridges, while the other towns were practically undefended.[14]

29 August

On 29 August Browning flew to France to confer with Montgomery and De Guingand,[15] and FAAA's outline plan for Linnet was sent to him.[16] The objectives were 'to assist the Northern and Central Army Groups to destroy the German Army by blocking withdrawal routes to the east', 'to assist the advance of the Northern Allied Army Group by seizing and area ahead of it, and holding a bridgehead over river Euscat at Tournai 9231', 'to create a diversion by landing in rear, and on the lines of communication, of the German Army' and 'to form a link between the Northern and Central Groups of Armies'.

It was thought that the Germans would fight a strong rearguard action to withdraw to a defensive line based on the Somme, Marne and Saone rivers. Intelligence estimated that the Germans had the equivalent strength of 30 divisions, consisting of five Panzer divisions and 25 infantry divisions. Of the divisions on the Western Front three Panzer divisions and seventeen infantry divisions were on the main front. Other divisions were in Southern France, Holland or had not been located. The Germans were estimated to be able to reinforce the Western Front by the equivalent of a division every week for the next six weeks, in addition to ad-hoc formations made up of personnel found in Germany.

The total German strength in the Linnet area was estimated at 28,550 men. It was thought that the Germans would be able to react to the airborne landings with two divisions during the first week. There were believed to be garrison troops in the area along with some corps troops. The fighting value of these troops was described as 'extremely low,' as was the amount of German armour in the area.

The flak defences along the French-Belgian border were the strongest in Western Europe, a legacy of the Allied bomber offensive of the past few years which frequently crossed the North Sea over Northern France and the Low Countries. There was an almost continuous belt along the coast with particularly heavy flak around the harbours. There was also flak on shipping in the Channel and North Sea ports and mobile railway guns. Light flak was sited to work in conjunction with coastal gun batteries and other coastal defences. V-Weapon launch sites in the area also had flak protection, particularly from the mouth of the Seine to St Omer. This belt was consisted of approximately 275 heavy guns and 800 light guns. Most of the railway marshalling yards, major bridges and airfields in the area also had flak. Throughout the Battle of Normandy there was a tendency for mobile flak to be drawn into the land battle as conventional and anti-tank artillery, and it was believed that the same thing would occur during Linnet. The choice of an air route was a compromise between avoiding as many flak areas as possible and the requirements of navigation, but with no consideration to the needs of the airborne forces once on the ground. The best air routes to the Linnet area would be across the northern French coast. This route was 20 to 40 miles shorter than flying further south, the flak was believed to be weaker and the shorter distance would mean a shorter time in the danger zone. Air support would be needed to neutralise the flak defences along the coast and around Lille, Roubaix and Courtrai.

It would be 'advisable' for the Allied air forces to neutralise the enemy defences and flak concentrations within the proposed corridor using medium and heavy bombers. As there was a risk that bombing might compromise the element of surprise it was decided that diversionary operations would be flown elsewhere. Heavy flak concentrations would be bombed on D-Day. Bombing would cease at H-Hour to enable troop carrier aircraft to fly in, turn around and return to base. Diversionary bombing and dummy para drops would also take place during the period. As soon as the bombing had ceases Allies fighter-bombers on the flanks of the airborne convoys would attack any batteries, guns or troops firing on the troop carrier aircraft. Fighter and fighter-bomber support would continue until nightfall.

Linnet would require a total of 1,291 parachute aircraft and 2,656 gliders of all types. It was estimated that a total of 1,542 transport aircraft were available made up of 1,100 American and 452 British. There were over 3,000 gliders available of all types. The major constraint for the Allies was aircrew – there were only enough crew available to operate every aircraft, with no spare crews available. In terms of glider crews the situation was even more acute, as there were only enough to fly just over half of the gliders available. The issue for the Allied air forces was that new aircraft were arriving regularly, but crews took time to train.

The first lift would see the 101st Division carried in by 432 aircraft of the 53rd Troop Carrier Wing, and the bulk of the 82nd in 432 aircraft of the 52nd Wing. The 1st British Division with the Polish Brigade would be taken in by 265 glider loads by 38 Group and 385 parachute aircraft of 50th Troop Carrier Wing and 46 Group. All the force's parachutists would be dropped in the first lift except for forty-two aircraft from 82nd Division. This was clearly a big air lift effort, particularly for a first drop.

Two air routes were proposed – a southern route below the Somme and flying around Amiens and a northern route crossing the coast between Dunkirk and Ostend. If the southern route was chosen 50th and 52nd Troop Carrier Wings would not be able to tow gliders due to the distance involved, and 53rd Wing would only be able to carry one lift in the afternoon. One feature of Linnet was that it was proposed to carry most of the gliders by double tow.

The mission of the airborne force was to capture a firm base in the general area of Tournai, Avelghem, Renaix and Montrouel Au Bous. It was also ordered to capture the bridgehead over the River Euscat at Tournai and control the roads leading through Tournai, Lille and Courtrai. It would also capture and prepare an existing airfield to enable resupplies to be flown in – the existing airfields at Vendeville, Wevelghem and Chievres were highlighted as particularly suitable.

The airborne force would come under the command of 21st Army Group, but if it was relieved by 12th Army Group it would come under its command instead until contact could be established with 21st Army Group. The situation was clearly very fluid, which did not aid planning.

Browning was authorised to carry out detailed planning in conjunction with Troop Carrier forces, which would be commanded by Major General Paul Williams of IX Troop Carrier Command. The target for completion of plans was 3 September, with D-Day to be announced later.

The Allies had studied the area between Renaix and Tournai and deduced that two airstrips could be constructed of 6,000ft in length by the Airborne Aviation Engineer Battalion. The first strip would be operational after 30 hours of work and the second after an additional 30 hours, with three additional strips requiring 48 hours each. Existing airfields at Chievres and Lille could be rehabilitated quicker than new airfields could be built.

Special Operations Executive involvement was also discussed.[17] On 29 August representatives from SOE visited Airborne Forces HQ to discuss the operation. Brigadier Walch confirmed that the Bardsea parties could land on the night of D and D+1.[18] While at Airborne Forces HQ SOE also discussed SAS operations with the Commander of SAS Troops – it was thought that 100 Belgian SAS Troops might be made available for operations in the Ardennes and that they should be used in parties of 25. The SAS wanted to send in one or two small reconnaissance parties soon but was keen to discuss this with Browning first before submitting a proposal for operations in the Ardennes to SHAEF on 30 August. Walch agreed to tell the Belgians that the Jedburgh parties were being despatched, but only that they were being sent on missions connected with the Allied advance and with no details of Operation Linnet. Airborne Forces did not want any statements to be made to Belgian, French or Polish authorities until the operation had begun, presumably for security reasons, and after being briefed on the operation Jedburgh parties would be 'locked up.' Resistance commanders close to the Linnet area would be informed that an officer with a 'special mission' – with V-Weapon sites as a cover story – would be dropped in their area from 3 September onwards, and they were asked to identify a safe house for them.

Preliminary instructions for Special Forces were issued on 29 August. It was assumed that the operation would involve 'about four divisions' and would take place in the area bounded by Ath-Perulwelz-Frontier up to Menin-Courtrai-Denyzze-Oudenarde. It would have the objectives of cutting the German line of retreat through Belgium and preventing the Germans from stabilising a defensive line west of Belgium. Linnet would be supported by the Monica organisation in the Lille area, as well as Belgian Resistance movements. Bardsea parties would be put into operation at 36 hours' notice. They had already been issued with detailed plans for operations in the same area and were to concentrate on dislocating enemy road and rail traffic moving towards the landing area, as well as disrupting enemy petrol and ammunition supplies. They would also pass intelligence on enemy movements and dispositions. Belgian Resistance inside the landing area would be ordered to remain quiet and take no action unless ordered by Allied forces, but to make contact as soon as possible with Special Forces representatives at divisional and corps headquarters. When required they would provide guides, gather intelligence, provide labour and possibly provide guards and patrols. Outside the Linnet area but within a radius of about 20km the Resistance was prepared to do likewise but would also be permitted to attack and harass enemy columns. In other parts of Belgium the resistance would be authorised to attack enemy movements, destroy fuel and ammunition dumps and harass enemy attempts to retreat through Belgium. These activities would be carried out in coordination with SAS parties.

Special Forces HQ would send representatives to divisional and corps headquarters to liaise with Resistance groups in the field. Airborne Forces HQ would send a liaison officer to Special Forces HQ to provide liaison with SAS units, and the French Forces of the Interior would provide an officer to liaise between French and Belgian Resistance. The Belgians would receive 'the greatest possible weight of stores' in the run up to Linnet. The Low Countries sections at Special Forces HQ would establish a war room at Norgeby House and an operations room would also be set up to support Linnet. Special Forces were arranging to send an officer familiar with SAS operations to Belgium to advise on suitable areas for the SAS to operate in. The Special Forces party at Airborne Corps HQ would consist of one GSO2 and two GSO3 from the Belgian Section, two wireless operators, one batman driver and a clerk. The parties with both 101st and 17th US Airborne Divisions would comprise one US officer, one Belgian officer and a wireless operator. The party attached to 1st British Airborne Division would be made up of one officer from the Belgian section, an officer from the Polish minorities section and a Belgian wireless operator. Uniquely for a brigade-level formation the Polish Parachute Brigade would have attached two Polish officers and a wireless operator. The 52nd Division would have attached a Jedburgh team of one US officer, one Belgian officer and a wireless operator.

Airborne Forces HQ's Operation Instruction No.1 for Linnet was written on 29 August.[19] The gliders carrying in what was described as the 'Corps HQ' would be landed north of Tournai. It would travel in the first glider lift and land in the 82nd Division area. There would be no corps artillery to augment divisional artillery resources as HQ Airborne Troops had never been intended to be an operational corps headquarters and had not been given the usual complement of corps troops. It was expected that Second Army would provide some artillery. 878th Battalion would receive instructions from the Commander Royal Engineers of 'British Airborne Corps' and divisional commanders were ordered to give priority of their engineer resources to the destruction of bridges. If any bridges had been prepared for demolition by the enemy then these charges were to be removed. Belgian and French civilians would be enrolled for labour through the Belgian Liaison Mission and would be issued with blue and white armbands. The Mission would also provide local experts to function as guides to operating locks, which would be important for maintaining water levels in the operational area. Requests from airborne divisions would be monitored by Corps HQ and prioritised 'only when necessary'. Each division would appoint one liaison officer who would travel with the divisional headquarters and take situation reports to Corps HQ after landing. GHQ Liaison Regiment – Phantom – would provide a patrol for Corps HQ and for each division. The Phantom patrol at Corps HQ would maintain direct contact with 21st Army Group.

An initial conference on the Air Support for Operation Linnet was held on 29 August.[20] It was attended by thirty-two officers from AEAF, USSTAF, FAAA, IX Troop Carrier Command, Ninth Air Force, Second Tactical Air Force, Bomber Command, 21st Army Group, SHAEF, 11 Group, ADGB and Eighth Air Force. Although most headquarters sent representatives their ranks varied widely – Major General Williams was the most senior officer attending but was the only representative from IX Troop Carrier Command, whereas AEAF was represented by numerous staff officers.

A meeting took place at Air Defence of Great Britain on 29 August to discuss Operation Linnet.[21] ADGB were considering asking for a postponement as they felt that the strategic bombing programme on D-1 when RAF Bomber Command would target airfields and the US Eighth Air Force would target flak defences could not be repeated on D-Day itself. For deception purposes any bombing attacks in the Linnet area would have to be replicated in another area. Eighth Air Force would attack flak position along the coast and inland, but only targeting defences that could interfere in the operation. It was stressed that if too much pressure was exerted on flak defences for too long a period the element of surprise might be lost, so a balance would clearly have to be struck. Ninth Air Force would isolate the Lille, Courtrai and Tournai area from H-Hour onwards from enemy air and ground opposition. 2nd Tactical Air Force would reinforce Ninth Air Force and as far as practicable cover First and Third US Armies, and assist ADGB with escort duties. They would also support 21st Army Group in effecting a link up with the airborne force. AGB would provide fighter cover and escorts for airborne lifts on D-Day and resupply missions, and would protect the landing zones at night. Bomber Command would drop parachute dummies on D-Day and at H-Hour north of Brussels, east of Charleroi, Arras, St Omer, Valenciennes, west of Lille and Cambrai. Bomber Command would also attack enemy fighter airfields from D-1. Achievres airfield would not be attacked to retain it for future use by the Allies.

On 29 August 21st Army Group Rear HQ Q Staff asked the US Army's Communications Zone to send representatives to their headquarters for a conference on the afternoon of 31 August to discuss ground maintenance for Operation Linnet. The conference would also be attended by XVIII Airborne Corps G4 Staff and Q Staff from FAAA.[22]

The addition of a Belgian Liaison Mission was in contrast to previous missions in France and future missions in Holland, where liaison with occupied countries was on a much reduced level. The Mission would be commander by Major R.L. Raemarker from Special Forces Headquarters and would be attached to Corps HQ where it would work closely with the SAS section. It would co-ordinate the activities of Jedburgh teams attached to airborne divisions and would also be responsible for briefing them before they reported to their Divisions. The Jedburgh teams at divisional level were instructed to contact Resistance groups and report to divisional HQ any information on enemy dispositions, headquarters and stores, as well as information on personnel available to provide guides, labour, local guards, medical assistance and nurses, police work for good order and protection of the civil population, and information on intended enemy demolitions, minefields, transport available, Gestapo agents and dangerous collaborators. They were to emphasise that no offensive military action would be allowed by Resistance groups within the Corps area and policy matters such as disagreements between leaders of the Resistance were to be referred to Mission Section before any action was taken.[23] The extensive liaison with the Belgians was in contrast to Market Garden, when the allies were mistrustful of the Dutch Resistance.

The Resistance organisation in Belgium, Troupes Secretes, was known to be highly organised, comprised of many former members of the Belgian Army and was divided into different zones. Each regional commander was in touch with London by radio. All Resistance action in Belgium since D-Day had been of a clandestine nature but there had been highly successful sabotage of rail and canal communications, and to a lesser extent on ammunition dumps, signals and other installations. It had not been possible to drop arms to the same extent as had been supplied to the French Resistance however, and stocks were getting very low. There was also a strong Polish resistance organisation around Armentières, Bethune, Arras, Cambrai and Valenciennes in Northern France where there was a large Polish population of up to 200,000. It was believed that the Poles would be keen to take part in offensive action. There were also considerable FFI forces in North East France.[24]

Instructions would be issued to Resistance groups from London after the airborne forces had landed. The Belgian Resistance would only be called on for overt action if it was likely that the area in which they were operating would be liberated by the Allies within 48 hours. At this point attacks on 'minor military elements' would be authorised including despatch riders, motorcycles, single motor cars and lorries. Armbands would be provided for Resistance troops working as guides, on guard duties or as labour personnel. Airborne forces were ordered to treat the Belgian Resistance with 'due consideration' and to respect their leaders and issue orders through them.[25]

30 August

On the afternoon of 30 August Montgomery visited Dempsey at Second Army and discussed Linnet.[26] On the same day Airborne Corps issued its Operation Order for Operation Linnet, accompanied by Planning Intelligence Summary No.1.[27]

Urquhart's orders for Operation Linnet were also issued on 30 August.[28] With 1st Polish Parachute Brigade under command the intention was to dominate the area around Renaix close to the Franco-Belgian border, particularly the crossings over the River Euscat. A firm base would be secured around Renaix, Escanaffles and Berchem, maintaining a frontage north of the Euscat and north-east of Renaix. Patrols would be pushed out three to five miles beyond the main front line. If the situation permitted one brigade was to be held in to reserve in order to exploit towards Courtrai to the west.

The division would take off in three lifts. The first would consist of the Divisional Tactical Headquarters, 1st Parachute Brigade, 1st Airlanding Brigade and most of the divisional troops. The second lift would deliver the 4th Parachute Brigade and the third lift would drop the Polish Parachute Brigade. In the first phase 1st Parachute Brigade and 1st Airlanding Brigade would land and occupy a firm base around Renaix. The Reconnaissance Squadron was given a significant task of seizing and holding Avelghem and the crossing over the Euscat at Escanaffles, and would also send out standing patrols south toward Carnois and patrols on the roads between Audenharde and Bossuyt and Renaix and Leuze. This coup de main role is similar to the one that it would be given during Market Garden.

In the second phase the 1st Parachute and 1st Airlanding Brigades would maintain their false front positions and push out patrols. 4th Parachute Brigade would land and go into divisional reserve only occupying its allotted main position if the situation required. A link up would be made with the US 82nd Airborne Division at Bossuyt. The Reconnaissance Squadron would continue to maintain standing patrols and would make a junction with the US 101st Division.

In the third phase the 1st Polish Parachute Brigade would land and occupy a position astride the road between Renaix and Leuze south of Carnais. The 4th Brigade would prepare to either seize Courtrai to the east or the exits on the road between Courtrai and Deyn Ze and between Courtrai and Bruges, effectively masking the town and denying its use to the enemy. Divisional Headquarters would be established at Les Fontaines. The leaving of a major objective such as Courtrai until the later phases of the operation bears similarities to the 82nd Airborne Division at Nijmegen being ordered to prioritise the Groesbeek Heights over Nijmegen Bridge.

Given the importance of river crossings, the divisional Royal Engineers were given detailed orders to either obstruct or prepare to demolish strategic road and railway crossings over the Euscat north of Berchem, near Escanaffles. The engineers were also to reconnoitre and prepare to destroy all bridges over the Euscat between Kerkhove and Bossuyt and remove all boats from the southern bank. All bridges over the canal between Courtrai and Bossuyt were also to be destroyed.

The division was given a tight turnaround to mount Linnet. Moves to transit camps would be completed the next day on 31 August and gliders would be loaded on 1 September. The first lift would take off on 3 September, the second on 4 September and the third lift on 5 September. All formations would be ready for take-off from Sunday 3 September and the final decision would be taken at midnight the night before, depending on the weather forecast.

The plan for Linnet shows a remarkable similarity to Operation Market. The division was to capture and dominate river crossings, albeit to deny them to the enemy rather than to facilitate an Allied advance. The intention of the operation was effectively to turn the River Euscat into a barrier to trap the retreating German forces. The division would be carried in by three lifts over three days, in the same loading as for Market. The Reconnaissance Squadron was to operate in advance of the main body of the division to capture strategic objectives, rather than to scout ahead of the infantry battalions.

On 30 August HQ Airborne Troops signalled 21st Army Group to suggest two interdiction lines to be implemented during Operation Linnet.[29] The purpose of these interdiction lines would be to destroy bridges and roads and prevent the Germans from getting reinforcements to the battle area. The priority line ran from the coast at Gravelines to Calais, St Omer, Aire, Bethune, La Bassee, Douai and Cambrai. The second priority line was from Bruges to Ghent, Malines and Louvain. The next day, however, 21st Army Group's BGS(Ops) Brigadier Belchem replied to Browning rejecting the suggested interdiction lines, as he felt 'after careful study' that they were not practicable. The lines were thought to be too long and would have involved destroying many bridges, which would not be possible even in clear weather. Belchem also suggested that destroying so many bridges might impede the advance of Allied troops. Therefore Belchem suggested that interdiction would be left to opportunistic fighter-bomber attacks on any movement located.

A copy of the Air Support plan in the AEAF files dated 30 August suggests that at one point a route from North Foreland in Kent to the mouth of the Scheldt was considered. This was crossed out and replaced in pencil by the route from Beachy Head to Le Treport. A note about bombing coastal defences was also crossed out and it was noted that if ADGB provided escort cover then fewer fighters would be available to cover bomber command missions. It was also planned to bomb Achievres airfield.[30]

SHAEF Operation Memorandum No.34 on Air Support was circulated on 30 August.[31] Although the aim was to outline how Army Groups would be supported by tactical air forces, it also contained covered how airborne operations might be supported. The Tactical Air HQ was to be located with the relevant Army HQ at all stages, a rule that SHAEF described as 'inviolable'. Air support tentacles might be delegated to work with lower formations and air formations could answer calls from them directly. The memo outlined that airborne operations would be launched 'as directed by the Supreme Commander', and that the actual launching and air support would be as specified by Leigh Mallory.

For Linnet it was agreed that priority of supply would be equal for each of the airborne divisions taking part. Resupply for 1st Airborne Division would be delivered by 38 Group with assistance from Ninth Air Force and for transport reasons British aircraft would take off from American airfields. The prioritising of supply drops would be different during Market Garden. On 30 August Brereton confirmed an amendment to the original plan in that all Allied troop carrying forces would be commanded by Williams and not by Hollinghurst. The Air Support plan for Operation Linnet suggested that aircraft taking off from the northern airfields would concentrate over March, cross the coast at Bradwell, turn at North Foreland before crossing the Continental coast west of Breskens, and then turn south to the landing area. Aircraft taking off from the central airfields would concentrate over Hatfield before following the same route, while the southern airfield forces would concentrate over Horsham and cross the at North Foreland before doing likewise. A map of the air routes suggests that they were designed to avoid the heavily defended London anti-aircraft area and the coastal anti-aircraft defences that ranged from Dover to Beachy Head.[32]

On 30 August Leigh Mallory transferred operational control of 38 and 46 Groups to Brereton, excluding aircraft which SHAEF required for special operations. Leigh Mallory also stated that 120 Dakotas from 46 Group would be required to go to Italy to take part in airborne operations in Greece shortly after Linnet had been completed.[33]

31 August

Brereton's diary entry for 31 August claims that Montgomery was pressing for Linnet to be cancelled saying: 'Their supply lines are badly overextended and they require air resupply. I [Brereton] directed that our targets be changed to the Aachen-Maastricht Gap. The troops will remain in the marshalling area.'[34]

On 31 August 21st Army Group G(Ops) circulated additional information regarding Linnet.[35] Interestingly the document noted that 'the G-3 Section of HQ FAAA are all airmen'. D-Day would be on 3 September with H-Hour at 0825. Contrary to earlier plans, it was anticipated that the whole force would land on D-Day, apart from the Polish Parachute Brigade and 52nd Division and that their arrival would be dependent on the weather, aircraft losses and the rate of resupply.

The decision to launch Linnet would be taken at FAAA at midnight before D-Day. FAAA would notify 21st Army Group, who would then notify army commanders and 12th Army Group. If 21st Army Group wished to postpone Linnet they would need to notify FAAA by 1800 the day before D-Day. In an emergency the operation could be called off up to an hour before the time of take-off, but by this time the bombing would already have started, which would have jeopardised the element of surprise.

The US Eighth Air Force would be responsible for anti-flak air support and would begin strafing attacks immediately and bomb flak installations on D-1. Bomber Command would also bomb flak positions on the night before D-Day and tactical air support would be provided by Ninth Tactical Air Force. The transport aircraft would cross the coast at Flushing at the mouth of the River Scheldt and then head due south.

On 31 August 21st Army Group G(Plans) forwarded details of Operation Linnet to British Second Army and Canadian First Army under the authority of De Guingand.[36] The intention was 'To present a major threat to the enemy's lines of communication, and hence to cause the enemy to divert, from the main battle, forces which he can ill afford, and thereby create opportunities for enveloping and destroying the maximum enemy forces by the combined action of airborne and ground forces.' At this point it was expected that the Airborne Force would come under the direct operational command of Montgomery, although it might later be delegated to Second Army.

21st Army Group's briefing for its army commanders estimated that the Airborne Corps would need to be prepared to hold out on its own for about 10 days. It is interesting that the longest estimate for the time that the airborne force would be isolated was not made known to the airborne forces themselves, only the ground forces that would be relieving them. The time that airborne forces would be expected to operate on their own changed for every operation, and it is not clear if there was a rationale for this flexibility.

The first troops would land at 0825. The troop carrier aircraft from the first lift would return to their bases in England at about midday and there would be a four hour interval before the second lift would begin. During this interval the heavy bombers would again attack flak positions and airfields. The first, second and third lifts would land Airborne Corps HQ, 1st, 82nd and 101st Airborne Divisions, the Polish Parachute Brigade, 878th Aviation Engineer Battalion and 2nd Airlanding Light Anti-Aircraft Battery. The fourth and subsequent lifts would carry supplies – up to approximately 350 tons per day per division – as a priority. The AFDAG would fly in as soon as an airstrip was available, where 52nd Division would be landed in C-47s.

101st Airborne Division was ordered to capture Tournai and hold the bridges over the Euscat in the town. They were also ordered to capture Chievres, Jurbise and Neumaison, and to contact 82nd Division around Mourcourt and Bois. 82nd US Airborne Division were ordered to capture the high ground north of Tournai around Fort St Aurbry, and to provide support to 101st Division if the town was attacked. The division was also ordered to capture Lille and Baysieux and to establish contact with the 1st Airborne Division at Bossuyt and at Courtrai. 1st British Airborne Division, with the Polish Parachute Brigade Group under its command, would capture the high ground at Fre le L'Enclus to the crossroads at Kirhove. The division would capture Courtrai and hold the roads leading out the town, including the important road to Bruges. They would capture the airfield at Bisseghem, west of Courtrai, and contact 82nd Division. 52nd Division would go into corps reserve upon landing. Special Forces and SAS operations would be co-ordinated with the airborne operation and supplies to Special Forces already in the area had been stepped up recently.

The artillery that the airborne force would have available sheds light not only on how lightly equipped the British airborne forces were compared to their American counterparts, but also how the British Airborne Corps was not equipped to act as a conventional corps on the ground. While the British Airborne Division had twenty-four 75mm howitzers, the US airborne divisions had forty-two. 52nd Division, by comparison, could land twenty-four 25-pounders with two other field regiments available to join by land. The British Airborne Corps had no corps artillery of its own. This was a critical error, not only because airborne divisions were so lightly equipped and needed firepower on call as soon possible, but also because the fighting during the Battle of Normandy had shown how important it was for a corps to have artillery on call. An assurance that it 'may be possible for Second Army to provide some artillery after junction has been effected' was unlikely to reassure the airborne forces.

The British and Polish seaborne echelons were already in France, having crossed the Channel for Operation Transfigure, and would be moved forward to the Second Army area as soon as possible ready to join up with their divisions. The seaborne echelon of 52nd Division would finish concentrating in France not later than 4 September. The seaborne echelons of the US airborne units would complete concentration in France by September.

Until the operational area was in range of Second Tactical Air Force, the US Ninth Tactical Air Command would provide tactical air support. FAAA would provide air support parties for the airborne divisions, XVIII US Airborne Corps and British Airborne Corps, and requests for air support and air reconnaissance would be submitted by divisions direct to IX Tactical Air Command. Requests would be monitored by HQ Airborne Corps and subsequently by HQ XVIII US Airborne Corps, who would exercise the right to amend of cancel requests as they considered necessary.

Linnet was eagerly awaited at the War Office and correspondence between Simpson, the Director of Military Operations, The Assistant Chief of the Imperial General Staff and Field Marshal Sir Alan Brooke, the Chief of the Imperial General Staff, suggests that there was much interest in its progress. Browning frequently copied Crawford, the Director of Air at the War Office, into his signals, who passed them on.[37] At one point during the planning process for Linnet, an officer in the Military Operations branch was told by his personal assistant 'I suggest you should keep this note in your historical archives. If not, I will!' On 31 August Whiteley at SHAEF phoned the War Office on behalf of 21st Army Group to ask for 52nd Division to be made available to take part in Operation Linnet. The division had been left out of the initial plan as it was not certain that it would be available. The message was passed onto Brooke and Simpson at the War Office. It is interesting that 21st Army Group asked Whiteley to request the division, rather than speaking to the War Office direct as it was entitled to do.

The Outline Plan for Linnet was published on 31 August and was also copied to the War Office.[38] The objectives were given as the seizure of the crossings over the Euscat River and canal around Tournai, holding Tournai, exploiting towards Lille and Courtrai, disrupting enemy communications in the area and to 'operate offensively and attack and destroy all enemy bodies attempting to escape Eastwards from the coastal belt within their range of operation.' The airborne forces were described as an 'Airborne Corps' commanded by Browning, which would be under the operational command of 21st Army Group. The airborne force would be in wireless contact with 21st Army Group Tactical Headquarters, Tac HQ Second Army and Tac HQ First US Army.

The target date was 3 September. The force was to be prepared to operate on its own for a week, supplied by air. The initial plan was for all paratroops of all airborne divisions to land in the first lift along with their glider elements in the early daylight of D-Day. The second lift would land the remaining gliders of all three divisions later the same day. D+1 would see the Polish Parachute Brigade landed.

Eisenhower had authorised planning for Linnet to be implemented on 28 August. 21st Army Group passed this authorisation on to FAAA and HQ Airborne Troops the same day, and stated that 52nd Division would be part of the airborne order of battle. The message from 21st Army Group on 28 August contained an undated Outline Plan. A map attached to the outline plan showed 1st Airborne Division landing south-west of Oudenarde, the Polish Parachute Brigade south of Renaix, the 82nd Division north of Tournai and the 101st Division south-west of Tournai. It was anticipated that the airborne force would dominate an area 20 miles by 10 miles, and the inter-Army Group boundary would run on a line Arras-Douai-Orchies-E of Tournai-S of Renaix.

FAAA Operation Memorandum No.3, published on 31 August, covered the scenarios of postponement or cancellation.[39] FAAA would make a decision at 2200 the night before D-Day. This decision would then be telephoned to the duty officers at HQ Airborne Troops (who would in turn relay to airborne formations), Eastcote for relay to troop carrier formations, Eighth Air Force and Bomber Command. FAAA would also inform 21st Army Group. An emergency signal confirming the cancellation or postponement would also be sent to Eisenhower,

Montgomery, Bradley, Ramsay and Leigh Mallory. It was believed that adverse weather may cause a delay of several hours. Postponement, on the other hand, would be for 24-hour periods. If no message had been received by FAAA or HQ Airborne Troops from 21st Army Group by 1800 on D-1, it would be assumed that Linnet would take place as planned the next day.

On 31 August De Guingand wrote to Dempsey at Second Army and Crerar at First Canadian Army.[40] This letter drew heavily on FAAA's Outline Plan but the few deviations and extra details are illuminating. De Guingand described the object of Linnet as to 'present a major threat to enemy lines of communication, cause enemy to divert from the main battle forces which he can ill afford, create opportunities for enveloping and destroying maximum enemy forces'. Once the airborne force came under the control of 21st Army Group command would pass in turn to Second Army. At the time that De Guingand was writing it was though that the airborne route would cross the coast at Flushing in Holland and then travel southwards to avoid flak around Lille. It was stressed, however, that the route may change if losses were experienced. In contrast to Browning's expectation that Second Army would provide artillery support De Guingand wrote more cautiously that this 'may be possible' after a junction had been achieved.

IX Troop Carrier Command's Field Order No3 was published on 31 August.[41] Maps showed the southern airborne route crossing the coast at Beachy Head then the French coast at Le Treport and that the airborne formations would assemble over March and Hatfield and pass over the North Foreland Lighthouse. Eureka and light beacons would be installed in all of these places as well as on a ship in the North Sea. By the time Linnet was launched the Allied ground forces were expected to be in the area of the Somme but it was hoped that small armoured and motorised columns might well be in advance of the main forces, particularly on the eastern flank in the area of the First US Army. It was estimated that if opposition on the British Second Army front was weak it would be more likely that 12th Army Group would operate to the north-east rather than to the east. During the outbound journey troop carrier aircraft would fly at 1,500ft, drop to 600ft above the terrain for the actual dropping operations and go up to 3,000ft for the return journey.

The final decision as to whether to proceed or postpone would be taken by Brereton at FAAA, and if there were any delays longer than an hour this would mean the cancellation of the second drop on D-Day. Linnet would require some formations from IX Troop Carrier Command to move to forward bases temporarily. The 442nd Troop Carrier Group would move to Ramsbury, the 439th to Balderton, the 440th to Fulbeck and the 441st to Langar respectively. 50th Troop Carrier Wing would take part in supply dropping missions for both US and British forces which would be flown from 38 Group airfields. The 437th Troop Carrier Group would move to Chilbolton for D-Day. Parachute aircraft would fly in nine-ship vee formations of serials of up to forty-five aircraft and gliders would fly in columns of up to forty aircraft, including in double-tow configuration. Glider tow ropes would be dropped immediately after clearing the landing zones. No paratroops or gliders would be allowed to return to the UK – aircrews were instructed that if they could not find the drop zone or landing zone paratroops or gliders would to be dropped in the assault area as close to their intended dropping place as possible. Aircraft were to maintain radio silence except in an emergency and were to take no evasive action during the run in to the drop zones. All pilots were ordered to continue to the target area even if they became detached from the main formation en route. US glider pilots, who were not trained as infantryman as British glider crews were, were ordered to report immediately to the nearest US Command Post and as soon as the situation permitted they would be evacuated to the headquarters of 82nd or 101st Divisions for further evacuation by air to the UK. Wing Commanders would be briefed on D-4, Squadron Commanders and other essential squadron staff on D-3 and combat crews on D-1. Resupply missions would take off from Greenham Common, Membury, Aldermaston, Welford and Ramsbury.

The intelligence estimate for IX Troop Carrier Command's field order was circulated on the same day. It predicted that there was a possibility of mist in valleys and smoke from industrial areas. The terrain was intensely cultivated with small farms and rolling fields and apart from occasional low rounded hills most areas were suitable for glider landings, with few obstacles. The proposed drop zones and landing zones were generally flat farmland 200 to 500m long, bounded by ditches, paths or small embankments.

The rapid Allied advance was thought to have disrupted the Luftwaffe who had been forced to regroup away from the front line. German fighter aircraft were being kept at least 75 miles back from the land battle as they were too vulnerable to Allied tactical air superiority. The Luftwaffe was believed to have 500 to 525 single-seat fighters, of which 200 to 275 were thought to be serviceable. Of these only 150 to 200 were available in the west, the rest were on the Eastern Front or defending Germany itself. They would only be able to assemble 100 for any operation. The Luftwaffe only had 25 Wild Sau night fighters of which only 10 to 15 were serviceable, only 300 twin-engined bombers available for night flying of which only 150 to 200 were serviceable, and only 30 fighter-bombers available, of which 15 to 20 were serviceable.

It was thought that the Germans would be able to find enough reserves to commit against the US Third Army – there was evidence that the Germans were removing Panzergrenadier divisions from Italy to oppose Third Army's advance. Once Third Army had taken Rheims they would have cut off the enemy's main communication link to the Seine and Somme, and if Patton were to swing north the Allies would have trapped the Seventh and Fifteenth Armies in a pocket. It was estimated therefore that the Germans would begin a slow withdrawal from the Seine and then the Somme so that German forces in the target area would probably, by the time of the operation, include first-line infantry and Panzer divisions. The coast was being held by the 712th Infantry Division, a low-grade formation that included a proportion of Russian troops. The Tournai area itself was garrisoned by approximately 2,400 troops, mostly composed of Landeschutzen and Ostbattalions.

101st Division's Field Order for Operation Linnet was published on 31 August 1944.[42] The divisions would land in the Tournai area with the principal mission of capturing Tournai itself and securing the bridges over the River Euscat in the town. It would land in two lifts, one on the morning of D-Day and the second in the afternoon of D-Day. The morning lift would consist of 432 parachute aircraft and 140 Waco gliders while the afternoon lift would comprise 764 Wacos.

The morning lift would see the three Parachute Infantry Regiments landing along with a small number of gliders. After landing the 501st and 506th Regiments would constitute Combat Command A and would be commanded by Brigadier-General Higgins, the Division's Assistant Commander who would have his command post in Tournai. 501st Parachute Infantry Regiment minus its 3rd Battalion which would land on Drop Zone B would land on Drop Zone A south of Marquain and capture it and the high ground to the south, with the intention of blocking enemy movement from Lille and Orchies. They were to contact 82nd Division at Marquain and with its 3rd Battalion at Willemeau. Regimental Headquarters would be at Orcq. 506th Parachute Infantry Regiment meanwhile would land on Drop Zone B south of Tournai and after assembling it would occupy the town west of the Euscat. Regimental headquarters would be in Tournai. It would be joined on Drop Zone B by divisional headquarters. The 3rd Battalion of the 501st Parachute Infantry Regiment would land on Drop Zone B and then capture St Maur. It would contact the rest of the Regiment at Willemeau and the 327th Glider Infantry Regiment at Chercq. The 502nd Parachute Infantry Regiment would land on Drop Zone C north-east of Tournai with C Company of the 326th Airborne Engineer Battalion under command. The Regiment less one Battalion would occupy the part of Tournai east of the Euscat. The remaining battalion would defend Landing Zone A. The Regiment would then move to the vicinity of Bois de St Martin and prevent enemy movement from the east. It was to send patrols out to the road between Renaix and Leuze and contact the 1st Airborne Division. It would also contact 82nd Division at Bourage and Mourcourt and would hold one battalion in divisional reserve east of Tournai. Regimental headquarters would be in the woods north-east of Rumillies. The glider elements of the first lift would land on Landing Zone W north-east of Tournai.

The afternoon lift would consist solely of glider units, which would land on Landing Zones W and I. The 327th Glider Infantry Regiment would land on LZ I south-east of Tournai, occupy the wooded area at Bourabraix and contact the 3rd Battalion of the 501st Parachute Infantry Regiment at Chercq and the 502nd at Marais. It would block enemy movement from the east and south and send patrols out towards Leuze and Thumaide. The Regimental Command Post would be in Vaulx. The divisional artillery, having landed on LZ I, would assume positions east of Tournai and would be prepared to support the element of the Division west of the Euscat in particular. Airborne Corps HQ would establish itself at Mont-Saint-Aubert, while the 101st Divisional headquarters were to be at Rumillies.

101st Division's Field Order also included an Intelligence Annex. At the time of issue the front line ran between Châlons, Rheims, Laon, Soissons and Paris and then along the Seine – apart from the 21st Army Group bridgehead at Vernon – to the sea. The 6th Parachute Division and the 17th Luftwaffe Division were immediately north of Paris while the 18th Luftwaffe Division, 49th, 344th, 711th, 272nd and 348th Infantry Divisions, 12th SS, 11th SS and 2nd SS Panzer Divisions and 2nd and 9th Panzer Divisions were north-west of Paris and east of the Seine. Along the Channel coast the 47th Infantry Division was four miles south-west of Calais, the 712nd Infantry Division and another unidentified division were around Bruges, the 70th Infantry Division – a 'stomach' division made up of troops who were less than fully fit – was at Antwerp and the 182nd Reserve Division was near Amiens. The Headquarters of the 16th Anti-Aircraft Division, which formerly commanded the flak defences of Paris, was in Lille. Local garrison troops were scattered throughout the area, including Landesschutz battalions of about 600 men, usually over 35 years old, and Ostbattalions consisted of about 600 men of foreign origin. The intelligence summary surmised that the Germans could either attempt to defend their existing positions, or withdraw to more suitable defensive lines along the Somme or further east. It was thought that a counter-attack would be unlikely. It concluded that it was likely that the enemy would continue to withdraw due to the American advance from Rheims, and would withdraw in greater strength to the north-east as a result. The Allies were aware that the German command in the west did not have complete control over its retreating personnel. The retreat was not being commanded as such and was being forced by the impending arrival of Allied troops everywhere. The general direction of the retreat was to the north-east. Intelligence suggested that the Germans had just under 25,000 troops in the wider area, including 14,500 in Bruges and along the Belgian coast. There were 2,570 troops in Tournai and 1,800 in Courtrai. As an indication of how chaotic the German retreat had been, the troops in Tournai came from six different battalions. One US corps had recently captured personnel from fourteen different German divisions in a single day.

Brigadier-General Gavin issued his orders to 82nd Airborne Division on 31 August. The division would land in daylight north of Tournai and capture and secure the general area of Tournai, Bossuyt and Clipet and hold the high ground around Mont St Aubert. They would also cut the enemy's lines of withdrawal or block counter-attacks. If the Germans attacked the 101st Division in Tournai the 82nd were to support them by holding the high ground and providing reserves if necessary.

The first wave – Force A – would land on D-Day beginning at dawn, including the divisional headquarters and signals company, the divisional artillery headquarters, 504th, 505th and 508th Parachute Infantry Regiments and 376th Field Artillery Battalion. The second lift would consist of the Glider Infantry Regiment and other support elements. 504th Parachute Infantry Regiment would land on DZ 4 and seize and hold ridge 30-40 and ridge 50. The regiment would also secure and mark LZ 4 for the glider landings of the second wave. It was also ordered to contact 1st Airborne Division at Bossuyt. 505th Parachute Infantry Regiment would land on DZ 5, and were ordered to capture and occupy several hills around Mont St Aubert and Mont de Trinite. They would secure and mark LZ 5 for the glider landings later on D-Day, and would establish contact with 101st Division. 508th Parachute Infantry Regiment would land on DZ 8 and occupy the ridge at Butor. They would secure LZ 8 for the glider landings on D-Day. 376th Parachute Field Artillery Battalion would land on DZ 8 and would support Force A.

On 31 August after a conversation between Browning and Hollinghurst it was confirmed that on D-2 and then on D+1 and D+12 at least eleven 38 Group aircraft would be allocated to SAS operations, with a higher priority than Linnet. From D+3 this would increase to 20 aircraft plus any other aircraft that might be available.[43]

The direct air support arrangements for Linnet were confirmed by 21st Army Group on 31 August. 21st Army Group's G(Air) Staff would arrange to reinforce the existing G3(Air) staff at the joint Ninth Tactical Air Command and US First Army headquarters with British staff to support Operation Linnet. Additional cipher personnel would also be provided to handle signals traffic. 21st Army Group intended for air support requests to be submitted directly by airborne divisions to Ninth Tactical Air Command. These would be monitored by British Airborne Corps or XVIII Airborne Corps as appropriate, who would have the right to amend or cancel requests. Air Support staff and communications previously centred on IX Tactical Air Command would then move to the joint Second British Army and 83 Group headquarters and continue to operate as before. This arrangement would continue until the airborne formations came under the command of Second Army.[44]

1 September

The appreciation of the German situation prior to Operation Linnet published by Second Army Intelligence on 1 September described the post-Operation Cobra period as a 'non-stop retreat', including the heavy defeat at Falaise and a general retreat to the Seine culminating in the fall of Paris.[45] The Allies had crossed the Meuse and after capturing Amiens and Arras were approaching Germany itself. The pursuit was so swift that enemy pockets were being bypassed. Intelligence suggested that the German army was in a state of confusion to the extent that the whereabouts of units was unknown to the command. Air reports spoke of a continual stream of traffic east and north-east from Amiens.

Intelligence predicted that the Germans would withdraw to a line roughly following the Somme from Dieppe to the Marne and then to the Swiss frontier by the night of 1 to 2 September, and form a defensive line to be held by 10 to 13 infantry divisions. The summary described the situation:

> Plans are meaningless. They are out of date at least by the time they are issued. Divisions are shadows of their war establishments, equipment is short, tanks are few – great administrative difficulties exist – HQs are

overrun, and reinforcements are non-existent unless they come from Norway, the Balkans and Italy . . . It is in these circumstances that the German High Command is required to make future plans.

It was predicted that although the Germans would have to seriously consider retreating to the German frontier they would be compelled to protect the V-Weapon sites around the Pas de Calais for strategic and propaganda reasons. Retreating to Germany would also bring the war to the door of the German people and would make it harder to hide the horrors of war from them. Intelligence estimated that there were thirteen infantry divisions retreating towards the Somme on 21st Army Group's front, along with the 9th and 10th SS Panzer Divisions which were described as 'all shadows of their former selves'. Further south on 12th Army Group's front were estimated to be eight Infantry Divisions, all described as being of very low strength. Seven low-category divisions from the Channel and North Sea coast or low grade units from Germany had been released and could join the battle north of Lille. Immediate opposition to Linnet was predicted to come from 712nd and 226th Infantry Divisions, as well as elements of other divisions that had been decimated but could reach the area to react to the landings. Armoured opposition was predicted to be 'negligible or even nil'.

Linnet was predicted to add to the confusion that already existed among the German armies and would be 'successful in every way.' It was predicted that the airborne forces could inflict a heavy defeat and would have no difficulty fighting off any German reinforcements which might reach the battle, and it was predicted that the speed of the British advance would be so swift that it would be unlikely that the airborne forces would have to operate on their own for 'more than a few hours'.

On 1 September Montgomery wrote to De Guingand, and appears not to have known the code name for the operation, 'I do not know what Linnet is, but if it is the drop of the Airborne Troops, it is definitely on for Sunday next'. Montgomery described Linnet as follows:

I have ordered Second Army to get itself by the evening of 2nd September into the area CARVIN-DOUAI-ARRAS-AUXI-LE-CHATEAU-ST POL-LENS, and not to go any further than that before 3rd September. Browning's troops will drop as arranged, and Second Army will go straight through them directed on ANTWERP, BRUSSELS and GHENT. I have instructed Second Army to move Browning's Corps Headquarters across the front of Second Army, and into the area COURTRAI-LILLE-YPRES, where it will be well placed to watch the left rear of Second Army. This move of the Airborne Corps is necessary because Canadian Army is hanging back somewhat, and Crerar tells me that he cannot use more than two divisions at present north of the Somme for maintenance reasons.

On 1 September Montgomery, Dempsey and Crerar met at Dempsey's headquarters to discuss Linnet.[46] Dempsey recorded in his diary that his proposed plan was agreed. The airborne corps would come under his command after landing and he would then move then into the area of Ypres, Courtrai, Roubaix and Lille. Later the same day Dempsey sent instructions to Browning to this effect. Browning's orders from Dempsey were to:

> Facilitate in every way possible the move of 30 Corps to BRUSSELS. This will include guarding all bridges in your area; policing all cross-roads in your area; and keeping all your own and civilian traffic off the roads which 30 Corps are using . . . You will secure complete control of the area YPRES-COURTRAI-ROUBAIX-LILLE. It is important that this should be done with the least possible delay.

On 1 September SHAEF's Air Defence Division signalled Montgomery, Browning, AEAF and FAAA to inform them that from first light on D-Day until the operation was complete Allied anti-aircraft fire would be limited to north and north-west of a line from the mouth of the River Seine to Les Andeleys, Gisors, Beauvais, Breteuil, Lamotte, St Quentin, Maubeuge and Mons. This was to prevent friendly fire hitting the transport aircraft of the troop carrier convoys and resupply flights.[47]

Late on 1 September De Guingand signalled Browning to tell him that Montgomery had decided that 52nd Division were not to be used during Operation Linnet due to the maintenance situation.[48] De Guingand also promised to send a liaison officer to Moor Park with the latest intelligence appreciation and Second Army's forecast of operations. He signalled FAAA on 1 September confirming the Operation Linnet was required and requested that it should take place on 3 September.[49]

During the planning of Operation Linnet thought was given to relations with the populations of occupied Europe, particularly in the parts of Belgium where Linnet would take place. A signal from SHAEF on 1 September – signed by Eisenhower – proposed sending communiques to the Belgian people in French and Flemish and with the voice of the Supreme Commander.[50] Resistance groups would be instructed to follow orders to prevent the Germans sabotaging important infrastructure and to engage the enemy 'according to rules of war'.The civil population would be instructed to remain quiet, to assist the resistance covertly and to avoid roads and junctions used by the enemy as these might be attacked by the Allied air forces. The Belgian Prime Minister would then read a short statement to the Belgian people. Eisenhower would address the Dutch population and request them to stay quiet and tell them that their time for liberation would come. This would be followed by a short statement from the Dutch Prime Minister. Eisenhower would also read a statement to Poles in the Lille area asking them to prevent the Germans sabotaging infrastructure and to obey Allied orders. This would be followed by a statement from the Polish Prime Minister.

On 1 September HQ Airborne Troops signalled the airborne divisions and 38 Group to inform them that if the weather was bad on the morning of D-Day but cleared later in the day the first lift would take off as soon as it could in daylight, followed by the remaining lifts 'as soon as possible'.[51] The decision over whether flight was possible would be taken by Brereton at FAAA. If, however, the weather was good then the first lift would take off at 0500 and drop at 0805. HQ Airborne Troops had also obtained agreement for 'minor cuts' to be made on all railway lines if these were minor enough to be quickly repairable so that the Allies could use them later.

On 1 September an internal SOE memo considered options for supporting Linnet.[52] Brigadier Mockler-Ferryman, the Director of SOE Operations in North-west Europe, had issued instructions verbally the same morning. In the event of the allies reaching the Linnet area before D-Day SHAEF agreed to Bardsea parties being despatched on the night of 2/3 September. The French Forces of the Interior would be informed, while Belgian Resistance groups would be ordered to mobilise bases, prepare to assist the Allies in moving forwards, capture German stores likely to be useful to the Allies, provide guides and prepare for sabotage plans, particularly around ports. SOE would establish a rear link for Special Forces staff and set up a war room. In the event of Linnet being cancelled four Jedburgh teams would be despatched within 36 hours of the cancellation being received, including one to Antwerp. These would be different to the Jedburgh units which had been attached to airborne forces for Linnet. The arrangements would be different if the operation would take place inside Belgium, no doubt as SOE was organised along country lines.

On 1 September Belchem wrote to Crerar, Dempsey and other branches of 21st Army Group HQ to inform them that as there would be insufficient time to warn forward troops of changes in routeing and timing of the airborne columns there would be no anti-aircraft fire under any circumstances during daylight from first light on 3 September until further notice, anywhere north of the Seine. Belchem had also referred a similar request for the US areas to SHAEF.[53]

In the early hours of 1 September Browning signalled to his divisions that if the weather was bad on the morning of D-Day but improved later in the day, one lift would be acceptable on D-Day, followed by the remaining lifts as early as possible. He explained that the decision regarding the lifts taking place rested entirely with Brereton.[54] Browning was increasingly out of the loop with decision making.

It was also decided on 1 September that Admiral of the Fleet Sir John Tovey, the Commander-in-Chief of The Nore, would be the coordinating naval authority for Linnet, as the airborne route over the North Sea passed over its area.[55]

On 1 September 21st Army Group signalled SHAEF G3 to request additional US Army units to join the 82nd and 101st Divisions to enable them to continue to operate on the ground.[56] These were in order of priority two Cavalry Reconnaissance Squadrons, two 105mm Howitzer Field Artillery Batteries, two 155mm Medium Field Artillery Battalions, two Tank Destroyer Battalions and a 4.2in Chemical Weapons Mortar Battalion. 21st Army Group also requested from SHAEF several US Army quartermaster units for First Allied Airborne Army. These included a Quartermaster Truck Group, two Grave Registration Platoons, one Collecting Company, one Evacuation Hospital, one Ambulance Company, one Cleaning Company and one Labour Company. Com Z had stated that they would not be able to provide them until D+6, but this would be unacceptable to First Allied Airborne Army as they would be required as soon as the airborne forces contacted Allied ground forces. 21st Army Group asked SHAEF to make the units available by the next day on 2 September. A thread was clearly emerging that airborne forces were not equipped to stay in the line indefinitely.[57]

Late on 1 September 21st Army Group confirmed to AEAF and FAAA that Operation Linnet would be required, with D-Day on 3 September.[58] Also on 1 September call signs were allocated to the Air Support Parties at airborne divisions.[59] 1st Airborne Division would be Jenson, 52nd Division Footsore, 101st Division Maestro, 82nd Division Forger, British Airborne Corps Whitehall and XVIII Airborne Corps Chinaboy. On the same day SHAEF signalled 21st and 12th Army Groups with details of anti-aircraft fire restrictions during Operation Linnet. Fire would be restricted to hostile aircraft north and north-west of the line from Les Andelys to Gisors, Beauvais, Breteuil, Lamotte, Maubeuge and Mons.[60]

As D-Day approached the Night Duty Office at AEAF was briefed that 21st Army Group had decided that Linnet was to take place. General Eisenhower might make several decisions, either to cancel Linnet and order a different operation around Liège-Aachen on 5 September, or to cancel Linnet entirely and commit the troop carrier forces into air supply of the American armies. A pencil note next to this point reads 'improbable'. They were also briefed that Brereton may decide to postpone the operation in consultation with General James Doolittle, the commander of the Eighth Air Force, on weather grounds. If any of these decisions were made the Night Duty Office was to inform FAAA, Bomber Command, Eighth Air Force, Ninth Air Force, Second Tactical Air Force, Air Defence of Great Britain, 11 Group, Anti-Aircraft Command, TCCP, the Admiralty, SHAEF, ANCXF, 21st Army Group and Leigh Mallory.[61]

2 September

On 2 September De Guingand signalled Montgomery to inform him that a decision would be made immediately on the weather for Operation Linnet. He told Montgomery that the Airborne Army had already been examining the feasibility of an operation in the Liège-Maastricht gap as an alternative. Brereton had informed De Guingand that if the operation was no longer essential that it might be better to keep the force and equipment to use later. This suggests perhaps that Brereton was lukewarm about Linnet. De Guingand seems to have shared Brereton's views, 'I do not know full implications but in view of delay and uncertain weather feel we should dispense with Linnet if possible and prepare similar operation to suit your future plans.'

Dempsey recorded in his diary that XXX Corps was moving elements forward in readiness for an advance with the twin objectives of capturing Brussels and Antwerp.[62] Against this objective it already seemed that the version of Linnet aimed at the Franco-Belgian border would be overtaken by events.

On 2 September Richardson wrote to De Guingand.[63] Richardson suggested that De Guingand's doubts should be made clear to Browning before the operation commenced, as 'it may be some time before the satisfactory communications are established either from Army Group or Second Army.' Richardson's perceptions of the operation had shifted, as he made clear to De Guingand:

> The object of the operation now seems to be to me to give added infantry strength to the Second Army right forward so that they can continue their thrust to Antwerp. The strength of Second Army's thrust is limited

by maintenance and hence to achieve our object their airborne force must be independent of ground supply.

Richardson recommend that Browning should be ordered to secure an airfield immediately after landing, probably the one at Chievres. Once it was secure it would be possible to 'pile in supplies and make the force an assistance to Second Army rather than a hindrance'. Richardson went as far as to suggest that the 101st Division should be dropped closer to Chievres to ensure its capture, as he felt that 'the tactical objections of dispersing his force is of much less consideration'. They also discussed the possibility of using airborne forces at Antwerp. Richardson suggested that as 'Linnet now becomes such a straightforward operation that General Browning may feel he can dispense with the Poles in the initial phase', presumably to keep them in reserve for future operations.

On 2 September Dempsey's instructions to Browning were sent to De Guingand. Second Army had two corps in the front line, having grounded VIII Corps in Normandy to release its transport. Second Army's plan would see XXX Corps around Carvin, Douai, Arras and Lens on the night of 2 September while XII Corps would be around St Pol, Frevent, Auxi and Hesdin. On 3 September the leading troops of XXX Corps would cross the Franco-Belgian frontier at 1100. XXX Corps' orders were to move direct to Brussels and Antwerp on an axis of Orchies, Tournai, Ath, Hal and Brussels and XII Corps would advance to the area of Merville, Le Bassee and Lilliers. On First Canadian Army's front the 1st Polish Armoured Division had been ordered to advance to the area of St Omer and Cassell while 3rd Canadian Division would aim for the area of Calais and Dunkirk. If the Canadians' advance was successful and Linnet was likewise, the Canadians would then be directed towards Ghent.

Dempsey confirmed that Browning's orders were to secure the area of Ypres, Courtrai, Roubaix and Lille 'with the least possible delay.' As an additional task Dempsey asked Browning to amend his tasking for his divisions to include an order to 'facilitate in every way possible' XXX Corps' advance on Brussels: 'This will include guarding all bridges in your area; policing all crossroads in your area; and keeping all your own and civilian traffic off the roads which 30 Corps are using.'

Finally, Dempsey asked Browning to inform him of the location of his headquarters as soon as it was established, along with the map reference of the nearest landing ground suitable for light aircraft. It is not beyond the realms of possibility that Dempsey might have intended to fly behind enemy lines to confer with Browning – he had previously crashed during the Normandy campaign while flying in an Auster light aircraft.

On 2 September AEAF HQ circulated a memo regarding Operation Linnet.[64] Eighth Air Force would be responsible for strafing any flak in the approaches to the landing area and would provide fighter escort cover to the airborne forces. During the day IX Tactical Air Command, supplemented if required by Second Tactical Air Force, would provide fighter cover over the assault area from shortly after the first drop to just before the start of the second drop. Cover would then be resumed after the second drop until last light. Air Defence of Great Britain would provide night fighter protection, a function that would be fulfilled by 125 Squadron and 456 Squadron of 11 Group. In the initial stages of the assault the Fighter Control Station at Hythe in Kent would control the fighters, with the codename of Gin Fizz. When over the operational area Ninth Tactical Air Command and Second Tactical Air Force would call Gin Fizz for instructions.

To control day and night fighters two Light Warning Sets had been provided for the airborne forces and each set would have two controllers in addition to technical and operational personnel. One set and its crew could be carried in two Horsa gliders. These would arrive in the second lift on D-Day and were scheduled to land at around 2100. It was thought that as they would be landing so late they would not be operational until the next day on D+1. As soon as a landing strip had been constructed in the airborne area an air transportable Ground Control Unit would be flown in a total of five Dakotas. This would then take over controlling air support in the area from the Light Warning Sets.

AEAF informed SHAEF that the route for Linnet had been changed and would now follow a line from Beachy Head, crossing the French coast at Le Treport, Abbeville, Doullens and Arras to the landing area.[65] The return flight would be made on the same route. AEAF asked for all anti-aircraft fire in the area to be suspended until 2200 on D-Day. TCCP at Eastcote informed 38 and 46 Group airfields that searchlights had been arranged at Bedford and Guildford from 0530 until dawn on 3 September, presumably as navigation aids in the half-light. In addition, a white occult light had been sited at Beachy Head which would flash from 0400 to dawn on 3 September and again from dusk until 2359 on 3 September.[66]

On 2 September HQ Airborne Troops informed their subordinate units that the air route had been changed to Beachy Head, Le Treport and Arras.[67] The drop zones and landing zones remained the same, but the formations would approach from the south-west instead of from the north and hence would be flying over Allied-held territory. All ground troops had been ordered not to fire north of the Seine during daylight until further notice. They were also informed that if weather conditions delayed the first lift it could take off up to 1600, which would have in turn delayed the second lift.

21st Army Group's plans section asked 12th Army Group to provide extra combat units for the US formations 'if divisions are needed to stay on and fight'.[68] These included a cavalry reconnaissance troop, a field artillery battalion each of 105mm self-propelled guns and 155mm howitzers, a self-propelled tank destroyer battalion, a chemical weapons battalion, a tank battalion and an anti-aircraft weapons battalion. 21st Army Group was clearly thinking about retaining the American divisions in the line after the airborne operation itself had been concluded. Later the same day SHAEF instructed 12th Army Group to make the units available with the addition of extra medical resources in the shape of a collecting company, a clearing company and a graves registration platoon for each division.

In the afternoon of 2 September several changes were made to the air plan for Linnet. Air Defence of Great Britain would no longer provide escort for the troop carriers and would be replaced by the US Eighth Air Force. The tactical air forces would be restricted to operating in a zone five miles adjoining each flank of the airborne route. At 1615 on 2 September AEAF confirmed that air attacks would only take place after H-Hour on request, and the Allied tactical air forces were restricted to only operating in a zone five miles either side of the airborne route under 8,000ft and in the landing area while the Eighth Air Force was operating.[69]

38 Group had worked up plans to make a Communications Flight available for the use of Browning as the Commander of the Airborne Force.[70] It would consist of six Austers crewed by two Flight Lieutenants, two Flying Officers and two Flight Sergeants with a small ground crew of two NCOs and six Airmen. All ranks were ordered to be prepared to 'live hard,' and to take only bed roll and personal kit as well as 'stout boots or shoes and thick socks'. That all ranks were ordered to be in possession of a knife, fork, spoon, mug, mess tin and water bottle and had to be told to wear battledress and a steel helmet perhaps suggests that they were not ready for active service in such a role and that the provision of a communications flight was a last-minute thought.

A shortage of glider crews meant that HQ Airborne Troops had to modify the intended airlift for Linnet on 2 September. The 2nd Airlanding Light Anti-Aircraft Battery was standing by at Tarrant Rushton to take off in the third lift, but due to a shortage of glider crews would not be able to take off until thirty-two glider crews had been evacuated back after their first flights. 38 Group were requested to tow these gliders as a top priority and without further orders, landing them close to the first landing strip to be completed.[71]

11 Group's Operation Instruction for Linnet was issued on 2 September.[72] Fighter protection would be provided for the airborne columns during the day between the UK coastline and the landing area, and fighter protecting of the operational area around Tournai by night. 11 Group would provide twenty-eight squadrons of Spitfires and Mustangs flying from North Weald, Bradwell Bay, Detling, Manston, Lympne, Hawkinge, Friston, Westhampnett, Brenzett and Deanland by day, and two squadrons of Mosquitos from Middle Wallop and Ford by night. Many of 11 Group's squadrons came from Allied countries and included French, Dutch, Belgian, Czech and Polish aircrews. By day eighteen squadrons would provide close escort for the airborne columns between Beachy Head and Tournai, with two squadrons over the Channel between Beachy Head and Le Treport, four squadrons between Le Treport and Doullens, six squadrons between Doullens and Douai and six squadrons between Douai and Tournai. This force would be divided into two parts, each of nine squadrons covering half of the patrol time each for the morning and evening drops. Six squadrons would be over the dropping area over Tournai during both the morning and evening drops, operating as two forces of three squadrons. Four squadrons of Mustangs would provide supporting patrols each of two squadrons throughout the dropping operations, with one patrol covering a line between Mons and Brussels and another between Neuzen and Brussels.

Close fighter escort for the transport aircraft would cover both flanks at a maximum of 2,000ft above the stream. Cover over the drop zones would be at between 5,000 and 8,000ft, or lower if the cloud base dictated. At night three night fighters from 125 and 456 Squadrons would be on continuous patrol over the airborne operational area around Tournai throughout each night of the operation. By day fighter cover would be controlled by 11 Group's usual sector control in England. Outside of the transport operations Ninth Air Force would protect the drop zone area. RAF Hythe would provide a running commentary to Ninth Air Force to warn them of any hostile or unidentified formations approaching from Germany. Night fighters would be controlled from Biggin Hill and Sandwich initially then handed over to the airborne operational area a soon as signals and a Ground Control Interception radar could be set up. However, later on 2 September it was confirmed that the US

Eighth Air Force would instead provide fighter cover rather than 11 Group, who would only provide night fighter cover and air-sea rescue.

In the afternoon a signal from Belchem at 21st Army Group to Dempsey and Crerar confirmed that the routeing for the air columns for Linnet had been modified to Le Treport and Arras.[73] AEAF confirmed that major changes had been made to the air plan.[74] The landing area had been made much smaller, with the landing and drop zones focused on Tournai. Close air support attacks would only take place upon request after the initial landings. The Allied tactical air forces would be barred from operating in a zone five miles either side of the airborne route under 8,000ft and in the landing area while Eighth Air Force were operating. A subsequent signal from AEAF to SHAEF indicated that with these changes it was likely that the tail of the airborne column would not return before nightfall. Therefore AEAF requested that all anti-aircraft fire should be suspended north and north-west of a specified line to prevent friendly fire casualties.

AEAF confirmed that on D-Day Gin Fizz, the Type 16 Station at RAF Hythe, would provide communications with fighter cover over the landing areas. Formation leaders were to call Gin Fizz on arrival and listen on that frequency whilst on patrol. After D-Day a control station would be set up in the airborne area, codenamed Programme.[75]

On 2 September the Air Ministry confirmed that it had arranged for Anti-Aircraft Command to show two searchlight cones over the assembly points at Guildford and Bedford to aid navigation. Each would consist of six searchlights in a circle of 750 yards radius with all lights flashing in continuous rotation.

At 2000 FAAA signalled that Linnet had been cancelled due to poor weather. Troops were ordered to remain at airfields at 36 hours warning for a new operation.[76] A signal from Belchem at 21st Army Group, sent at 2140 on 2 September, read 'In view of delay and weather problem C-in-C regrets op Linnet must be cancelled'. This suggests that the cancellation was Montgomery's decision.[77] At the same time TCCP at Eastcote signalled to 38 and 46 Group airfields that they were to stand down until 1200 on 3 September, and from then onwards to be at two hours' notice. This presumably meant that had the operation taken off on 3 September only one lift could have been delivered that day.[78] Just after midnight on 2 September AEAF signalled that Operation Linnet had been cancelled, but that it was possible that a similar operation might be ordered in the near future.[79] Dempsey was informed of its cancellation at 2215.

Late on 2 September Montgomery sent a personal message to Dempsey. He made clear that the cancellation of Linnet would have consequences on Dempsey's plans, and suggested that he might wish to delay his advance towards Ghent and Brussels or decide to not advance beyond that line.[80]

Late the same evening on 2 September De Guingand wrote to Montgomery and informed him that FAAA had planned an alternative operation to capture bridges between Maastricht and Liège.

3 September

On 3 September De Guingand wrote to Montgomery that the weather had been worse than FAAA had forecast, and that in his opinion 'it is a very good thing that Linnet did not take place'. De Guingand had also received a signal about morale issues in 52nd Division connected with them not being used in operations:

> I enclose a signal I got from Browning about 52 Division. He is obviously worried about the effect upon the Division in the event of their not being used. It is a bit rough on them one knows, but it cannot be helped and it is up to him to see they understand the position. In the meantime, we are going to make use of some of their transport which is over here waiting for them to 'hot up' our maintenance.

Later that day Montgomery signalled De Guingand that he had met with Bradley who informed him that he did not need an airborne operation around the Maastricht-Liège area. They had therefore agreed that the Troop Carrier aircraft should be dedicated to transporting supplies to keep up the momentum of the advance.

De Guingand informed Montgomery that an airborne operation at Liège-Maastricht could take place the next day on 4 September, and described the plan as having 'certain merits'. He had discussed the operation with SHAEF and Brereton and proposed that if Linnet did not take place then the troop carrier aircraft should be used for supply work, and that the Allies should only plan for 'small air-borne drops to undertake such tasks as securing the islands off Antwerp etc'.

At 1145 on 3 September Brereton signalled Montgomery, Bradley and Eisenhower informing them that what he described as an 'alternate target Operation Linnet' could take place on 4 or 5 September.[81] He informed them that the airborne route would cross the Channel at Beachy Head, cross the French coast at Le Treport and then follow a line approximately south of Charleroi to the Landing Zones in the Liège area. Although Brereton 'requested you take all necessary action to protect troop carrier aircraft from friendly fire,' it is not hard to imagine that switching an operation at such short notice left scant time to inform anti-aircraft units in order to prevent friendly fire incidents.

The same day Brereton met with Eisenhower and Tedder at SHAEF Advanced HQ.[82] Brereton's diary records that both were in favour of Linnet take place in the Aachen-Maastricht Gap, and suggested that the Supreme Commander had delegated the decision to Bradley and Montgomery. Later the same day Brereton also met Browning at FAAA HQ at Ascot where Brereton told his subordinate that Linnet II 'would be mounted tomorrow or not at all'. Browning understandably objected to the operation being mounted at such short notice, because maps of the area could not be distributed to the airborne units in time to allow them to be briefed on the areas in which they would be operating. Brereton replied that in the circumstances of the chaotic state of the German forces in western Europe, 'chances had to be taken', and that the operation would only be cancelled because of bad weather or if called off by SHAEF. Browning was concerned enough to remain behind after the conference, when he told Brereton that in his opinion the operation was not feasible at such short notice and that he would be submitting a written protest, along with those of his divisional commanders. Browning then left.

However, Browning made a critical error of judgement. Brereton immediately called General Ridgway, who assured Brereton that the commanders of the 82nd and 101st Divisions – Gavin and Taylor – would not 'protest the execution of any decisions handed down to them', and that even if they expressed opinions during the planning of an operation they carry out the operations and 'make a 100 percent job of it.' Expecting Browning's protest, Brereton ordered Ridgway to prepare to take over command of Linnet.

Later that evening Brereton received a letter from Browning, which concluded that because of their sharp difference of opinion he felt that he could no longer continue as Deputy Commander of the First Allied Airborne Army, and therefore tendered his resignation. His later withdrew his resignation, but the disagreement caused significant friction between the two.

FAAA signalled 38 Group and other addresses late on 3 September cancelling Linnet, but stated that the operation would be moved to an alternative target.[83] An earlier message at 1130 the same day had stated that the alternative target for Linnet might be subject to an operation 4 or 5 September, with the landing area around Liège.

On 3 September Brereton signalled AEAF from 9th Air Force HQ regarding the alternative for Operation Linnet. The signal outlined a route from Beachy Head, crossing the French coast at Le Treport, flying over Charleroi to the landing areas at Dogxebras and Lovexbras around Liège. The operation might take place on either 4 or 5 September.[84]

Meanwhile airborne plans in the Mediterranean were threatening to reduce the allocation of troop carrier aircraft. 46 Group had been committed to move to Italy from 4 September and to be away from Britain for 10 days, and FAAA was therefore warned on 3 September not to count on the involvement of its 100 aircraft in Linnet. Later the same day however, it was confirmed that the Chief of the Air Staff and the Air Ministry had agreed that 46 Group was to take part in Linnet before leaving for overseas. The Allied air forces in the Mediterranean objected as this would leave little time for 46 Group to train with the 2nd Parachute Brigade in Italy before a planned operation. They wanted all of 46 Group's aircraft to arrive in their theatre at least seven days prior to a planned operation, which would require then to reach Italy by 8 September. Brereton signalled to SHAEF on 2 September that all the Dakotas of 38 and 46 Groups were essential for Linnet and were already loaded for the mission. Aside from the oversight that 38 Group did not have any Dakotas Brereton stressed that the release of sixty aircraft to Italy would cause a serious delay to Linnet. He therefore asked for the move to be postponed until D+2.[85]

4 September

When HQ Airborne Troops signalled 38 Group at 0525 on 4 September to confirm that Linnet had been cancelled the message stated that units under the command of British Airborne Corps were to remain in their present locations ready for another operation on 6 September. The 82nd and 101st Divisions were to return to their billets and reverted to the command of XVIII Airborne Corps. Planning staffs were ordered to return to Moor Park by 1800 on 4 September.[86]

Linnet II

As early as 1 September Brereton had written to Browning suggesting an alternative target area for Linnet.[87] In what could be described as a terse letter, Brereton ordered that an alternative target area had been selected, with the mission of seizing a firm base in the area Liège-Maastricht, seizing and utilising an existing airfield for airborne supply, and capturing the bridge over the Meuse between Liège and Maastricht inclusive.

Linnet II was Brereton's idea. It is probable that he felt under pressure to use the airborne forces, as SHAEF had been under pressure from

Washington, in turn FAAA was being pressed for action.[88] Browning and HQ Airborne Troops also felt that the lack of planning time would lead to a ragged drop.[89]

A signal from HQ AEAF at 1630 on 3 September to AEAF advanced HQ on the Continent stated that an alternative operation Linnet was being planned against Aachen. Ninth Air Force had had responsibility for air support in the original Linnet plan, but as it had been diverted to operations around Brest it was proposed that 2nd Tactical Air Force would support. It was later decided that 2nd Tactical Air Force would be out of range.

The Operation Instruction for what would later be known as Linnet II was issued by Browning on 3 September.[90] Linnet II was designed to capture and hold the main bridges over the Meuse between Maastricht and Liège and prevent their demolition. Linnet II would be cooperating exclusively with 12th Army Group. Third Army was driving east towards the Rhine, while the First Army was stated to be driving north towards the Maastricht-Liège area. Second British Army was believed to be directed on Brussels and Antwerp while the Canadian Army was in the Pas de Calais towards Dunkirk. 1st Airborne Division would land west of Maastricht and secure high ground from Waltwilder to Grand Spauwen, capturing the two road bridges over the Meuse in Maastricht, and linking up with the 82nd Division at the crossroads of the road between Tongres and Maastricht. The 82nd Division would land around Tongres and capture the high ground from Galgenburg to Wihogne and deny the Germans the use of roads in the area. They were to capture and hold the road bridges over the Meuse at Vise and west of Dalhem, and would link up with the 101st Division at Viernay. The 101st Division would land west of Liège and capture the high ground and dominate roads passing south-east and east through the area from Viernay to the bridge over the Meuse at Kessale. It was to capture the bridges at Kessale and immediately north of Bressoux. Airborne Corps HQ would land with 82nd Division.

Early on 4 September the Chief of Operations at AEAF signalled SHAEF Forward Headquarters, forwarding on a message that have been received from Brereton:

> . . . weather requires delay in mounting in Linnet tomorrow second army will be in area by time airborne can land. Have talked with Chief of Staff Northern Group of Armies and stated in my opinion Linnet should be cancelled. Can drop and seize Meuse crossings Liège Maastricht inclusive on 36 hours' notice. This as last strategic objective within

range of present bases. I consider any other targets in present range as secondary to Meuse crossings unquote.[91]

Linnet II exposed the tensions in the command structure of the First Allied Airborne Army. Dismayed that the units taking part in the operation would lack maps and aerial reconnaissance photographs, Browning threatened to resign. He later retracted his resignation after the cancellation of Linnet II, but that it was offered at all highlights that relations between Brereton and Browning were far from cordial. It has been argued that having threatened to resign once Browning was far less likely to object in future and therefore had limited leverage regarding the planning of future operations. Buckingham has suggested that the prospect of being replaced – Ridgway was a potential and more experienced alternative – made Browning more compliant in future.[92]

On 4 September Brereton went to HQ British Airborne Corps at Moor Park for a 'frank talk' with Browning about their exchange the previous day.[93] Brereton told Browning that as he had been appointed deputy commander of FAAA by Eisenhower his resignation would have to be forwarded to the supreme commander. Brereton intended to forward Browning's resignation with his comments, and he invited Browning to add his own. However, Brereton found that Browning had reconsidered overnight:

> Browning, who had cooled off considerably after writing his letter, was quite willing to have his resignation withdrawn. He realized that under the circumstances that General Ridgway would command the airborne forces in Operation Linnet II. After a frank talk I felt that we understood each other.

At 0450 on 4 September Brereton signalled SHAEF, Browning, Bradley and other headquarters and formations that the 'Operation on alternate target to Operation Linnet' had been cancelled.[94] However, Brereton's diary suggests that Linnet II was not cancelled until 5 September.[95]

On 5 September Bradley signalled Patton, Lieutenant General Courtney Hodges at US First Army and Lieutenant General William Simpson at US Ninth Army regarding Operation Linnet. He stated that moving Linnet to an alternative target was possible although not probable. If it did take place in the Liège area the airborne force would cross the Channel at Le Treport, then flying over Charleroi to the landing area. From first light on D-Day until the operation finished anti-aircraft fire would be restricted to engaging aircraft which actually committed hostile acts, north and north-west of a line from the Seine at Les Andelys to Gisors and Beauvais.[96]

That Brereton mentioned Ridgway in explaining Browning's change of heart is telling, and Linnet II also affirms how Browning's star had fallen. Had he expected Montgomery to defend him? Brereton outflanked him by threatening to go straight to Eisenhower. There were clearly issues between Brereton and Ridgway on the one hand and Browning on the other. The British had pushed for Browning to be appointed to what would later become Brereton's command, but Ridgway and Browning had pre-existing tensions stretching back to the Mediterranean theatre. In summary, FAAA was not a harmonious headquarters and was certainly not an advert for alliance warfare. The argument between Brereton and Browning suggests that the FAAA leadership had fundamental relationship issues.

OPERATION INFATUATE

Not for the first or last time during the campaign in North-west Europe the capture of Antwerp had raised the spectre of water obstacles. Whilst the capture of the city and port on 4 September was a significant achievement for the Allies, the docks themselves were useless unless the vast Scheldt estuary could be cleared of enemy presence. Otherwise, any Allied shipping would have been extremely vulnerable. And the Allied logistical situation in late August and early September meant that shipping was seen as a priority, albeit to differing degrees by different generals.

On 2 September Richardson wrote to De Guingand and explained that he had been studying 'the problem of Antwerp'. Allied intelligence indicated that it could be flooded in 48 hours and that therefore it was essential that the Allies try and 'bounce' the place. He went on to recommend that the Polish Parachute Brigade, which was at that time scheduled to land during Operation Linnet, should instead be held back to be dropped in advance of a thrust to Antwerp. Richardson identified key locations at Aalst and Boom where the brigade could be dropped, and he suggested to De Guingand that the operation should be put to FAAA. Richardson felt that Linnet might be such a straightforward operation that Browning might feel able to dispense with the Polish Brigade. Richardson also rejected the possibility of an airborne operation to capture Rotterdam and recommended that securing Antwerp early would be of 'paramount importance'.[1]

Later the same day De Guingand signalled Montgomery. He informed his chief that he had discussed the possibility of dropping a 'small force' at Antwerp to prevent inundations. Browning however thought that it would be too late to mount an operation to do this and that the problem might be best tackled overland.[2]

On the morning of 7 September De Guingand again signalled Montgomery. De Guingand had discussed a range of matters with

Whiteley at SHAEF, among them airborne operations and the issue of opening Antwerp:

> Whiteley's opinion is that we could have two US airborne divisions in accordance with Ike's directive allotting airborne army to 21st Army Group. They might be employed for capture of Walcheren Island which might be right? to speed up use of Antwerp and should not affect greatly air supply as after capture divisions could be immediately withdrawn. Project being examined.[3]

Unfortunately Montgomery does not seem to have recorded his opinion of De Guingand's ideas, but his chief of staff was increasingly an advocate for an airborne operation on the Scheldt. His letter to Montgomery dated 8 September suggests as much:

> The more I consider the use of the American airborne divisions for the capture of Walcheren Island, the more I like it. It would perform the twofold object of clearing the way for the opening of Antwerp and will block the German escape route from the Pas de Calais. I have told Charles Richardson to get on to the Airborne Army about it, and when we receive your decision we will take the necessary action. I understand the air are keen on it because the air commitment for neutralising the Island will be a big one.

Richardson signalled First Allied Airborne Army the same day to request that they examine the possibility of an airborne operation to capture Walcheren:

> Request you examine feasibility of airborne operation to capture Walcheren. Operation required early as possible. Artillery support might be given from mainland by First Canadian Army and after capture force will be at once withdrawn. Early capture of island will permit use of Antwerp and speed up progress of whole campaign. Request early reply.[4]

It is worth noting that Richardson 'requested' FAAA to examine the suggestion, rather than ordering them as 21st Army Group would have been able to do to Browning and HQ Airborne Forces earlier in the campaign.

Only a day later Brereton wrote to Montgomery stating his objections to using airborne forces at Walcheren.[5] He explained that no airborne units would be available as all available divisions were allocated to operations elsewhere. If British troops were withdrawn it would take a minimum of seven days to unload, reorganise and plan the new operation. He also identified heavy flak defences on Walcheren Island and that these would inflict heavy losses on the transport aircraft. The small size of the island would also risk the drowning of many troops who might be dropped in the water. Finally, rain would make the landing of gliders impossible, which would prevent the landing of motor transport, artillery and anti-tank weapons, effectively leaving the airborne force immobile and without heavy weapons. Brereton also suggested that the terrain would be unsuitable for parachute landings.

Brereton signalled Montgomery regarding Walcheren the next day on 10 September restating his earlier objections.[6] He again argued that an airborne operation on the island would not be feasible for a number of reasons. No airborne troops would be available, 1st British Airborne and the 82nd and 101st US Divisions having already been earmarked for Market Garden, unless the US airborne divisions in reserve were not used in support of Bradley's Army Group on the axis of Aachen-Koln.

Despite his objections Brereton's diary entry of 11 September suggested that Operation Infatuate, the codename for a landing on Walcheren Island, was one of ten airborne operations under consideration at that point in time. Brereton recorded that he refused Infatuate because of: '. . . intense flak on Walcheren, difficult terrain which would prevent glider landing, excessive losses likely because of drowning, non-availability of U.S. troops, and the fact that the operation is an improper employment of airborne forces'.[7]

Putting aside that the 'proper and improper' use of airborne forces was clearly a matter of debate, the same diary entry alludes to other reasons why Brereton may have rejected Infatuate.[8] It is hard to escape the conclusion the Brereton was simply not interested in helping to make an airborne operation on Walcheren possible.

Montgomery's directive M525 issued on 14 September explained that although Antwerp had been captured the Allies could not make use of the port as the Germans still controlled the Scheldt.[9] Clearing the estuary would be the priority of the Canadian Army. However Montgomery went on to elaborate that 'Our real objective, therefore, is the Ruhr. But on the way to it we want the ports of Antwerp and Rotterdam, since the capture of the Ruhr is merely the first step on the northern route of advance into Germany.'

Directive M525 subsequently went on to state that 'The whole energies of the Army will be directed towards operations designed to enable full use to be made of the port of Antwerp. Airborne troops are available to co-operate. Canadian Army will take over the Antwerp area from Second Army beginning on 17 September.'

The prospect of an airborne operation at Walcheren did not end with Brereton's refusal in early September, and a conference held on 21 September to discuss Operation Infatuate was attended by Crerar, Ramsay and De Guingand.[10] Crerar envisaged that Infatuate would entail an advance westward into South Beveland, probably co-ordinated with a waterborne assault on the harbour at Hoedekenskerke, and assisted by airborne troops 'if able to participate in the securing of the initial bridgehead'.

At the same conference Crerar said that it would be 'highly desirable' to flood Walcheren, and the conference discussed whether flooding the island would eliminate any prospect of using airborne troops, probably due to the risk of large numbers of troops drowning. Crerar explained that he saw the most suitable tasks for airborne forces as being the securing of a small bridgehead on South Beveland to the west of the canal to make early use of the harbour at Hoedekenskerke and to possibly secure the causeway to Walcheren. After Crerar and De Guingand departed the conference Belchem at 21st Army Group telephoned Mann, Crerar's chief of staff, and informed him that airborne troops would not be available for Infatuate.

On 23 September a conference took place at the Headquarters of First Canadian Army to discuss Operation Infatuate. Among the attendees were Cutler from FAAA. Crerar outlined four alternatives: an airborne landing, an approach via South Beveland, a river crossing across the Scheldt, or a seaborne assault on the south-west or north-east corners of Walcheren. Crerar conceded that the possibilities of an airborne operation were, at that stage, remote. Cutler told the conference that if the Canadian Army were able to put up a 'really good case' then Eisenhower might reconsider his decision regarding the employment of airborne troops at Walcheren. Cutler also promised that FAAA would examine the possibility of an airborne operation in the South Beveland Isthmus. However the suitability of Walcheren for airborne operations still remained doubtful, particularly as at the same conference Crerar and Simonds discussed bombing the sea walls at Walcheren to flood the island.[11]

The planning of the subsequent operations that took place on the Scheldt and Walcheren sheds light on how an airborne operation there might have transpired. A report by 21st Army Group's Intelligence Staff on 22 September examined the Dutch mainland on the south bank of the Scheldt, Walcheren Island and South Beveland.[12] The Allies had the advantage of local knowledge, including from the Chief of Engineer of the Dutch Department of Public Works and Transport and a Warrant Officer in the Royal Netherlands Army who was a former tug master on the Scheldt.

The drainage of Walcheren was controlled by thirty-two sluices and two locks on the Beveland Canal. The canal was a metre above the surrounding land and would add to flooding if the dykes on either side were breached. It was estimated that the Germans would be able to flood the entire island to a depth of 1m to 2.5m by opening and closing control points at the right states of tide. The island would be flooded to a maximum depth in five to seven days, although parts of the island below sea level would be flooded in two and a half days. The neck of land between the island and mainland could be easily and quickly flooded. Most roads would be submerged, and the main roads would only be a quarter of a metre above the water level.

Walcheren was made up of Polderland and rough pasture, and the average level of land was 1.2m above Mean Low Water Spring. By opening and closing control points at the right state of tide and breaching the dykes of canal it would be possible to flood the island in three days. The whole of the island would be flooded with the exception of the sand dunes on the south-west and north-west sides of the island and a few high points in the centre. The average depth of the flooding would be 0.5m to 2m.

The discussions regarding an airborne operation as part of Infatuate, however brief, suggest that it would have been extremely hazardous due to the terrain of Walcheren. Although the opening of Antwerp would have met the Allied need for strategic objectives, the risk of many airborne troops drowning would have been significant. It might however have made sense to use airborne troops to assist in the opening of the Scheldt, if not on Walcheren, possibly by helping to seal off the isthmus north of Antwerp and trapping the German forces on the North Sea coast.

OPERATION COMET

3 September

After the cancellation of Linnet Montgomery continued to look for opportunities to use the First Allied Airborne Army during 21st Army Group's advance into the Low Countries. Although previous airborne plans had included river crossings as objectives, particularly Axehead and Linnet, even a cursory glance at the map confirms that the many rivers and canals in Holland and Belgium would inevitably become obstacles to the Allied rate of advance.

On 3 September Montgomery's directive M523 stated his intention to 'advance eastwards and destroy all enemy forces encountered. To occupy the Ruhr, and get astride the communications leading from it into Germany and to the sea ports.'[1] At this point the British Second Army was advancing to secure the area of Brussels, Ghent and Antwerp while the Canadian Army was further south across the Somme around Abbeville. The boundaries that Montgomery set for his and Bradley's Army Groups suggest that he was thinking far ahead, with 21st Army Group's boundary being Opladen, Warburg and Brunswick inclusive, well into Germany. On 6 September Second Army was to advance eastwards from the general line of Brussels and Antwerp. In Montgomery's own words 'The western face of the Ruhr between Dusseldorf and Duisburg will be threatened', while the main weight of Second Army would be directed towards the Rhine between Arnhem and Wesel. After crossing the Rhine Second Army would be directed on the general line of Osnabruck, Munster and Rheine. The Ruhr itself would be bypassed to the north, to link up with a southward thrust through Hamm. The Canadian Army was ordered to clear the Channel and North Sea coast and then remain in the general area of Bruges and Calais. Montgomery hoped that one division, or if necessary a corps, would be sufficient to clear the western Netherlands around Rotterdam and Amsterdam. He predicted that 12th Army Group would direct US First Army to move with its left flank in contact with 21st Army Group,

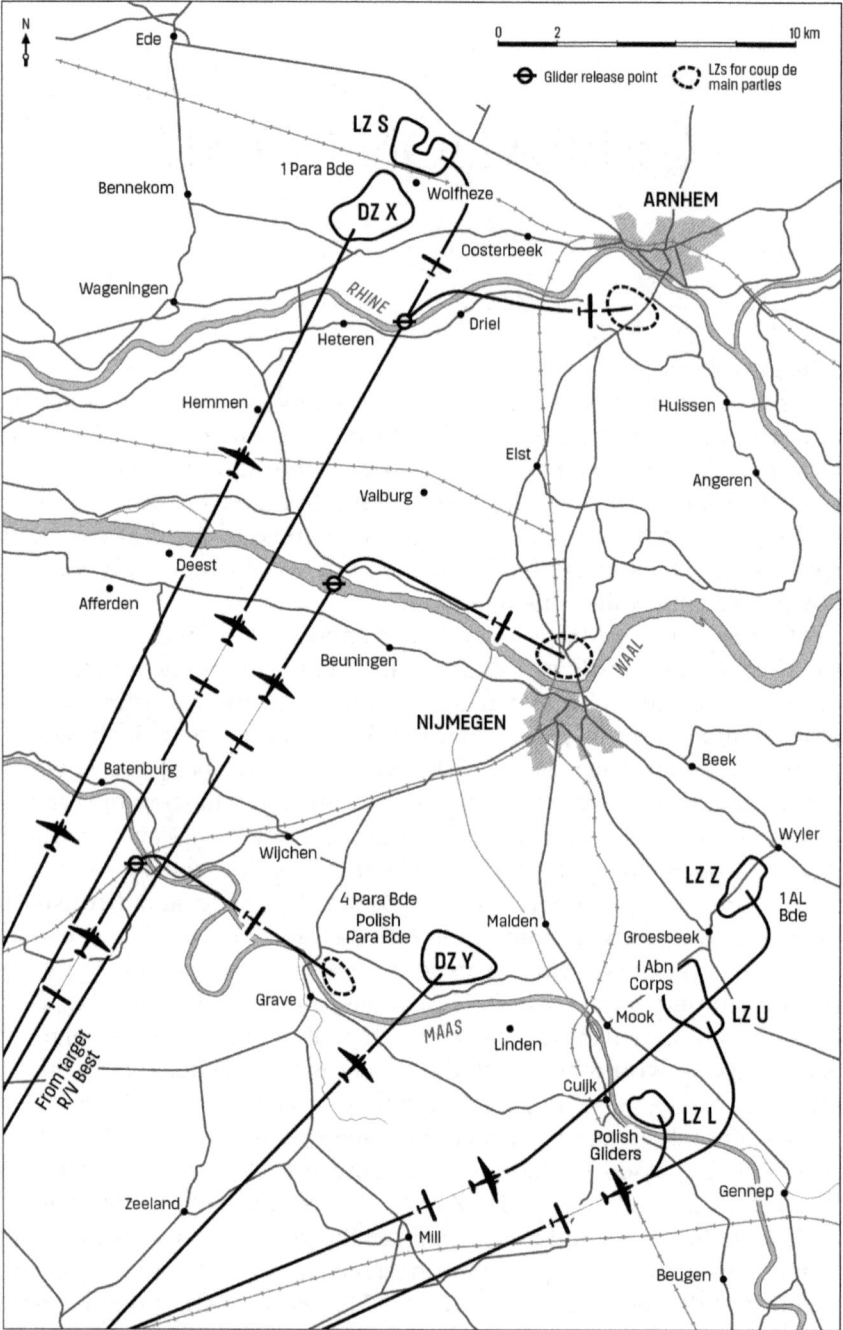

Map 7: Operation Comet. (Source: TNA WO 219/3065)

and that two of its corps would be given the objectives of Maastricht and Liège, Sittard and Aachen then Cologne and Bonn.

The objectives in M523 suggest just how ambitious the Allied command was in the first few days of September 1944. Boundary lines all the way to Brunswick, and thinking that one division would be sufficient to clear the western half of Holland, was either based on thinking that German resistance had all but ceased, over-optimism or a combination of both. It is notable from M523 that Montgomery originally hoped that the advance from Belgium into Holland would begin on 6 September.

Although airborne operations were not mentioned in M523, on the same day that it was issued Montgomery met with Dempsey to discuss an as yet un-named airborne operation between Nijmegen and Wesel, suggesting that the specific crossing over the Rhine that would be the objective had not been decided. In the evening of 3 September Montgomery signalled De Guingand and ordered him to meet him on the Continent, saying 'Consider we may want considerable airborne drop to make certain of getting over Meuse and Rhine. Order Browning to come to see me tomorrow and you come too.'[2] The US Air Force Historical Study suggests that Arnhem was selected around this time as the flak was stronger around Wesel.[3]

After the war Belchem argued that the choice of Arnhem over Wesel was influenced by a signal from Nye, the Vice Chief of the Imperial General Staff, on behalf of the War Cabinet on 9 September asking when the Rotterdam, Utrecht and Amsterdam area would be cleared. He thought that Montgomery had not been certain about aiming for Arnhem and that 'all of us,' including Dempsey and Browning, had been in favour of Wesel. Belchem suggested that there had been virtually no Germans between the front line and Wesel on 9 September, something that was also pointed out by General Siegfried Westphal who was chief of staff to Field Marshal von Rundstedt, the German commander in the West. Montgomery did not tell Belchem, who was acting as chief of staff in the absence of De Guingand who was on sick leave, why he had changed his mind. Belchem also felt that threating the Ruhr was not in conflict with securing the Scheldt and that threatening the German homeland would lead to units being withdrawn from the coast.[4]

4 September

On the evening of 4 September Dempsey met with Browning, De Guingand and Graham at Second Army Headquarters, where Dempsey's diary records that they discussed plans for the capture of Nijmegen and Arnhem. Dempsey recalled that he had planned to launch the operation from Antwerp on the morning of 7 September, led by XXX Corps, and that the Airborne Corps of 'two or three Brigades' would land on the morning of the same day 'to get the bridges'.[5]

Also on 4 September a staff conference was held at First Allied Airborne Army Headquarters to plan what Brereton described as 'the Arnhem operation'.[6] It has been suggested that as Comet was a 'British operation' Brereton and Parks did not involve themselves in the planning of the operation itself.[7] The accuracy and impact of this is not clear, but the directive for Comet was still issued to Browning by FAAA and not 21st Army Group.[8]

5 September

On 5 September Dempsey issued a directive to Lieutenant General Brian Horrocks at XXX Corps and Browning containing his orders for the coming operations.[9] Dempsey predicted that the Germans would expect the Allies' main effort to be further south between the Meuse and Strasbourg on the American front. He summed up the Allied plans as 12th Army Group advancing towards Frankfurt while 21st Army Group and US First Army advanced towards the Ruhr. Dempsey predicted that First Army would be directed south of the Ruhr before turning north-east while Second Army would be directed north of the Ruhr before turning south-east, with its right flank directed towards Brunswick. This directive was completely in harmony with Montgomery's directive M523.

Second Army was given two tasks by Dempsey – to prevent the Germans 'breaking out of the bag' and to gain a bridgehead over the Rhine. Dempsey predicted that Second Army's operations may take time as its ability to advance would depend upon the speed of the Canadian Army's movements on its left. He also stressed that speed would be important to catch the Germans whilst they were still off balance after their defeat in Normandy. Not for the first or last time Dempsey showed a more astute judgement of the situation than he has been credited with by historians.

Operations to trap the Germans would begin on 7 September. XXX Corps would advance to Aalst and Antwerp and XII Corps to Lille and Ghent, and airborne operations to gain a bridgehead over the Rhine would begin after 14 September to allow enough bridging equipment to be brought forward. After landing and linking up the Airborne Corps would come under XXX Corps and would then revert to command of Second Army. XXX Corps was ordered to capture crossings over the Albert Canal beginning on the morning of 7 September. At the time of Dempsey's directive XXX Corps was around Antwerp and would be relieved by XII Corps before moving to the Dutch-Belgian border, and Dempsey stressed that the speed of XXX Corps' advance towards Nijmegen would depend upon the administrative situation. The airborne operation would take place on the evening of 7 September and the morning of 8 September, while 52nd Division would begin landing on the morning of 10 September.

Before the airborne operation was to take place the formations on Second Army's left flank – 11th Armoured Division, 50th Division and 8th Armoured Brigade – would be directed from Antwerp towards Breda, Tilburg and s'Hertogenbosch. The right flank – consisting of the Guards Armoured Division – would be directed from Louvain towards Eindhoven, Nijmegen and Arnhem, with one regiment being ordered to capture the ferry over the Rhine at Emmerich. The objective was to capture a start line on Eindhoven, Tilburg and Breda. Horrocks' plan for the ground advance to link up with the airborne landings involved capturing a start line that would link Eindhoven, Tilburg and Breda. This plan would have given the ground offensive towards Arnhem stronger flank protection. Montgomery himself suggested that it would not be possible to drop the airborne forces on the Rhine until the Second Army was in Eindhoven.[10] This begs the question, if Eindhoven was considered as the minimum start line for Comet, why was the start line so far south for Market Garden when the German defences had stiffened?

On 5 September Montgomery wrote to Simpson at the War Office: 'We have reached a vital moment in the war, and if we now take the right decision we could be in Berlin in 3 weeks and the German war would be over . . . I have given my views very clearly . . . I fear very much we shall have a compromise, and so prolong the war.'[11] However as we have seen, the Allies already had a compromise in the shape of the First Allied Airborne Army. And of Montgomery's qualities, Allied diplomacy was not often one of them.

6 September

On 6 September Eisenhower confirmed that the First Allied Airborne Army would support what he described as the Northern Group of Armies, 'up to and including crossing of the Rhine and then be prepared to operate in large scale operations into Germany'.[12]

IX Troop Carrier Command's Warning Order for Comet was published on 6 September.[13] Command and control of the air transport operation would be conducted from the TCCP at Eastcote and the decision to postpone or cancel would be made by Brereton at First Allied Airborne Army in sufficient time to inform all units concerned. The air route for Comet would cross the Dutch coast over Schouwen island south of the Rhine delta and then fly up the flat river plain of the Maas, Waal and Rhine towards Nijmegen and Arnhem, a route selected to avoid known enemy concentrations of flak.[14] It was thought that it would be extremely unlikely that the Allies would be able to achieve tactical surprise as the approach of the air formations would be obvious and the Germans were likely to be alerted by radar or visual reconnaissance. They would not, however, be able to determine the exact landing areas due to the direction changes during the route.

The air planning for Comet drew upon a detailed flak defence map. There was believed to be a large concentration of hundreds of flak guns around Rotterdam and the adjoining North Sea Coast, including nineteen light flak guns on Walcheren Island alone. This flak belt is not surprising given the sustained Allied bomber offensive over the previous few years. Closer to the landing area there were believed to be six heavy and sixteen light guns at Deelen airfield with a range that included the planned landing zones at Arnhem. Closer to Arnhem there were thought to be six heavy and one light flak guns at the bridge itself. At Nijmegen bridge there were thought to be five heavy and eighteen light guns, although these were out of range of the planned drop zones.

The northern route would cross the English coast at Aldeburgh after forming up over March, while the southern route would form up over Hatfield and cross the coast at Bradwell. The Arnhem drop zones would be LZ S north of Wolfheze and DZ X south-west of Wolfheze. Those at Nijmegen would be LZ L at Middelaar, LZ U at Groesbeek, LZ L north of Groesbeek and DZ Y at Overasselt. The supply dropping zones would be on the south bank of the Rhine opposite Oosterbeek and north of Boskamp. Aerial photographs of the landing zones and drop zones would be issued to headquarters for planning purposes. Even though Comet would see smaller forces landing around each objective most of the landing zones were still at some distance from the bridges – the landing areas designated for Comet were approximately five miles from Arnhem and Nijmegen respectively. Landing Zones S, U, Z and L were approximately eight miles south and south-east of Nijmegen. Although the drop zones for Market Garden are often thought to have been selected after 10 September most of them had been identified for Comet.[15]

The first day of Comet would consist of two lifts. The first aircraft would begin taking off at 0606 carrying the 1st Airborne Division. It would begin dropping at 0800, finish by 0832 and return to base in Britain at 0949. The second lift consisting of the Polish Brigade and a resupply drop would start taking off at 1554. The second drop would commence at 1745 and be completed by 1819, with the aircraft landing back in Britain by 1931. On the second day a third lift would take in the 878th Airborne Engineer Aviation Battalion and an Airfield Control Unit. It would take off at 0821 and begin landing in Holland at 1000, returning to Britain by 1119.

The Luftwaffe was thought to have around 500 single-engined fighters in East Holland and North-west Germany. Around 200 to 275 of these aircraft were serviceable with crews available, and of these it was estimated that no more than 150 to 200 could be used to defend against the airborne operation. The Germans possessed 175 twin-engined fighters of which 100 to 120 were serviceable. It was thought unlikely that they would be used as they were likely to be held back as night fighters. The Germans had as few as 15 to 20 serviceable fighter-bombers and 175 serviceable twin-engined bombers. In summary, the Luftwaffe was not thought to present any discernible threat to the operation.

In terms of enemy ground forces the 347th, 719th and 70th Infantry Divisions were reported to be around the Arnhem and Nijmegen area. The 347th and 719th were training and coastal divisions respectively and were thought to have moved north-east from Antwerp. It was not known if they were to remain in Holland or retire to the Siegfried Line. The only known garrison troops in the area were thought to be static flak battalions in the towns.

1st Parachute Brigade's orders for what was referred to as 'Operation Fifteen' were given by Lathbury verbally on 6 September and as had become customary were then followed up with a confirmatory note. The operation would be carried out in two lifts. The first lift would begin landing at 0430 when a glider coup-de-main party consisting of a company from the 2nd South Staffords would land and capture Arnhem bridge.[16] A platoon from the 21st Independent Company would land at 0730 and mark the drop zone for the rest of the Brigade which would begin landing at 0800.

The 2nd Parachute Battalion, in an echo of their role in Market Garden, would despatch a coup-de-main party of one company on its own route as soon as possible to move as fast as possible to relieve the company of South Staffords at the bridge. They would then assume a defensive position within the town facing west. The 3rd Battalion would also send a coup-de-main party to relieve the South Staffords and would then take up a defensive position in the town facing east.

The 1st Battalion meanwhile would send one company to hold the landing zone for the glider lifts. After remaining at the drop zone to protect the troops collecting supply containers, the battalion was to escort the second glider lift into the defensive perimeter around the town. Once there the battalion was to go into brigade reserve, but with one company holding the southern end of Arnhem bridge.

What happened during Market Garden when Arnhem bridge could not be captured and held by a reinforced division makes it difficult to see how the 1st Brigade would have undertaken the same objective with a brigade. German opposition might not have been as stiff if Comet had been launched, but the capture of Arnhem bridge by a brigade would have been a risky business at best, but and at worst even more of a disaster than Market Garden. The brigade commander, Brigadier Lathbury, was probably hoping to make up for the lack of reconnaissance by ordering each parachute battalion to despatch a 'coup-de-main' company to head into the town. Given the distance from the drop zone it is questionable whether these companies would have been able to make quicker progress than the rest of their battalions, and certainly not with the speed that reconnaissance jeeps might have been able to. It is also intriguing – and has never been satisfactorily explained – why a glider coup-de-main assault on Arnhem bridge was considered feasible for Comet but not for Market Garden.

38 Group's Operation Order for Comet was issued on 6 September and provides the bulk of the detailed information regarding how the operation would be transported and landed.[17] 38 Group's orders also contained much information on the ground situation. The Germans were assessed as 'making every effort to withdraw his troops, even in scattered parties, back to Germany. Crossings over the R.Rhein are a vital factor in his escape routes. The bridges will be held and the main ones certainly prepared for demolition.'

Meanwhile Second British Army was said to be driving north-east through Belgium and Holland towards the Rhine, directed on the main river crossings at Nijmegen and Arnhem. The Airborne Corps' objective was summarised as '. . . seize and hold the bridges crossing the R.Rhine at Nijmegen, Arnhem and Grave to facilitate the speedy advance of 30 British Corps'. The 1st British Airborne Division would land around Grave, Nijmegen and Arnhem and seize the bridges over the Rhine and secure them pending the arrival of XXX Corps. The US 878th Aviation Engineer Battalion would then land and construct landing strips while Airborne Corps HQ would also land in the area.

The troop carrier aircraft were to be ready for take-off from Friday 8 September. If no cancellation or postponement were received from 21st Army Group by 1800 the previous day and if the weather was suitable the operation would commence according to flight timings. A final decision would be made at midnight by Brereton and would be passed through the TCCP at Eastcote to RAF station commanders and through British Army channels by GSO1s (Air) to the airfields. A duty officer at HQ Airborne Corps would notify the duty watchkeeper at 21st Army Group Main Headquarters by telephone and wireless. The selected routes had been cleared with the Allied naval and ground forces.

The glider coup-de-main parties would be towed by eighteen Stirlings of 38 Group to the bridges at Arnhem, Nijmegen and Grave. The first main lift would begin with 12 Stirlings dropping the pathfinders of the 21st Independent Parachute Company and shortly afterwards 269 aircraft of IX Troop Carrier Command would drop elements of 1st Airborne Division. The first glider lift would comprise 130 aircraft of 46 Group and 210 aircraft of 38 Group, both carrying units of 1st British Airborne Division. The second lift would consist of 114 aircraft from IX Troop Carrier Command carrying paratroops and 110 and 206 aircraft from 46 and 38 Groups respectively towing gliders. Within that number 38 Group would also be towing gliders carrying Airborne Corps Headquarters.

The third lift, on the morning of D+1, would see 157 aircraft of IX Troop Carrier Command towing gliders carrying elements of 878 US Aviation Engineer Battalion and Airfield Control Units. Meanwhile at the same time 100 aircraft of 38 Group would drop supplies for 1st Airborne Division and 26 aircraft of 38 Group would tow gliders carrying elements of 878th US Aviation Engineer Battalion and 1st Polish Parachute Brigade. Further resupply missions would be flown from D+2 onwards as requested by the forces on the ground through HQ Airborne Corps to the TCCP at Eastcote.

The Allies' overwhelming air superiority meant that significant measures were planned to counter German reactions to the landings. On D-Day all flak positions along the airborne corridor would be attacked by the Eighth US Air Force and Air Defence of Great Britain immediately before and during the drop. The airborne formations would be provided with a light fighter escort from Air Defence of Great Britain over the North Sea and the heaviest possible cover over the rest of the route. After the airborne forces had landed the Ninth US Air Force would provide an umbrella of fighter cover over the landing areas during daylight and after nightfall fighters would be provided by Air Defence of Great Britain. Ninth Air Force would provide tactical air support, particularly harassing the enemy and preventing the arrival of reinforcements. Photographic reconnaissance would be provided by Mosquitos of 2 Group RAF who would film selected stages of the operation on D-Day. Aircraft of 34 Wing – part of 2nd Tactical Air Force – would photograph the drop zones and landing zones on D-Day one hour after the first lift had landed and after the second lift had arrived.

The coup-de-main parties would comprise six gliders each carrying troops from the South Staffords, King's Own Scottish Borderers and Border Regiment respectively, piloted by specially selected glider crews and all taking off from RAF Harwell. The coup de main troops were to be ready to emplane at 0145 in time to land at 0545. The Border Regiment were allocated to Grave Bridge, the King's Own Scottish Borderers to Nijmegen Bridge and the South Staffords to the Bridge at Arnhem. The coup-de-main glider serials would rendezvous over the landing zone at 0427 at 6,000ft and land at 0430. The South Staffords at Arnhem would land immediately south of the road bridge after being released from their tugs over the Rhine west of Driel. The King's Own Scottish Borderers would land immediately north of the Nijmegen road bridge.

The parachutists forming the first lift – from the 1st and 4th Parachute Brigades – were to be ready to emplane from 0315 in time to drop at 0730. The first-lift gliders, carrying the 1st Airlanding Brigade and divisional troops, were to be ready for emplaning from 0240 in time to begin landing at 0715. The 1st Parachute Brigade would land on DZ X and the 4th Parachute Brigade and divisional headquarters on DZ Y. The second parachute lift – of the Polish Parachute Brigade – was to be ready to begin emplaning from 1400, in time to drop at 1745. The second lift gliders, meanwhile, would include twenty-two gliders from HQ Airborne Corps. This was more than for previous operations but less than the 30-plus that would be used for Market Garden.

The airborne movement would incorporate four lifts – eighteen gliders forming three coup-de-main parties landing at 0430 on D-Day, the first main lift landing from 0715, the second lift landing at 1750, and the final lift on D+1 landing from 1000. Bomber Command would carry out a diversionary mission on the night before the operation on the night of 7/8 September which would be co-ordinated with FAAA. Air Defence of Great Britain would provide protection from night intruders, while the US Eighth Air Force would attack German night fighter airfields. Air Defence of Great Britain would also organise an air sea rescue service over the North Sea.

7 September

A message from AEAF HQ on 7 September described Comet as an: 'Airborne operation is planned for 8 and 9 September to seize the bridges in the vicinity of Nijmegen-Arnhem. It involves the movement of approximately 1 ½ divisions from UK to DZ/LZ in above area.'[18]

8 September

At midday on 8 September Dempsey met Horrocks at Brussels airport where the latter reported that his attempts to advance out of the bridgehead over the Albert Canal north of Diest had been strongly resisted. Dempsey noted in his diary that 'The time has clearly not yet come when we can drop 1 Airborne Div in the ARNHEM area, and I told commander 30 Corps to postpone it until 9/10 Sept at the earliest.'[19] The Allies may have started to feel that the window of opportunity had passed, as at 1042 on 8 September Brereton signalled SHAEF that Comet had been postponed for 24 hours and 45 minutes.[20]

On 8 September HQ Airborne Troops issued an order of priority in which units should be left behind if there were many aircraft casualties on the first lift and it was not possible to take all the second lift. Airborne Troops suggested the following order of priority for rejection – the remainder of Airborne Corps HQ, the Polish Brigade, Administrative, 181 Field Ambulance, 1st Airborne Division HQ, 10 Horsas from HQ Airborne Troops, the Anti-Tank Batteries, 1st Airlanding Light Regiment, units of 1st Airlanding Brigade, units of 4th Parachute Brigade and finally units of 1st Parachute Brigade. It is not known if this order of priority was discussed with Urquhart, the commander who would have been fighting the battle. The remainder of the Airborne Corps HQ was afforded a low priority – if this was the case why was such a large headquarters being taken at all? – and it is also interesting that the Polish Brigade, one-quarter of Urquhart's infantry strength, was relatively high priority for exclusion.[21]

9 September

At 0328 on 9 September Brereton signalled SHAEF that H-Hour for Comet had been postponed for an additional 24 hours 'on account ground situation' and had been rescheduled for 0800 on 10 September. At 2325 on the same day the operation was postponed for an additional 24 hours.[22] In the afternoon of 9 September Dempsey met again with Horrocks at the latter's headquarters at Diest. XXX Corps' attempts to break out of their bridgehead were still being strongly opposed, and as a result Dempsey told Horrocks to postpone the airborne landings until the night of 11 and 12 September 'at the earliest'.[23]

An argument broke out between AEAF and SHAEF over whether the landing areas could be restricted to other air traffic during the operation. On 9 September SHAEF Forward HQ's Air Division ordered that the landing zones would become restricted areas to other air formations. Later the same day AEAF Rear HQ at Stanmore replied that no request to restrict flying around the landing areas had been received from FAAA who were the formation responsible for planning the operation. AEAF also suggested that these restrictions would prevent resupply missions, and that they would '. . . only lead to considerable confusion and danger to friendly personnel and aircraft.' Accordingly AEAF requested that SHAEF's earlier signal should be cancelled immediately. It is not clear whether the landing zones would have been restricted during Operation Comet, but AEAF's more than assertive response to SHAEF indicates the level of control that the air forces had over airborne operations.[24]

Late on 9 September – at 2330 to be exact – Browning wrote to XXX Corps asking for information on which airfields around Vokel, Eindhoven and Gelze-Fijn would be available first to fly in 52nd Division in C-47s. His headquarters would land on the evening of D-Day and take up position in the area south-west of Nijmegen, rather than the Groesbeek Heights which it would occupy in Market Garden.[25]

10 September

Early on 10 September Montgomery met with Dempsey at 21st Army Group. They agreed that given the increasing German strength in the Arnhem-Nijmegen area that one division would not be adequate for the proposed operation. Dempsey recorded in his diary that he obtained Montgomery's agreement to instead use three airborne divisions to achieve the same objectives.[26] This again suggests that Dempsey played a more active role in the evolution of Comet into Market Garden than has previously been thought.[27]

Brereton's message cancelling Comet was not sent until 0559 on 11 September, almost 24 hours after Montgomery, Dempsey and Browning had begun planning its replacement. In the same message Brereton stated that that new operation – referred to as Market – was scheduled for 'not earlier than September 14th'. On 11 September 21st Army Group advised SHAEF that what was referred to as 'Revised Op Comet' could not take place before 23 September.[28] Brereton's diary also confuses the chronology of Comet and Market Garden – his diary entry of 11 September refers to Operation Comet as being one of ten operations being planned, even though Comet had been cancelled the day before.[29]

Conclusion

As Comet was in effect a prototype of Operation Market Garden, it is the one planned operation in this series that can be assessed with some reflection on how the later operation transpired. Comet features strongly in the post-war recollections of veterans. As the divisional commander Major General Urquhart was perhaps under more pressure than most:

> My division was to carry out the same plan with my division that I was now only part of in a corps . . . There was no doubt that the Germans had had a hell of a battering and they were going backwards. If only everything had happened about two or three weeks before we could have got away with it, because they were on the run. But, you see, Germans are very professional people, and they reacted extremely quickly, they always did.[30]

Brigadier John Hackett commanded the 4th Parachute Brigade, and later recalled the planning for Comet:

> I remember a conference for one operation, that thank god never came off, which was Operation Comet. For Operation Comet, believe it or not, the 1st Airborne Division with the Polish Brigade under command was going to take on the crossing of the three rivers, which turned out to be too much for three airborne divisions in Market Garden – we were going to do the lot with one. I remember, in disbelief, old Sosabowski in his rough, gruff voice, when the plan was disclosed him saying 'but the Germans, General, the Germans!' He knew, I knew too.[31]

Major Tony Hibbert was the Brigade Major of the 1st Parachute Brigade and would therefore have been involved in detailed planning for operations. He viewed Comet in a more positive light, pointing out that it would have taken place in a slightly different context than Market Garden:

> I think probably almost certainly it could have succeeded . . . because the Germans were still off balance, and, it sounds ridiculous, but it could have worked if Second Army had been ready to move fast enough. Certainly Von Zangen's [15th] Army hadn't escaped from Antwerp and the German morale at that stage was absolutely rock bottom. I think this supercharge, as it were, could have just ridden through.[32]

It is noticeable, however, that more junior officers viewed Comet very much through the lens of Market Garden, perhaps as they were privy to less of the planning. Captain Peter Wilkinson was a Battery Command Post officer serving with the 1st Airlanding Light Regiment Royal Artillery:

> This operation was called off, and we were actually loaded for that into our aircraft. That was the last one that was frustratingly called off. The reason I don't know, but it was very fortunate that it was because the strength of the force that was planned to go in was quite insufficient to cope with the situation.[33]

Jack Reynolds, who commanded the 2nd South Staffords Mortar Platoon at Arnhem, viewed Comet in a similar light:

> We were due to go to the place the Yanks went to in Holland. Nijmegen. We were originally going there, that was the intention. But they got that one, which was a pushover. And we got Arnhem, because Monty was desperately keen to show Patton that he could cross the Rhine first. We were a plaything for him.[34]

A common thread among post-war recollections is a feeling that the casualty rate for Comet would have been much worse as the forces allocated to each objective were much less than for Market Garden. Francis Moore commanded a troop of the 1st Airlanding Anti-Tank Battery:

> About 10 days before we went to Arnhem we were down at the airfields, at Down Ampney in Gloucestershire, and we were briefed on an operation in which the 1st Airborne Division was going to do the whole of what turned out to be Operation Market Garden . . . This was cancelled, thank heavens, as I don't think anybody would have survived.[35]

The planning for Comet shows Dempsey playing a much more active role in the co-ordination of operations than is often thought. Comet – and indeed other airborne operations – go some way to challenging the assumption that Montgomery micro-managed Dempsey. The plan for Comet would have also seen XXX Corps assuming command of the Airborne Corps as soon as a link-up was made, which suggests that the airborne corps headquarters was superfluous. The presence of coup-de-main parties in Comet is also in stark contrast to their absence in Market Garden, but suggests that the element of surprise was prioritised during the planning of the earlier operation.[36]

It has been pointed out by one historian that Comet would have used brigades for tasks that divisions would struggle with during Market Garden.[37] Comet was devised during a period when the Germans were in full retreat and lacked command and cohesion. However, German units and troops had been drilled to respond swiftly to airborne landings, and there was clear evidence that the front line had started to congeal. Market Garden would show just how quickly the Germans could react.

As Market Garden was really a modification of Comet, events that took place after 10 September also shed light on airborne planning prior. On 6 October 1944 Browning wrote to Hollinghurst, the commander of 38 Group. Browning told him that he thought that everyone 'from the Supreme Commander downwards' had been caught out by the German recovery. Browning suggested that the formation of his Corps Signals 'a bare three weeks' before taking off for Market Garden as the reason that communications broke down with 1st Airborne Division, and that he was always 36 to 48 hours behind in information. This is certainly true, but it begs the question why this deficiency came as such a surprise and have not been foreseen. Browning's letter also suggested that there may have been some unspecified difficulties between himself and Hollinghurst, to the extent that he had to try to reassure him that he 'did not believe that that had been the case'.

Air Vice Marshal Kingston-Mcloughry, one of the senior officers at 38 Group, told his audience at a lecture at the RAF Staff College in 1950 that the location of commanders and headquarters spread over the UK and the Continent meant that communications were 'shocking'. This highlighted, he argued, the need for close contact between commanders and planners at all levels and for good communications. Two years later in 1952 Kingston-Mcloughry told Hollinghurst that he thought that the First Allied Airborne Army had been set up to have another American senior commander. He also thought that FAAA was 'very much in the midst of their teething troubles when airborne operations, and difficult ones at that, were thrust upon them'. He felt that important lessons from Normandy had been ignored as a result and that 'staff work at Airborne Army HQ was not faultless'.[38]

In 1978 Belchem told Noble Frankland, the then Director of the Imperial War Museum, that although he was standing in for De Guingand who was ill in hospital, the planning for Comet and Market Garden was not done at 21st Army Group and had been delegated to

Dempsey, Browning and Horrocks. This marks a striking departure from Montgomery's normal way of running the battle, which was much more hands-on from 21st Army Group.[39] Belchem also said that he personally would not have accepted the 'restrictive conditions' imposed by the air commanders to the extent that he would have referred it to Eisenhower for adjudication, as had happened with the American airborne operation in Normandy. Belchem was at a loss to explain why Browning had not appealed to Montgomery, if necessary via Dempsey, as he was certain that Montgomery would have referred the problem to Eisenhower. It was possible, Belchem thought, that Browning was being loyal to his superior Brereton – although Belchem may not have known at the time about Browning's threat to resign over Linnet II, which had certainly used up much of his influence. Another problem Belchem foresaw was that Eisenhower might have referred the problem to Tedder, an airman, who would not have been predisposed to support Montgomery given their previous enmity.

Belchem also suggested that if 21st Army Group had been involved in planning Market Garden they would have insisted on the airborne troops being landed as close to their objective as possible, and cited the examples of German operations to capture the Corinth Canal Bridge, the Allied landings at Primasole in Sicily and Pegasus Bridge in Normandy. In the event the staff at 21st Army Group only found out about the distance between the drop zones and the bridge when it was too late. Belchem also questioned the air force intelligence assessment of flak around Arnhem bridge and at Deelen and felt that reports from Bomber Command were perhaps 'old hat.' Documents from the planning of Linnet and Comet suggest that the risk of flak was taken extremely seriously, perhaps overly so.

Belchem also criticised Browning for not challenging the Air Forces:

> With respect to the Arnhem plan, I fear one is obliged to put the onus on General Boy Browning, for accepting Allied Air Force restrictions. At HQ. 21st Army Group level we did not know the details in time to offer any helpful suggestions. The decision to make Arnhem the objective (in preference to the Emmerich-Wesel area) was only made on 10 Sept, and the last date for making modifications to the plan was 12 Sept., owing to the time needed for briefing (e.g. there were 4,500 aircraft involved on D-Day 17 Sept). Of course some preliminary planning had been done on alternative objectives, but I do not know how far it had gone.

Belchem felt that if the airborne commanders had 'made a fuss' Eisenhower might have intervened in a similar manner to how he did in Normandy, and that although Brereton was 'not an easy character' that Eisenhower could have dealt with him.

It is hard to escape the conclusion that if these difficulties existed for Market Garden they would also have had a dire effect on Comet, particularly as that operation would have taken place with a third of the airborne forces and without any drops around Eindhoven.

THE RECKONING

When reflecting on the range of operations that were proposed between D-Day and Arnhem, the most obvious challenge is not allowing what transpired during Operation Market Garden to influence our thinking unduly. However, the profile of both battles means that many of the participants were forthright with their opinions after the war.

Belchem thought that appointing Browning as the deputy commander at FAAA was 'manifestly wrong', as his status as a British commander in a predominantly American formation meant that he was obliged to accept conditions that no US airborne commander would have. Browning's position as deputy commander to Brereton meant that a vital link to 21st Army Group was not as strong as it could have been. Belchem even thought that the shortcomings of the plan were not reported to Montgomery as the short timescales involved left no time for discussion.

Belchem also thought that it was a 'grave mistake' to appoint the 'unfortunate Urquhart' to command 1st Airborne Division. Although he was competent and experienced, Belchem argued, his lack of airborne experience coming into such a demanding command meant that the air commanders easily outmanoeuvred him. Belchem also stated that Urquhart was at 'near exhaustion' by the time Market Garden took off, which suggests that the gruelling schedule of the previous three months since D-Day had taken a toll on him.

Belchem also criticised the airborne signals arrangements. He felt that it was 'incomprehensible' why the problem of airborne signals had not been solved, and that 1st Airborne Division had no contact with Browning, the UK or the tactical air forces for four days. He compared the failings with the Royal Armoured Corps' mastery of signals. Internal communication problems also made coordination on the ground impossible. Belchem also thought that the airborne division had not exercised or trained around likely scenarios, including signals problems, and that senior officers must bear responsibility for this oversight.

Brigadier Walch's papers include several reports after Market Garden, which given the similarities between the two operations also pose useful reflections for Comet. The intelligence report on British Airborne Corps after Market Garden stated that detailed interrogation of prisoners of war could not be carried out as normal at corps level as there was no prisoner-of-war cage. The Airborne Corps had no special wireless section, unlike other corps. There was also a lack of counter-intelligence personnel. The artillery evaluation after Market Garden also concluded that more powerful radio sets were needed 'for a link up of this type,' and that the airborne signals needed to have trained with the ground signals beforehand.[1]

The air support notes after Market Garden were even more critical. The Air Support Signals Unit with 1st Airborne Division had not managed to establish communications, and some demands had been sent to the tactical air forces via the artillery net link to 64th Medium Regiment. Communications had never been established with Second Army, nor with any aircraft in the air. An RAF control car attached to Airborne Corps HQ had no authority to call up aircraft for two days. The close wooded country also meant that the air forces were unwilling to engage targets without a six-figure grid reference. The report concluded that an Airborne Corps should have its own Air Support Section as part of its Corps Signals set up, consisting of a Forward Control Post for the Corps HQ and two sets to each division, two sets linked to Army HQ and one to the RAF Ground Control Centre. It was also suggested that operators should be able to practice working together as a group over operational distances. Airborne Corps also wanted to fly in an RAF controller with a CHF set with Corps HQ on future operations. Airborne Corps also felt after Market Garden that amongst the hurried planning the Air Forces had not been informed of their commitments quickly enough, which did not leave them enough time to prepare and brief personnel.

HQ Airborne Corps' evaluation of Market Garden stated that it had always been 'quite clear that once a firm junction with XXX Corps had been made, the division would have to be administered entirely by XXX Corps as, except for the AFDAG organization, Airborne Corps had no administrative resources of any kind. To this end a close A/Q and Service liaison with XXX Corps had been established during the week preceding the operation.' Again, this suggests that the Airborne Corps was not established for the role that it was asked to perform. If it had to reply on XXX Corps for so many things, what was it contributing?

The communications report on Market Garden makes for equally depressing reading. The small available Airborne Corps Signals had only just been formed and was completely untrained. It had been designed on a minimum basis for one of the planned operations in Brittany and was increased in size by 'hurried improvisation' for Operation Market Garden. Signals had to be provided for a mixed British and US airborne force. Owing to the lack of training, and the lack of any suitable common British and American airborne cipher, it was necessary to add a considerable US element to the Corps Signals. This element was also provided hurriedly and was untrained. Due to a lack of British air support tentacles, and because the force was largely American, it was decided to use US Air Support Parties. This was also hurriedly improvised, the operators were inexperienced and were working in difficult conditions. No time was available for developing a suitable signals plan. As one of the key roles of an operational corps is to co-ordinate formations in the field, this was always going to be more difficult without a suitable signals set up.

The XXX Corps report on Market Garden is not any more positive. 101st Airborne Division came under XXX Corps on landing, thus meaning that the Airborne Corps only commanded two divisions. XXX Corps had found the marshalling for Market Garden 'unique', due to the serious bottlenecks on the single road leading to Arnhem. This was even more congested due to the need to have two vulnerable groups up front in the advance – bridging engineers and the seaborne tail of airborne units, which between them consisted of 7,000 vehicles. XXX Corps found the breakout difficult due to the small bridgehead. There were few roads and the woods either side of the road were heavy, making it difficult for armoured vehicles to move off the road. Horrocks therefore decided to break out with a very heavy artillery barrage supported by tactical air support, relying on weight of firepower. XXX Corps was an experienced headquarters, and even it found the Market Garden campaign challenging.

The political angle to FAAA's formation influenced how its role was perceived. Even while Market Garden was taking place Eisenhower clearly felt pressure to highlight that FAAA had already been a success. On 19 September he sent a personal message to Brereton congratulating him on the performance of FAAA during Operation Market Garden:[2]

The initial major operation of the Allied Airborne Army has already proceeded sufficiently far to confirm the wisdom of the decision to organize all our airborne forces under a single command. Individually your divisions have previously exhibited unexcelled skill, courage and resolution. But the current operation marks the first attempt in warfare to utilize a number of airborne divisions against a single major objective.

The perfection of your staff work is demonstrated by the complete coordination between air, ground and airborne forces, and this coordination has resulted in maximum tactical effect. I congratulate you and your Deputy, General Browning, together with all officers and ranks serving under you.

Best wishes and good luck for the future to every man of the Allied Airborne Army.

Brereton replied to Eisenhower's message the same day:

Your message of congratulations and good wishes to the First Allied Airborne Army has been received with great pleasure I have transmitted it with my personal thanks to the officers and men of all ranks whose tireless and courageous devotion to duty is responsible for the results you have been so kind as to command.

It is a source of pride to us all that our Army is now a member of your fighting team and we shall endeavour to our utmost to continue to merit the honour.

On 22 September, while Market Garden was still being fought, Arnold in Washington sent a congratulatory message to Eisenhower and Brereton

The information on the initial successes of your command in its first operation received here with great joy . . . Decisive role of large scale airborne operations in military doctrine of future is view held here. Brilliant work of all Command and Staff Echelons in the planning and execution of your assault is fully appreciated . . . Please express my sincere pleasure to all concerned for a job well done.[3]

This message sheds much light on Arnold and Marshall's determination for their concept of airborne operations to be a success, even to the extent of sending such a message before it was clear whether Market Garden had worked. Eisenhower was clearly under great pressure from across the Atlantic.

On 27 September Parks wrote to Marshall, giving a description of Market Garden.[4] Parks stressed that when the first lift landed on 17 September, it was only 46 days since FAAA had been authorised on 2 August. He described the formation of the headquarters as having 'picked up personnel here and there and scraped together a working staff', but that in his opinion FAAA had an 'extremely able and well-balanced team'. Interestingly, he told Marshall that the British had been slow in providing their quota of staff officers. 'There has not been a dull moment for us, because the situation has moved so rapidly that we were striving all the time to keep abreast of it. The problems involved have been varied and complex, but I am very proud of the way the staff have been able to meet them.'

It is hard to describe Parks's letter as anything other than a self-written glowing reference for FAAA and Brereton:

General Brereton deserves great credit for his versatility, courage and determination. He conceived the plan of fighters and bombers to beat down the flak on our flights to the targets and didn't waver in his confidence that it would be effective, even when experienced air officers on a high level were ready to back out. Our losses of less than 2% prove him correct.

Parks told Marshall that he felt that the 82nd and 101st Divisions had achieved their objectives – even though in the same letter he also states that it was too early to evaluate the operation. He also criticised Second Army's breakout.

I feel that we accomplished the airborne mission fully and that the 2nd Army mission would have been completed as well if there had been more forces back of our spearhead. A little better break in the weather might have helped that, but the fact remains that the Arnhem bridge was reached too late by the 2nd Army.

Parks also described the advance from Nijmegen as 'painfully slow', even though he was 'not in possession of all the facts'. 'Thank you for giving me the opportunity to partake in this operation. I have enjoyed it thoroughly – never worked harder in my life, but it has been worth every effort.'

Communications between SHAEF and FAAA even while Market Garden was taking place suggest that the latter headquarters was not yet fit for its role.[5] On 23 September, a message from SHAEF Main, signed by Eisenhower, to SHAEF Forward suggested that better communication links were needed with FAAA. The message suggested investigating a direct link from FAAA HQ in England to SHAEF Forward on the Continent. On 25 September FAAA proposed moving to Europe with a headquarters of 365 personnel, and were planning to establish in the vicinity of SHAEF in Paris or Rheims, with the troop carrier aircraft in the Le Mans and Rennes area. And on the same day

Brereton messaged SHAEF G3 to suggest that a representative come to FAAA to study the personnel requirements of the headquarters, stating that 'Essential that operational needs of this headquarters be studied at first hand by your representative'. On 12 September, only five days before Market Garden began, Eisenhower had approved the placing of an advanced liaison group of three to four officers from FAAA at his forward headquarters. He affirmed, however, that no authority existed to equip the headquarters of FAAA for field service.[6]

It was not until January 1945 that FAAA began to assume a more substantial establishment. The Main Headquarters – codenamed Midnight Main – was billeted around Ascot, Winkfield, Camberley, Bagshot, Windsor, Wentworth, Northwood, Paddington and Weybridge. It was staffed by 192 officers and 96 other ranks. By this point Browning had already moved on and Major General Richard Gale, who had commanded 6th Airborne Division in Normandy was now Brereton's deputy. By January 1945 the headquarters included signals, public relations, finance, naval, weather, medical and dental, chaplains, motor pool and postal sections.[7]

The small Forward Headquarters was codenamed Midnight Forward, and by January 1945 it was co-located with SHAEF in Paris. Headed by Cutler, it consisted of twenty-seven officers and twenty other ranks. It included small elements from the plans and G1 to G4 sections, Adjutant-General staff, Engineers, Medical, quartermaster and signals sections and a French liaison officer.

Walch recalled in his memoirs that Corps HQ had to deal with twenty different operations, none of which took place. Not all operations reached 1st Airborne Division, as Airborne Corps handled much of the initial planning. Walch described this policy as 'saving their time being wasted', but it is hard to escape the conclusion that this also meant the division was detached. Indeed, Walch mentions in his memoirs that as few as 'one or two' operations were mentioned to Urquhart and his staff:[8]

> These constant ideas, usually too late and sometimes woolly, were a real worry and their cancellation, time after time, wasn't good for morale. 1 Airborne Division thought they were being persecuted when we passed on to them only about two or three possibilities which looked likely; they had no idea of the worries we saved them at Corps HQ.

Walch also felt that although the existence of the Airborne Army posed a very real threat to the Germans, the cancelled operations had a detrimental effect on the airborne formations waiting in England, particularly 1st Airborne Division:

However the advance of the Allied ground forces was so rapid that the objectives were captured before the ideas for airborne intervention matured. 1 Airborne Division, longing to get into action and being continually frustrated, were getting restless and in some ways morale suffered.[9]

Walch recalled in his memoirs that Airborne Corps HQ consisted of a Forward HQ, a Rear HQ and a Base HQ. The Forward element, he thought, was untested. This was by no means surprising as it was formed late and had not been exercised. The signals element of the headquarters was poorly equipped and trained. The War Office had taken a long time to provide a signals establishment, Walch thought because the Corps HQ was a low priority because it was not intended to operate in the field.[10]

The US Air Force Official History of airborne operations in the Second World War concluded that although Arnold was pressing for more and larger airborne operations the means were not available. It also concluded that airborne plans were made too slowly and the objectives were too close to the front line. Although Market showed the risks of going far beyond the front line, the author thought that 'big rewards' were 'worth gambling for'.[11]

It is important to stress that although the received wisdom is that the airborne forces waiting in the UK – particularly 1st Airborne Division – went through the whole planning process for each operation, the evidence suggests that this was not the case. Not all of the operations reached the division, and even then not all of these went as far as the troops assembling at their take off airfields. At the time most of the personnel of the division would only have known about the existence of several of the plans.[12]

Considering the rollercoaster of airborne planning between D-Day and Market Garden, and how the roots of what transpired at Arnhem can be so clearly seen emerging as the campaign progressed, shows how crucial it is to consider Normandy and Arnhem as part of the same campaign. The air forces' emphasis on flak increased as the summer wore on, as did the distances from drop zones to objectives. Arnhem did not just happen.

It is perhaps a roundabout compliment that the campaign was eventually successful despite the tensions that hampered the Allied command. British influence was clearly declining, as shown by the imposition of the First Allied Airborne Army, which was imposed on Eisenhower in turn by Washington. It is hard not to see the Airborne Army as un-necessary militarily, but politically expedient.

Browning does not come out of this period well. Having not commanded in action since the First World War, he appears out of his depth and for a senior Allied commander was consistently inconsistent with his advice, for example around the length of time that airborne forces could fight before being relieved. By contrast his subordinate, Urquhart, was marginalised and did not have the freedom that his American counterparts had.

There is certainly scope for more research on airborne operations that were planned after Market Garden. Several plans were considered to support the Rhine crossing, including Operation Naples which would have seen an airborne landing at Cologne, and Operation Choker would have taken place at Worms. Operation Arena would have landed airborne forces 100 miles behind the Rhine, and Operation Eclipse, meanwhile, would have been an airborne landing on Berlin.

Perhaps the last word should be given to the effect that a summer of cancelled operations had on the men of the 1st Airborne Division in particular. Bill Higgs was a Glider Pilot:

> It should have been Antwerp, it should have been in the bocage, it should have been in Brussels, it should have been all sorts of places. But he [Montgomery] was getting there first you see.[13]

Ronald Adams commanded the Mortar Platoon in the 156th Parachute Battalion:

> Very frustrating indeed. I don't think it adversely affected our morale, it was just irritating and annoying, and I think it also put pressure on senior officers to sort of keep the spirits up. Because there we were, we wanted to be in. Come September of course we were all anxious to get there before the war ended. It [Arnhem] wasn't the first preparation that we had been briefed for. We had been briefed for 3 or 4 before. And usually, as the saying went then, if we had landed they would advance so quickly that the only thing we could have dropped with would have been collecting tins for the Airborne Securities Fund.[14]

The wide range of testimonies found in veterans' accounts, many of whom were interviewed long after the war, illustrates how complex it is to assess the effect that this period had on morale and effectiveness. We have seen when examining individual operations, the psychological effect on personnel in the airborne forces depended very much on their part in the planning.

APPENDIX

AIRBORNE CORPS UNITS FOR OPERATION TRANSFIGURE

Unit	Source	Personnel	Vehicles including trailers and excluding motorcycles
HQ Airborne Troops		200	18
1 Airborne Div		12,500	1,890
Polish Ind Para Bde		2,500	318
Corps Troops			
8 HQ Forward Maintenance Centre		12	2
2 Detail Issue Depot	9 Beach Group	36	0
35 Casualty Clearing Station		120	9
2 Field Dressing Station	7 Beach Group	79	14
25 Field Dressing Station	10 Beach Group	79	14
24 Field Transfusion Unit	10 Beach Group	4	1
37 Field Transfusion Unit		4	1
46 Field Surgical Unit		11	3
47 Field Surgical Unit	9 Beach Group	11	3
Det Medical Stores Unit		11	2
One Forward Maintenance Ammunition Section (from 36 Ordnance Beach Detachment)	9 Beach Group	14	3

(Continued)

203

Unit	Source	Personnel	Vehicles including trailers and excluding motorcycles
One Forward Maintenance Ammunition Section (from 36 Ordnance Beach Detachment)	9 Beach Group	4	3
One Forward Maintenance Supply Section (from 36 Ordnance Beach Detachment)	9 Beach Group	13	2
176th Infantry Brigade Light Aid Detachment Type B (non-Armoured)	59th Division	12	4
Detachment Workshop REME (from 148 Light Aid Detachment)	39th Armoured Brigade	38	6
One Section from 242 Beach Provost Company	7 Beach Group	16	0
One Section from 243 Beach Provost Company	9 Beach Group	17	0
Det Postal Unit (from 21st Army Group Postal Unit	21st Army Group	3	1
277 Pioneer Coy		290	3
Total		**15,984**	**2,297**

Source: TNA WO 205/691: 21st Army Group G Plans, Operation Transfigure: air support, outline plans, Aug 1944.

NOTES

Part I – First Allied Airborne Army: August-September 1944

1 TNA WO 219/106: Organisation: First Allied Airborne Army, Jun-Dec 1944.
2 Lewis Brereton, *The Brereton Diaries: The War in the Air in the Pacific, Middle East and Europe, 3 October 1941 – 8 May 1945* (New York: William Morrow & Co, 1946), p.332.
3 TNA WO 219/106.
4 Ibid.
5 TNA WO 219/4975: SHAEF First Allied Airborne Army, Organisation and functions of the H.Q, Aug 1944-Jul 1945.
6 Brereton, *Diaries*, pp.330–1.
7 Ibid., p.331.
8 TNA WO 219/106.
9 Ibid.
10 TNA WO 219/552: SHAEF AG, 1 Allied Airborne Army: organisation and order of battle. Establishment of Combined Airborne Headquarters, Aug-Dec 1944.
11 TNA WO 219/106.
12 Roger Cirillo, *The Market Garden Campaign: Allied operational command in northwest Europe* (Cranfield University PhD thesis, 2001), p.201.
13 Brereton, *Diaries*, p.333.
14 Cirillo, *The Market Garden Campaign*, p.196.
15 Ibid., p.197.
16 Ibid., p.198.
17 IWM Documents.9487: The Private Papers of Brigadier AG Walch OBE. Browning's Chief of Staff, Walch, described in his memoirs how Montgomery and 21st Army Group still went directly to Browning and copied FAAA in.
18 TNA WO 32/10927: Policy and Functions of First Allied Airborne Army.
19 Ibid.
20 TNA WO 219/2860: Formation of 1 Allied Airborne Army, May 1944-May 1945.
21 Cirillo, *The Market Garden Campaign*, p.204.
22 TNA WO 219/260: SHAEF Operations Overlord and Neptune: post-operational planning, Sept 1944.
23 TNA WO 219/552.
24 TNA AIR 37/776: Air Commander-in-Chief, AEAF: 1st Allied Airborne Army formation and employment, 1944.
25 TNA WO 219/4975.
26 TNA WO 32/10927.
27 TNA WO 219/552.
28 Brereton, *Diaries*, p.339.

29   TNA WO 32/10927.
30   TNA WO 219/2864: SHAEF G3, 1 Allied Airborne Army chain of command, Apr-Sept 1944.
31   Cirillo, *The Market Garden Campaign*, p.196.
32   TNA WO 219/552.
33   TNA WO 219/4975.
34   William F. Buckingham, *Arnhem 1944* (Tempus, 2004), p.63.

Part II – Breakout

Operation Lucky Strike

1   TNA WO 219/2504: Operations Lucky Strike, Hands Up and Beneficiary: planning for a drive towards the River Seine after capture of ports in Brittany, Jun-Jul 1944.
2   TNA WO 205/5B: 21st Army Group Communications between Commander in Chief and Chief of Staff, Jun 1944-Mar 1945.
3   TNA WO 205/8: 21st Army Group, Operational plans submitted to the Chief of Staff, Jun 1944-Feb 1945.
4   TNA WO 219/2504.
5   Ibid.
6   TNA WO 205/668: 21st Army Group G Plans, Operation Lucky Strike: planning papers: appreciation of possible development of operations, Jun 1944-May 1945.
7   TNA WO 205/672: 21st Army Group G Plans, Operation Lucky Strike: notes on assault across the River Seine, engineer appreciation, Jun-Jul 1944.
8   TNA WO 205/668.
9   TNA WO 219/2504.
10   Ibid.
11   TNA WO 219/3069: SHAEF G4, Operation Lucky Strike: estimate of the administrative situation, Jul-Jul 1944.
12   TNA WO 205/668.
13   TNA WO 205/670: 21st Army Group G Plans, Operation Lucky Strike: major considerations affecting the extent of support, Jun-Jul 1944.
14   Ibid.
15   TNA WO 205/668.
16   TNA WO 205/671: 21st Army Group G Plans, Operation Lucky Strike: administrative appreciation, Jun-Jul 1944.
17   TNA WO 205/672.
18   TNA WO 219/2504.
19   TNA WO 205/671.
20   TNA WO 205/672: 21st Army Group G Plans, Operation Lucky Strike: notes on assault across the River Seine, engineer appreciation, Jun-Jul 1944.
21   TNA WO 219/2504; TNA AIR 51/417/9: AEAF Air Staff Lucky Strike, Jun-Jul 1944.
22   TNA WO 205/669: 21st Army Group G Plans, Operation Lucky Strike: employment of airborne forces, July 1944.
23   TNA WO 205/671.
24   Ibid.
25   TNA WO 205/670.
26   TNA WO 205/672.
27   TNA WO 205/670.
28   Cirillo, *The Market Garden Campaign*, p.137.
29   Ibid., p.143.

30 TNA WO 285/2.
31 Brereton, *Diaries*, pp.323–4.
32 TNA WO 285/2.
33 Ibid.
34 TNA WO 171/369: HQ Airborne Troops Main War Diary, Jan-July 1944.
35 Cirillo, *The Market Garden Campaign*, p.103.
36 Ibid., p.104. Cirillo suggests that a number of US historians have downplayed the importance of Lucky Strike in Allied strategy. Forrest Pogue relegated Lucky Strike to a footnote and Martin Blumenson did not mention it at all.
37 Ibid., p.265.

Operation Transfigure

1   IWM Documents 1838 Simpson.
2   TNA WO 205/428: 21st Army Group G Ops Air, Operation Transfigure: air support, outline plans, Aug 1944.
3   TNA AIR 37/1057: SHAEF (Main and Rear): AEAF: historical record June-Aug 1944.
4   Brereton, *Diaries*, pp.323–4.
5   John C. Warren, *Airborne Operations in World War II, European Theater* (USAF Historical Division, 1956), p.94.
6   TNA WO 171/370: HQ Airborne Troops Main War Diary, Aug-Dec 1944.
7   TNA WO 205/691: 21st Army Group G Plans, Operation Transfigure: air support, outline plans, Aug 1944.
8   Ibid.
9   Ibid.
10 Brereton, *Diaries*, p.324.
11 TNA AIR 37/291: 38 Group, Operation Transfigure, 1944.
12 Brereton, *Diaries*, p.329.
13 TNA WO 205/691.
14 Ibid.
15 TNA WO 171/392: 1st Airborne Division G Staff War Diary, Jan-Aug 1944.
16 TNA WO 205/691; TNA WO 205/428: 21st Army Group G Ops Air, Operation Transfigure: air support, outline plans, Aug 1944.
17 Ibid.
18 TNA AIR 37/1057.
19 TNA WO 171/370. It is not clear why Urquhart was not at this meeting.
20 TNA AIR 37/295: 38 Group Operation Transfigure, 1944.
21 Ibid.
22 TNA WO 205/691. They would remain in France until Market Garden took place.
23 TNA WO 205/428.
24 TNA WO 171/370.
25 Buckingham, *Arnhem*, p.230.
26 TNA WO 205/691.
27 Ibid.
28 Ibid.
29 Ibid.
30 Ibid.
31 TNA WO 205/428.
32 Ibid.
33 Ibid.
34 TNA AIR 37/291.

35   TNA AIR 37/295.
36   TNA AIR 37/291.
37   TNA WO 205/691.
38   TNA WO 205/428.
39   TNA WO 171/370.
40   AIR 37/295.
41   WO 218/200: Special Services, Operation Transfigure: report, Aug 1944.
42   TNA WO 205/691.
43   Ibid.
44   TNA AIR 37/295.
45   Ibid.
46   TNA WO 205/428.
47   TNA WO 205/691.
48   Ibid.
49   TNA WO 205/428.
50   Ibid.
51   TNA WO 205/691.
52   Ibid.
53   TNA WO 171/392.
54   TNA WO 171/370.
55   Brereton, *Diaries*, p.333.
56   TNA AIR 37/295.
57   TNA WO 218/200.
58   TNA AIR 37/1057.
59   TNA WO 205/428.
60   TNA WO 171/592: 1st Parachute Brigade War Diary, Jan-Dec 1944.
61   TNA WO 171/594: 4th Parachute Brigade War Diary, Jan-Sept 1944.
62   TNA WO 171/370.
63   TNA WO 218/200.
64   TNA WO 205/691.
65   On 16 August SHAEF signalled Bradley that as there was an FFI representative
      at HQ Airborne Troops, they did not want a special forces team with 101st
      Division. Why is not clear.
66   TNA WO 205/691.
67   TNA WO 171/392.
68   TNA WO 218/200.
69   Brereton, *Diaries*, p.334.
70   TNA WO 171/392.
71   TNA AIR 37/901: AEAF Operation Transfigure, 1944.
72   TNA WO 205/691.
73   TNA AIR 37/295.
74   Ibid.
75   TNA WO 205/691.
76   IWM Documents 10866: The Private Papers of Air Chief Marshal Sir Leslie
      Hollinghurst.
77   TNA AIR 37/295.
78   TNA WO 171/392.
79   TNA WO 205/691.
80   Ibid.
81   Warren, *Airborne Operations*, p.94.
82   Brereton, *Diaries*, p.334.

83   TNA WO 171/392.
84   TNA WO 171/592.
85   TNA AIR 37/295.
86   Ibid.
87   TNA WO 205/428.
88   TNA AIR 37/291.
89   IWM Oral History 20136: John Waddy.
90   IWM Oral History 22133: Peter Wilkinson.
91   IWM Oral History 22381: Harry Gibbons.

Operation Axehead
1   TNA WO 205/142: 21st Army Group G Ops, Crossing of Water Obstacles, Oct 1943-Sept 1944.
2   Ibid.
3   Ibid.
4   Ibid.
5   TNA WO 205/662: 21st Army Group G Plans, Operation Axehead: outline plan, appreciation and maps, Mar-Jun 1944. Unless otherwise stated, references to Operation Axehead are taken from this source.
6   TNA WO 205/142.
7   TNA AIR 37/621: 2nd Tactical Air Force, Operation Axehead, 1944; and TNA WO 205/662.
8   TNA AIR 37/621.
9   Ibid.
10   TNA WO 171/369: HQ Airborne Troops Main War Diary, Jan-July 1944.
11   TNA WO 205/195: 21st Army Group G Ops, Airborne operations plans, May 1944.
12   TNA WO 171/392.
13   TNA WO 219/3062: SHAEF G4, Operation Axehead: appreciation of movement problems, Jun 1944.
14   TNA WO 219/3062.
15   TNA WO 205/5B.
16   TNA WO 205/672.
17   The crossing of the Seine eventually took place at Vernon.
18   TNA WO 171/370.
19   Ibid.

Operation Boxer
1   Warren, *Airborne Operations*, p.96.
2   Brereton, *Diaries*, p.334.
3   TNA WO 285/2.
4   TNA WO 219/4980: SHAEF First Allied Airborne Army, Operation Boxer, Aug 1944.
5   TNA AIR 37/293: 38 Group Operation Linnet, 1944.
6   Warren, *Airborne Operations*, p.96; Cirillo, *The Market Garden Campaign*, p.211.
7   Brereton, *Diaries*, p.336.
8   TNA WO 285/2.

Part III – The Low Countries

Operation Linnet

1   Cirillo, *The Market Garden Campaign*, p.209.
2   TNA WO 171/370; TNA WO 205/869: 21st Army Group Operational Reports, Operation Linnet: instructions and correspondence, Aug 1944.
3   Ibid.; Warren, *Airborne Operations*, p.96.
4   Brereton, *Diaries*, p.335.
5   TNA WO 205/869.
6   TNA AIR 37/509: AEAF Operation Linnet, 1944.
7   Warren, *Airborne Operations*, p.96.
8   TNA AIR 37/293.
9   TNA WO 205/197: 21st Army Group G Operations: Airborne Plans, Jul-Aug 1944.
10 TNA AIR 37/509.
11 TNA WO 285/2.
12 TNA AIR 37/509.
13 Ibid.
14 TNA WO 205/868: 21st Army Group Operational Reports: Operation Linnet defence overprints, Aug 1944.
15 TNA WO 171/370.
16 TNA WO 205/197.
17 TNA HS 6/239: Special Operations Executive Support for military and naval operations: Overlord and Linnet, 1944.
18 Operation Bardsea comprised Polish personnel who had been trained to parachute and take part in special operations, performing a similar role to Jedburgh parties. Fifteen Bardsea groups landed behind enemy lines during Operation Overlord.
19 TNA AIR 37/293.
20 TNA AIR 37/509.
21 Ibid.
22 Ibid.
23 TNA AIR 37/293.
24 Ibid.
25 Ibid.
26 TNA WO 285/9: General Sir Miles Dempsey personal war diary, Jun-Sept 1944.
27 TNA WO 171/370.
28 TNA WO 171/392.
29 TNA WO 205/197.
30 TNA AIR 37/509.
31 IWM Hollinghurst papers.
32 TNA AIR 37/292: 38 Group Operation Linnet, 1944.
33 TNA AIR 37/292.
34 Brereton, *Diaries*, p.335.
35 TNA WO 205/197.
36 Ibid.
37 TNA WO 208/93: War Office Directorate of Military Operations and Intelligence, Operation Linnet: outline plan, Aug-Sept 1944.
38 Ibid.
39 TNA AIR 37/292.
40 TNA WO 205/869.
41 TNA AIR 37/509.
42 TNA WO 219/605: SHAEF AG, Airborne operations: Field Order 3 for Operation Linnet, Aug 1944.

43 TNA AIR 37/292.
44 TNA WO 205/869.
45 TNA WO 205/197.
46 TNA WO 285/9.
47 TNA WO 205/197.
48 Ibid.
49 Ibid.
50 Ibid.
51 Ibid.
52 TNA HS 6/239.
53 TNA WO 205/869.
54 Ibid.
55 TNA AIR 37/509.
56 Ibid.
57 Ibid.
58 Ibid.
59 Ibid.
60 Ibid.
61 Ibid.
62 TNA WO 285/9.
63 TNA WO 205/197.
64 Ibid.
65 Ibid.
66 TNA AIR 37/292.
67 TNA WO 205/197.
68 Ibid.
69 TNA AIR 37/292.
70 Ibid.
71 Ibid.
72 TNA AIR 37/293.
73 TNA WO 205/869.
74 Ibid.
75 Ibid.
76 TNA AIR 37/292.
77 TNA WO 205/869.
78 TNA AIR 37/292.
79 TNA AIR 37/509.
80 TNA WO 285/2: General Sir Miles Dempsey Papers, Letters and directives from General Montgomery C in C 21st Army Group, Mar 1944-Apr 1945.
81 TNA WO 205/197.
82 Brereton, *Diaries*, p.337.
83 TNA AIR 37/292.
84 TNA AIR 37/509.
85 Ibid.
86 TNA AIR 37/292.
87 Ibid.
88 Cirillo, *The Market Garden Campaign*, p.221.
89 Ibid., p.219.
90 TNA AIR 37/292.
91 TNA AIR 37/509.
92 Buckingham, *Arnhem*, pp.76–7.

93   Brereton erroneously suggested that the conference concerned Operation Market. Given the date, it was almost certainly related to Operation Comet.
94   TNA WO 205/197.
95   Brereton, *Diaries*, p.338.
96   TNA AIR 37/509.

Operation Infatuate
1   TNA WO 205/197.
2   TNA WO 205/5B.
3   Ibid.
4   TNA WO 205/197.
5   Ibid.
6   TNA WO 205/194: 21st Army Group G Ops, Airborne operations plans, Sept 1944-Apr 1945.
7   Brereton, *Diaries*, pp.340–1.
8   Ibid., p.340.
9   TNA WO 285/2.
10   TNA WO 205/238: 21st Army Group G Ops, Operations Vitality and Infatuate: planning papers, minutes of conferences of Chiefs of Staff. Part I, Sept-Oct 1944.
11   Ibid.
12   TNA WO 205/650: 21st Army Group G Plans, Operation Infatuate: intelligence data and maps, Sept 1944.

Operation Comet
1   TNA WO 285/2.
2   TNA WO 205/5B.
3   Comet represents the first Allied airborne operation in which flak played a significant part in planning. The influence of potential losses – it was estimated that aircraft losses could be as high as 40 per cent – alludes to the role that fear of flak would play in the selection of drop zones.
4   IWM Documents. 19517: Montgomery Ancillary Collection: Major General R.F.K. Belchem.
5   TNA WO 285/9.
6   Brereton, *Diaries*, p.338.
7   Cirillo, *The Market Garden Campaign*, p.348.
8   Ibid., p.350.
9   TNA WO 285/14: General Sir Miles Dempsey Papers, Advance from Caumont to Dutch frontier: notes and directives, Aug-Sept 1944.
10   Cirillo, *The Market Garden Campaign*, p.381.
11   IWM Documents 1838: Montgomery Ancillary Collection: General Sir Frank Simpson.
12   IWM Simpson papers.
13   TNA WO 205/850.
14   Ibid.
15   The landing areas around Wolfheze and Oosterbeek would be used during Market Garden.
16   The coup de main was rejected for Market Garden.
17   TNA WO 219/3065.
18   Ibid.
19   TNA WO 285/9.
20   TNA WO 219/3065.

21 Ibid.
22 Ibid.
23 TNA WO 285/9.
24 TNA WO 219/3065.
25 TNA WO 205/869.
26 TNA WO 285/9.
27 Ibid.
28 TNA WO 219/3065.
29 Brereton, *Diaries*, p.340.
30 IWM Oral History 21034: Robert Elliot Urquhart.
31 IWM Oral History 12022: John Hackett.
32 IWM Oral History 21040: Tony Hibbert.
33 IWM Oral History 22133: Peter Wilkinson.
34 IWM Oral History 32510: Jack Reynolds.
35 IWM Oral History 21583: Francis Moore.
36 Cirillo, *The Market Garden Campaign*, p.356. Cirillo has argued that Browning advocated for coup de main parties and that they had to take place at night time, but that Leigh Mallory objected.
37 Buckingham, *Arnhem*, p.75.
38 IWM Hollinghurst papers.
39 IWM Belchem papers.

The Reckoning

1   IWM Walch papers.
2   TNA WO 219/106.
3   TNA WO 219/552.
4   TNA WO 219/4975.
5   TNA WO 219/106.
6   Ibid.
7   IWM Walch papers.
8   Ibid.
9   Ibid.
10 Ibid.
11 Warren, *Airborne Forces*, pp.205–07.
12 Buckingham, *Arnhem*, pp.65–7.
13 IWM Oral History 22095: Bill Higgs.
14 IWM Oral History 13668: Ronald Adam.

BIBLIOGRAPHY

Archive Sources

Imperial War Museum
Documents:
1838: Montgomery Ancillary Collection: General Sir Frank Simpson.
9487: The Private Papers of Brigadier A.G. Walch OBE.
10866: The Private Papers of Air Chief Marshal Sir Leslie Hollinghurst.
19517: Montgomery Ancillary Collection: Major General R.F.K. Belchem.

Oral History:
12022: Brigadier John Hackett, 4th Parachute Brigade.
13668: Ronald Adams, 156th Parachute Battalion.
20136: Major John Waddy, 156th Parachute Battalion.
21034: Major General R.E. Urquhart, GOC 1st Airborne Division.
21040: Major Tony Hibbert, 1st Parachute Brigade.
21583: Francis Moore, 1st Airlanding Anti-Tank Battery Royal Artillery.
22095: Bill Higgs, Glider Pilot Regiment.
22133: Peter Wilkinson, 1st Airlanding Light Battery Royal Artillery.
22381: Harry Gibbons, Glider Pilot Regiment.
32510: Jack Reynolds, 2nd Battalion South Staffordshire Regiment.

The National Archives, UK
AIR 37/291: 38 Group, Operation Transfigure, 1944.
AIR 37/292: 38 Group Operation Linnet, 1944.
AIR 37/293: 38 Group, Operation Linnet, 1944.
AIR 37/295: 38 Group Operation Transfigure, 1944.
AIR 37/509: AEAF Operation Linnet, 1944.
AIR 37/621: 2nd Tactical Air Force, Operation Axehead, 1944.
AIR 37/776: Air Commander-in-Chief, AEAF: 1st Allied Airborne Army formation and employment, 1944.
AIR 37/901: AEAF Operation Transfigure, 1944.
AIR 37/1057: SHAEF (Main and Rear): AEAF: historical record June-Aug 1944.
AIR 51/417/9: AEAF Air Staff Lucky Strike, Jun-Jul 1944.

HS 6/239: Special Operations Executive Support for military and naval operations: Overlord and Linnet, 1944.

WO 32/10927: Policy and Functions of First Allied Airborne Army.

WO 171/369: HQ Airborne Troops Main War Diary, Jan-July 1944.

WO 171/370: HQ Airborne Troops Main War Diary, Aug-Dec 1944.

WO 171/392: 1st Airborne Division G Staff War Diary, Jan-Aug 1944.

WO 171/592: 1st Parachute Brigade War Diary, Jan-Dec 1944.

WO 171/594: 4th Parachute Brigade War Diary, Jan-Sept 1944.

WO 205/5B: 21st Army Group Communications between Commander in Chief and Chief of Staff, Jun 1944-Mar 1945.

WO 205/8: 21st Army Group, Operational plans submitted to the Chief of Staff, Jun 1944-Feb 1945.

WO 205/142: 21st Army Group G Ops, Crossing of Water Obstacles, Oct 1943-Sept 1944.

WO 205/194: 21st Army Group G Ops, Airborne operations plans, Sept 1944-Apr 1945.

WO 205/195: 21st Army Group G Ops, Airborne operations plans, May 1944.

WO 205/197: 21st Army Group G Operations: Airborne Plans, Jul-Aug 1944.

WO 205/238: 21st Army Group G Ops, Operations Vitality and Infatuate: planning papers, minutes of conferences of Chiefs of Staff. Part I, Sept-Oct 1944.

WO 205/428: 21st Army Group G Ops Air, Operation Transfigure: air support, outline plans, Aug 1944.

WO 205/650: 21st Army Group G Plans, Operation Infatuate: intelligence data and maps, Sept 1944.

WO 205/662: 21st Army Group G Plans, Operation Axehead: outline plan, appreciation and maps, Mar-Jun 1944.

WO 205/668: 21st Army Group G Plans, Operation Lucky Strike: planning papers: appreciation of possible development of operations, Jun 1944-May 1945.

WO 205/669: 21st Army Group G Plans, Operation Lucky Strike: employment of airborne forces, July 1944.

WO 205/670: 21st Army Group G Plans, Operation Lucky Strike: major considerations affecting the extent of support, Jun-Jul 1944.

WO 205/671: 21st Army Group G Plans, Operation Lucky Strike: administrative appreciation, Jun-Jul 1944.

WO 205/672: 21st Army Group G Plans, Operation Lucky Strike: notes on assault across the River Seine, engineer appreciation, Jun-Jul 1944.

WO 205/691: 21st Army Group G Plans, Operation Transfigure: air support, outline plans, Aug 1944.

WO 205/850: 21st Army Group Operational Reports: Operation Comet, Sept 1944.

WO 205/868: 21st Army Group Operational Reports: Operation Linnet defence overprints, Aug 1944.

WO 205/869: 21st Army Group Operational Reports, Operation Linnet: instructions and correspondence, Aug 1944.

WO 208/93: War Office Directorate of Military Operations and Intelligence, Operation Linnet: outline plan, Aug-Sept 1944.

WO 218/200: Special Services, Operation Transfigure: report, Aug 1944.

WO 219/106: Organisation: First Allied Airborne Army, Jun-Dec 1944.

WO 219/260: SHAEF Operations Overlord and Neptune: post-operational planning, Sept 1944.
WO 219/552: SHAEF AG, 1 Allied Airborne Army: organisation and order of battle. Establishment of Combined Airborne Headquarters, Aug-Dec 1944.
WO 219/605: SHAEF AG, Airborne operations: Field Order 3 for operation Linnet, Aug 1944.
WO 219/2504: Operations Lucky Strike, Hands Up and Beneficiary: planning for a drive towards the River Seine after capture of ports in Brittany, Jun-Jul 1944.
WO 219/2860: Formation of 1 Allied Airborne Army, May 1944-May 1945.
WO 219/2864: SHAEF G3, 1 Allied Airborne Army chain of command, Apr-Sept 1944.
WO 219/3062: SHAEF G4, Operation Axehead: appreciation of movement problems, Jun 1944.
WO 219/3065: SHAEF G4, Operation Comet: warning order and cancellation, Sept 1944.
WO 219/3069: SHAEF G4, Operation Lucky Strike: estimate of the administrative situation, Jul-Jul 1944.
WO 219/4975: SHAEF First Allied Airborne Army, Organisation and functions of the H.Q, Aug 1944-Jul 1945.
WO 219/4980: SHAEF First Allied Airborne Army, Operation Boxer, Aug 1944.
WO 285/2: General Sir Miles Dempsey Papers, Letters and directives from General Montgomery C in C 21st Army Group, Mar 1944-Apr 1945.
WO 285/9: General Sir Miles Dempsey personal war diary, Jun-Sept 1944.
WO 285/14: General Sir Miles Dempsey Papers, Advance from Caumont to Dutch frontier: notes and directives, Aug-Sept 1944.

Unpublished Sources
Cirillo, Roger, *The Market Garden Campaign: Allied operational command in northwest Europe* (Cranfield University PhD thesis, 2001).

Published Sources
Belchem, Major General David, *All in the Day's March* (London: Collins, 1978).
_____, *Victory in Normandy* (London: Chatto & Windus, 1981).
Bennett, David, *Magnificent Disaster: The Failure of Market Garden, The Arnhem Operation September 1944* (Greenhill, 2008).
Blumenson, Martin, *Breakout and Pursuit* (Washington: US Army Centre of Military History, 1993).
Brereton, Lewis, *The Brereton Diaries: The War in the Air in the Pacific, Middle East and Europe, 3 October 1941 – 8 May 1945* (New York: William Morrow & Co, 1946).
Brooke, Field Marshal Lord Alan, *War Diaries 1939-1945* (London: Phoenix Press, 2002).
Buckingham, William F., *Arnhem 1944* (Stroud: Tempus, 2004).
Buckingham, William F., *Paras: The Birth of British Airborne Forces from Churchill's Raiders to 1st Parachute Brigade* (Stroud: Tempus, 2005).
Buckley, John, *Monty's Men: The British Army and the Liberation of Europe* (Yale University Press, 2014).

_____, and Preston-Hough, Peter (eds), *Operation Market Garden: The campaign for the low countries autumn 1944: Seventy years on* (Solihull: Hellion, 2016).

Clark, Lloyd, *Arnhem: Jumping the Rhine 1944 and 1945* (Headline, 2008).

Delaforce, Patrick, *The Black Bull: From Normandy to the Baltic with the 11th Armoured Division* (Stroud: Sutton, 1993).

_____, *The Fighting Wessex Wyverns: From Normandy to Bremerhaven with the 43rd Wessex Division* (Stroud: The History Press, 2003).

_____, *Churchill's Desert Rats in North-west Europe* (Barnsley: Pen and Sword, 2010).

D'Este, Carlo, *Decision in Normandy: the Unwritten Story of Montgomery and the Allied Campaign* (Harper Collins, 1983).

Eisenhower, Dwight D., *Crusade in Europe* (London: Heinemann, 1948).

Ellis, Major L.F., *Victory in the West: Vol I, The Battle of Normandy* (London: HMSO, 1962).

_____, *Victory in the West: Vol II, The Defeat of Germany* (London: HMSO, 1968).

Ford, Ken, *Assault Crossing: The River Seine 1944* (Barnsley: Pen and Sword, 2011).

Fraser, David, *And we shall shock them: The British Army in the Second World War* (London: Hodder and Stoughton, 1983).

French, David, *Raising Churchill's Army* (Oxford: University Press, 2002).

Frost, Major General John, *A Drop too Many* (Buchan and Enright, 1982).

Fullick, Roy, *Shan Hackett: The pursuit of exactitude* (Barnsley: Pen and Sword, 2003).

Gavin, General James M., *On to Berlin* (New York: Bantam, 1978).

Greenacre, John, *Churchill's Spearhead: the Development of Britain's Airborne Forces during World War II* (Barnsley: Pen and Sword, 2010).

Hamilton, Nigel, *Monty: Master of the Battlefield 1942-1944* (London: Hamish Hamilton, 1983).

_____, *Monty: The Field Marshal 1944-1976* (London: Hamish Hamilton, 1986).

Hibbert, Christopher, *Arnhem* (London: Phoenix, 2003).

HMSO, *By Air To Battle: The Official Account Of The British Airborne Divisions* (London: HMSO, 1945).

Holland, James, *Normandy '44: D-Day and the Battle for France* (London: Bantam, 2019).

Horne, Alistair and Montgomery, David, *Lonely Leader: Monty 1944-1945* (Pan, 2002).

Horrocks, Sir Brian, *A Full Life* (London: Collins, 1960).

_____, *Corps Commander* (London: Sidgwick and Jackson, 1977).

Keegan, John (ed.), *Churchill's Generals* (London: Warner, 1991).

_____, *Six Armies in Normandy* (Random House, 1992).

Kent, Ron, *First in! Parachute Pathfinder Company* (London: Batsford, 1979).

Kershaw, Robert J., *'It never snows in September': The German View of Market Garden and the Battle of Arnhem, September 1944* (Hersham: Ian Allan, 1990).

Kessell, Lipmann, *Surgeon at Arms* (Barnsley: Pen and Sword, 2011).

Kite, Ben, *Stout Hearts: the British and Canadians in Normandy 1944* (Solihull: Hellion, 2014).

Lamb, Richard, *Montgomery in Europe 1943-45: Success or Failure?* (London: Buchan and Enright, 1983).

Magry, Karel, *Operation Market-Garden Then and Now Vols 1 and 2* (After the Battle, 2002).

Mawson, Stuart, *Arnhem Doctor* (The History Press, 2000).

Mead, Richard, *General 'Boy': The Life of Lieutenant General Sir Frederick Browning* (Barnsley: Pen and Sword, 2010).

Mead, Richard, *The Men Behind Monty* (Barnsley: Pen and Sword, 2015).

Middlebrook, Martin, *Arnhem 1944: The Airborne Battle* (London: Penguin, 1994).

Montgomery, Bernard, *The Memoirs of Field Marshal Montgomery* (Collins, 1958).

Neillands, Robin, *The Battle of Normandy 1944* (London: Cassell, 2002).

———————, *The Battle for the Rhine: Arnhem and the Ardennes: the campaign in Europe* (London: Cassell, 2005).

Newton-Dunn, Bill, *Big Wing: The biography of Air Chief Marshal Sir Trafford Leigh Mallory* (Shrewsbury: Airlife, 1992).

Nicol, John and Rennell, Tony, *Arnhem: The Battle for Survival* (London: Penguin, 2011).

Otway, Lieutenant Colonel Terence, *Airborne Forces of the Second World War* (London: HMSO, 1951).

Peters, Mike and Buist, Luuk, *Glider Pilots at Arnhem* (Barnsley: Pen and Sword, 2009).

Pogue, Forrest C., *George C. Marshall: Organizer of Victory* (Viking, 1973).

———————, *The Supreme Command* (Washington: US Army Centre of Military History, 1989).

Powell, Geoffrey, *The Devil's Birthday: The Bridges to Arnhem 1944* (Buchan and Enright, 1984).

———————, *Men at Arnhem* (Barnsley: Pen and Sword, 2003).

Richardson, General Sir Charles, *Flashback: A Soldier's Story* (London: William Kimber & Co, 1985).

Ritchie, Sebastian, *Arnhem: Myth and Reality* (Ramsbury: Hale, 2011).

Rostron, Peter, *The Military Life & Times of General Sir Miles Dempsey GBE KCB DSO MC* (Barnsley: Pen and Sword, 2010).

Ruppenthal, Roland G., *Logistical Support of the Armies, Vol I: May 1941-September 1944* (Washington: US Army Centre of Military History, 1995).

Ryan, Cornelius, *A Bridge Too Far* (Wordsworth Editions, 1999).

Sims, James, *Arnhem Spearhead* (Imperial War Museum, 1978).

Stacey, Colonel C.P., *The Victory Campaign: The Operations in North-west Europe 1944-1945* (Ottawa: Queen's Printer and Controller of Stationery, 1960).

Terraine, John, *The Right of the Line* (Ware: Wordsworth, 1997).

Urquhart, Major General R.E., *Arnhem* (London: Cassell, 1958).

Warner, Philip, *Horrocks: The General who led from the front* (Barnsley: Pen and Sword, 2005).

Warren, John C., *Airborne Operations in World War II, European Theater* (USAF Historical Division, 1956).

Webster, David Kenyon, *Parachute Infantry* (London: Random House, 2014)

Wilmot, Chester, *The Struggle for Europe* (Ware: Wordsworth, 1997).

INDEX

Note – operations that are the subject of chapters are only indexed where they appear outside of those chapters

Admiralty 156
AEAF (Allied Expeditionary Air Forces) 6, 8, 15, 17, 33–4, 49–50, 54, 75, 82–3, 99, 129, 131, 137, 141, 153, 155–6, 158–9, 161, 163, 165, 185–6
AFDAG (Airborne Forward Delivery Airfield Group) 37–8, 53, 56–7, 61, 66–7, 73, 78, 80, 143, 194
Air Ministry 4–5, 15, 161, 164
Antwerp 169–72, 178
Anvil, Operation 5, 40–1
ANXF (Allied Naval Expeditionary Forces) 6, 33, 79, 82, 92 , 156
Arnhem xvi, 109
Arnold, General Henry 'Hap' 3, 5, 9, 17, 196, 199
Axehead, Operation 9, 28, 35, 41

Bardsea, Operation 135, 154
Bedell Smith, Lieutenant General Walter 3–4, 8
Belchem, Brigadier David 47, 140–1, 154–5, 161, 172, 177, 189–90, 193
Beneficiary, Operation 35, 49
Bird, Lieutenant Colonel 15
Bonesteel, Colonel Charles 35, 39
Bradley, General Omar 17, 25, 42–3, 45, 49, 51–5, 56, 60, 67, 71, 75, 79, 86, 128, 129, 145, 162–3, 166, 175

Brereton, Lieutenant General Lewis 3–4, 6, 9–10, 13, 15, 49–50, 52, 71, 79, 82, 84, 107, 111, 123, 125–6, 141–2, 146, 154–6, 162–7, 170–1, 178, 180, 183, 185–6, 190–1, 195–7
British Army:
  21st Army Group 7, 9–10, 14–16, 21–23, 26–27, 29–31, 33–4, 38, 41–2, 44, 47–9, 51, 53, 56–9, 63, 68, 73, 77–80, 84–5, 89, 92, 97, 102–03, 107, 109, 117–18, 123, 126, 128–9, 134, 142, 145–6, 149, 154–6, 158, 170, 172, 175, 178, 179, 183, 186, 189
  Second Army 21, 23, 25, 28–9, 33, 54, 92, 98, 100, 108, 111, 125, 127, 129, 142–6, 151–3, 156–7, 165, 175, 177, 179, 182, 187, 194
  First Canadian Army 21, 23, 25, 28, 33, 54, 92–3, 96, 100, 102–03, 105, 111, 118, 127, 142, 153, 157, 165, 170, 172, 175, 178
  Anti–Aircraft Command 156, 161
  I Corps 41
  Canadian II Corps 41, 101–02
  VIII Corps 41, 157
  XII Corps 41, 157, 179
  XXX Corps 41, 153, 157, 178–9, 182, 185, 188–9, 194–5
  1st Airborne Corps 10, 53, 78, 87, 108, 128–30, 139, 143–5, 152, 165, 178, 182–4, 194
  HQ Airborne Troops 4, 6, 10, 13–14, 16, 30–1, 35, 38, 47, 51–3, 55–8, 60–1, 63–4, 67–8, 73, 77–8, 80–1, 83–4, 92, 107–08, 128, 146, 154, 158–9, 164